SQUEEZING TH

HENRY BLOFELD

Squeezing the Orange

blue door

First published in Great Britain in 2013 by
Blue Door
An imprint of HarperCollins*Publishers*
77–85 Fulham Palace Road,
Hammersmith, London W6 8JB

www.harpercollins.co.uk

This paperback edition 2014

A catalogue record for this book is
available from the British Library

ISBN: 978-0-00-750640-8

Printed and bound in Great Britain by
Clays Ltd, St Ives plc

MIX
Paper from
responsible sources
FSC **FSC™ C007454**
www.fsc.org

For Valeria, whose love, interest, humour and enthusiasm has made all the difference.

CONTENTS

Preface

I find the older I get the more time I spend thinking back to my early life which I suppose turned me into the person I have become. I have found also that by looking back on this period at the age of seventy-three, I am able to look at it from a much more relaxed perspective than when I last wrote about it fifteen years ago.

The nasty bits don't hurt or matter as much as they did and the best bits seem to have become even more fun. There is no point in trying to blame anyone but yourself. It is much better to throw your head back and have a thoroughly good laugh. As a result, maybe, I find my first thirty-odd years much more interesting than the rest of it, when effectively the die has been cast.

My early upbringing, strange by today's standards; my traditional education which, after a homesick start, I enjoyed hugely; a nasty accident; Cambridge; the City and then my two extraordinarily lucky starts in both journalism and broadcasting have all left their mark. I have, therefore, written at some length about my early life and tried to bring alive some of the more remarkable characters who had an influence on me as I started out.

I have spent a life unashamedly in pursuit of fun and this book is meant to be a reflection of that. I know I have been horribly self-indulgent and hedonistic and altogether pretty selfish, but I hope also that I have communicated a fair measure of enjoyment and pleasure and it is this with which I am trying to deal now.

After describing how it all began, I decided not to go on in this vein in case it developed into a boring chronology of cricket tours and matches. I have talked about our commentary box and its inhabitants and one or two important occurrences along the way, but without, I hope, failing to see the funny side of it all.

If I have developed a philosophy, it is ridiculously simple. I regard every day as an orange, from which I try and squeeze every last drop of juice before moving on to tomorrow's. This book is an attempt to bring a glass or two of that delicious juice back to life and hence the title.

Henry Blofeld
London, 2013

ONE

Grizel and Shelling Peas

According to my mother – who had drawn the short straw at the font when she was christened Grizel – my birth was less eventful than my conception. Grizel did not muck around: she was always earthy and to the point. When my wife and I were first married, she encouraged us to waste no time in starting a family, as she felt that delay might have a discouraging effect on procreation. 'I was lucky,' she told me, 'because I bred at the shake of a pair of pants' – adding, with emphasis, 'Which was just as well, as it was all I ever got.' That, I hope, was not entirely fair on Tom, my father, who may not have been one of Casanova's strongest competitors, but I am sure he had his moments. In any case, this particular pair of pants must have shaken with vigour, no doubt as part of the Christmas festivities, in 1938, as late in the evening of the following 23 September I made a swift and noisy entrance into this world. Tom will have been sitting in the drawing room dealing with a whisky and soda and *The Times* crossword puzzle while Dr Bennett conducted the events upstairs. I dare say this was not too arduous a production for him, for on another occasion Grizel said, 'I found that having babies was as easy as shelling peas. I can never understand what all the fuss is about.' So that was that.

Tom and Grizel were fiercely Edwardian in their beliefs

about bringing up children, and the three of us – Anthea was ten years older than me, and John seven – had a tougher time of it than children have now. Of course we were all born with whacking great silver spoons in our mouths, but I don't know how you can choose your parents. You've got to get along with what you've got. I'm sure Anthea and John had a stricter start to life than I did. In the thirties nannies and nurserymaids abounded, and Tom and Grizel will have been even more remote figures for the other two than they were for me. I probably had an easier time of it because during the war Nanny had to go back home to Heacham in west Norfolk to look after her sick mother. As a result, Grizel, with the help of any temporary nurserymaid she could lay her hands on, had to roll up her sleeves and do much of the dirty work herself, so she and I had a closer relationship than she did with Anthea and John. I am sure the love between parents and children was just as strong then as it is now, but in those days it was not the upfront jamboree that it has become. In fact, when you look back at it all those years ago, it seems harsh and at times almost cruel. My friends were brought up in much the same way – that was just the way things were done. I should think my parents' generation felt that life was easy for us compared to the way they themselves had been brought up in the years immediately after Queen Victoria had died. It is all part of the ever-going evolutionary process which has brought us now to the age of the free-range child. So what seemed perfectly normal to us at the time may seem shocking from today's considerably more relaxed perspective.

While Tom and Grizel were sticklers for keeping us on the straight and narrow, they were, in their own way, loving parents who did their best to make sure that we had as happy a childhood as possible, within the constraints of the time.

They were always there for us, to help and give support, although if the fault was mine, as it usually was, they did not hesitate to say so, and seldom minced their words. For years they remained a staunch last resort, and like all offspring I went running back when in need of help, usually in the form of cash, although with only modest success, as Tom and Grizel were never that flush, and guarded their pieces of eight with a solemn rectitude.

I remember when I had reached the pocket-money stage going along to my father's dressing room to collect my weekly dose. Sometimes I arrived a little ahead of schedule and caught him in his pants, socks and attendant sock suspenders, which was an awe-inspiring sight. It was like looking at a pole-vaulter as things went wrong. There was great excitement one morning when I found I had graduated from a twelve-sided threepenny bit (a penny of which had to go into the church collection) to a silver sixpence. The handover of the coin or coins was carried out with a formality which almost suggested that the Bank of England was involved. Tom kept his loose change in the top drawer of a tiny chest with three little drawers which perched alongside his elderly pair of ivory-backed hairbrushes, which had a strong smell of lemon from the hair oil he got from his barber. As my father made a coot look as if it was in urgent need of a haircut, this all seemed a rather pointless exercise.

While he solemnly located the appropriate piece of small change in this magical drawer, I stood by the door. I don't think it would have occurred to Tom that he was a frightening figure to a small boy. This had something to do with his height – he stood six feet six inches tall in his stocking feet – as well as his monocle and the sock suspenders, which so fascinated me. His lighter side was harder to find than Grizel's, and his was naturally a more formal manner. The staff, in the house and on the Home Farm, treated him with a watchful respect. When crossed or let down he could be extremely angry, and would have made common cause with some of those grumpy Old Testament prophets.

Tom regarded the ancien régime as the only possible way forward, while Grizel, if left to herself, would have been happy to allow her more extravagant natural instincts to come to the surface. While Grizel laughed in a bubbling, jolly sort of way, Tom's merriment seemed to rumble up with more control from the bottom of his throat, and the source of his humour was often harder to fathom than his wife's. Grizel had a strong sense of loyalty to her husband, and she was always more than aware of her position as Tom's wife, and played the role pretty well. She was a snob, but I remember it as a snobbery as of right, rather than as a contrivance. Looking back on my parents and my childhood now, it comes to me like a black-and-white, but seldom silent, movie, and from this distance I find it highly entertaining.

The Blofelds have always been a restless lot. At some long-ago point, now lost in the mists of time, they moved from north Germany to Finland, and then shot across the North Sea with the Vikings before finally being grounded on the north Norfolk coast somewhere near what is today called Overstrand, then pushing a few miles inland and setting up shop in a small village called Sustead. Three or four hundred years whizzed by before they up-anchored again, moving twenty-odd miles south-east to Hoveton, which at that time was owned by some people called Doughty. Having a shrewd eye for the main chance, a Blofeld married a Miss Doughty, who was to become the sole surviving member of that distinguished family. Hoveton therefore soon became the Blofeld stronghold, and has remained so ever since.

Discipline – good manners, politeness, the pleases and thank yous of life – was all-important in my childhood. I can't remember how young I was when I was first soundly ticked off for not leaping to my feet when my mother came into the room, but young enough. Dirty hands, undone buttons, sloppy speech or pronunciation, and the use of certain words were all jumped upon. Throwing sweet papers or any other rubbish out of the car window was also not popular. Goodness knows what my parents would have made of mobile telephones, and their frequent and disturbing use. Table manners were rigidly enforced. No one sat down before Grizel was in place, and you were not allowed to start eating until everyone had been served. If toast crumbs were left on a pat of butter, there was hell to pay, your napkin had to be neatly folded before you left the dining room, and you ate what was put in front of you and left a clean plate.

The nursery was presided over by Nanny Framingham, who was nothing less than a saint. Cheerful, enthusiastic and always smiling, she put up with all sorts of skulduggery. On one occasion I all but frightened her to death. My father's guns and cartridges were kept in the schoolroom, which was next to his office. I always took a lively interest in the gun cupboard, although it was forbidden territory, and when no one was around I used to go and have a good look round. I loved the smell of the 3-in-One oil which was used to clean the guns. There was also something irresistible about the cartridges. I would steal one or two of them, take them back to the nursery and cut them up to see how they were made. One afternoon Nanny came into the room unexpectedly while I was engaged in this harmless pastime, and the sight of the gunpowder and loose shot lying all over the table terrified her – she saw us all going up in an enormous explosion, and was quick to run off and enlist help. Within a matter of minutes Tom burst into the nursery, looking and sounding a good deal worse than the wrath of God. My cartridge-cutting activities came to an immediate halt, and I was probably sent up to my bedroom for an indefinite period, possibly with a clip over the ear or a smack on the bottom as well. Corporal punishment was always on the menu.

The schoolroom lived up to its name, for it was there, along with my first cousin, Simon Cator, and Jane Holden, an unofficial sister and lifelong friend who lived nearby at Neatishead, that we were given the rudiments of an education by the small, bespectacled, virtuous, austere and humourless Mrs Hales. I often wonder, looking back, what she and Mr Hales – who I'm not sure I ever met – got up to in their spare time. Not a great deal, I should think. They lived at Sea Palling, and she turned up each morning rather earlier than was strictly necessary in her elderly Austin Seven, which, in spite of often making disagreeable and unlikely noises, kept going for many years. On the occasions when we got the better of Mrs Hales and were rather noisily mobbing her up, the door from the schoolroom into my father's office would burst open, Tom's thunderous face would appear, and order would be instantly restored. Our lessons were fun, and we learned to read and write and do some basic arithmetic. Mrs Hales must have done a good job, because when I went away to boarding school I found I was able to hold my own.

Tom was an imposing figure. In addition to his height, he had a small moustache which was more a smattering of foliage on his upper lip than anything else. He said he grew it to avoid having to shave his upper lip, which, as he used a cut-throat razor for most of his life, may have been a tricky operation. He had a huge nose, which he blew and sneezed through with considerable venom while applying a large and colourful silk handkerchief to the enormous protuberance.

His monocle hung from a thread around his neck, and dangled down in front of his tie. This was impressive, unless, as a small boy, I was summoned to his office for my school report to be discussed. I would tread apprehensively down the long corridor, past the cellar and the game larder, and through the schoolroom for this ghastly meeting. It never had a happy outcome, because away from the games field I was an out-and-out slacker. Tom, sitting behind his desk while I perched apprehensively on the leather bum-warmer around the fireplace, would read out all the hideous lies those wretched schoolmasters had written about me. Not only that, he would believe every single word of them. Both he and Grizel invariably took the side of my persecutors, something it seems parents seldom do today. Having read out the details of whichever crime it was that I was supposed to have committed, there would be a nasty tweak of the muscles around his right eye. The monocle would fall down his shirt front, indicating that it was my turn to go in to bat. I was then invariably bowled by a ball I should have left alone.

When I had reached the age when I was more or less house-trained, I was allowed to join my parents in the drawing room for an hour or so before going to bed. Nanny would open the drawing-room door in the hall to let me in, and Grizel would always greet me with the words, 'Hello, ducky.' I loved these visits, for Grizel usually had something fun or interesting for me to do. She taught me card games, starting with a simple two-handed game called cooncan. I graduated from that to hearts, which needed four people, and piquet, which I played with Tom. Grizel also taught me the patiences she would play while Tom was reading and I loved the one called 'trousers'. We played Ludo and Cluedo, and occasionally Monopoly. Tom would make up the numbers for these, too, but I don't think Monopoly was really his sort of thing. When he had bought the Old Kent Road he was never quite sure what to do with it.

When I was a touch older, Tom would read aloud to me, and I have always been eternally grateful for this. I think he started me off with Kipling's *Just So Stories* – I adored 'The Elephant's Child'. I know I have never laughed at any story more than Mr Jorrocks's adventures in R.S. Surtees' *Handley Cross*. Tom was brilliant at all the different accents: his imitation of huntsman James Pigg's Scottish vowels was special. Then there were John Buchan's Richard Hannay books, *The Thirty-Nine Steps* and so on, and Dornford Yates's stories about Jonathan Mansell and the others discovering treasure in castles in Austria. I was introduced to Bulldog Drummond, Sherlock Holmes and Dorothy Sayers' detective Lord Peter Wimsey who became a great hero of mine. Tom adored P.G. Wodehouse, and wanted to read me some of the Jeeves books, but Grizel couldn't stand them, and they stayed on the shelves. We all have awful secrets which we hope will never slip out. One of mine is that I had a mother who didn't like Wodehouse or Gilbert and Sullivan. This still surprises me, because I would have thought Grizel would have enjoyed the fantasy world of Wodehouse. Tom's reading would finish in time for the weather and the six o'clock news. After the news headlines, Tom would invariably tell Grizel to turn off the wireless. He dismissed the rest of the news as 'gossip'. Then it was drinks time for them and bedtime for me.

I am sure Tom never played cricket, judging from his one performance in the fathers' match when I was at Sunningdale. But he enjoyed the game, and each summer he and two of his friends, Reggie Cubitt (who was his cousin) and Christo Birkbeck, would go up to London for the three days of the Gentlemen v. Players match at Lord's. They stayed at Boodle's, and I dare say it was as close as any of them ever came to letting their hair down, which probably meant no more than having a second glass of vintage port after dinner. It is unlikely that they would have paid a visit to the Bag o'Nails after that. Reggie and Christo were a sort of social barometer for Tom and Grizel. If, in the years I still lived at home, I was intending to embark upon some rather flashy adventure, Grizel would caution me by saying, 'What would Reggie and Christo think?'

Just before the end of the war there were some German prisoners-of-war working on the farm at Hoveton. It was said that if Germany had played cricket it might never have gone to war, so it was ironic that these PoWs were put to work turning a part of the old parkland up by the little round wood at Hill Piece into a wonderfully picturesque cricket ground. The village team, Hoveton and Wroxham, played there, and for several years later on I organised a two-day game in September between the Eton Ramblers and the Free Foresters, which was highly competitive and great fun. It was a lovely ground in a wonderful setting, but sadly it has disappeared for a part of it has now been planted over with trees.

Tom could be great value. He had a wonderful turn of phrase. He and Grizel would go to bed every night at around ten o'clock. Sitting in the drawing room at the Home Farm, or later in the hall at Hoveton House, he would shut his book, half stretch, and say, 'Well, I think it's time for a bit of a lie-down before breakfast.' Another splendid offering would come when a visitor was over-keen to make a favourable impression. When asked what he thought about whoever it was when he had gone, Tom would say, 'Awfully nice. I do just wish he wouldn't fart above his arsehole quite so much.'

There was one incident when I was young for which I never forgave Tom. I always ate with Nanny in the nursery, but I was allowed to have lunch in the dining room with my parents on the last full day of the school holidays – I was sent to boarding school at Sunningdale when I was seven and a half. And not only that: I was allowed to choose the pudding. One year Grizel came by a stock of tinned black cherries, and whenever I tasted them I didn't think I would ever get much closer to heaven. Goodness knows where she found them. Anyway, on this occasion I said I would like some black cherries as the pud, and to my surprise my wish was granted. We sat down to lunch at one o'clock – mealtimes were immutable, and if you were late it was considered to be a major crime. Tom carved the cold beef. They had cold roast beef six days a week, or so it seemed, and to ring the changes, hot roast beef on Sundays. A woman called Joan, who ferried these things around in the dining room, put my plate in front of me, and when everyone had been served, we tucked in. Our empty plates were collected, and then it was time for the cherries.

They were brought in by Joan on a large brown tray, and put down on the sideboard. As well as the big glass bowl brimful of cherries, there was another full of junket, that ghastly milk jelly which I detested with a passion. Tom got up to serve us, and in addition to a pretty useful pile of cherries, I was given two big spoonfuls of junket. We were brought up to 'eat level', which meant that junket and cherries had to be eaten together. But on this occasion I threw caution to the winds and, feigning great enthusiasm, got stuck into the junket, which I finished in record time. My undisturbed pile of cherries was now gleaming up at me from my plate. The next five minutes looked promising. But Tom had been watching.

'Joan,' he said, for she was still lurking by the sideboard, 'Master Henry' – I was always Master Henry as far as the staff were concerned – 'clearly does not like his cherries. Will you please remove them.' Which is what she did, and I have only just stopped crying. Life could be bloody unfair, or so it seemed. But I had broken the rules.

In the fifties Tom bought an old Rolls-Royce from a chap who lived in the neighbouring village of Coltishall. It was a bespoke model, and was thought to be one of the last Rolls made with a red 'RR' on the front of the bonnet – the change to black was made in 1933, for aesthetic reasons. It was a huge, pale-grey car with a soft roof which never came off, as far as I know. There was a window between the back and the front seats which could be wound up by those in the back so the chauffeur couldn't do any eavesdropping. As Tom always drove it himself this window remained down and was not to be touched. I thought it was the sexiest car ever, because it had no fewer than three horns. One was a gentle toot for warning an old woman against crossing the road; the next was a bit stronger, in case she had already started; and the third was a klaxon which yelled at her just as she was disappearing under the wheels. 'Bloody fool,' Tom would mutter after he had pressed it.

My father used the Rolls as his main car for at least ten years, and it always caused my school chums great amusement when he drove it down to Eton. He was the Chairman of the Country Gentleman's Association, and the number plate was CG 1000, so he was known by my friends as 'Country Gent One Thousand'. As it was such a big car he sometimes had difficulty negotiating the smaller streets in London, but it was such an imperious-looking machine that almost everyone got out of the way. If not, there was much hooting, which occasionally got to the klaxon stage. Although parking in those days was a great deal easier than it is now, it still presented problems in the busy parts of London. But Tom, whose appearance was nothing if not distinguished, had the answer to that. He would drive slowly down, say, Bond Street, and when he saw two coppers walking along the pavement – as one did in those far-distant days – he would stop the car, get out and shut the door, saying to the nearest one, 'Officer, look after my car for me. I shall only be about ten minutes,' and walk off. When he returned they would indeed be looking after his car. I always wondered who they thought he was.

In many ways Grizel was the antithesis to Tom. She was short, although there was a fair bit of her in the horizontal sense, and she packed a pretty good punch. She went around like a battleship under full steam, with a siren to match. A woman of the most forthright and damning opinions, with a fund of common sense, she did not tolerate what she described as nonsense in any shape or form, and was quick to spot anything remotely bogus. In turn, you had to accept her as she was. She was very bright, and had a marvellous sense of humour. She was a reasonably devout Christian, and church – where Tom read the lessons, and was joint patron of the living together with the Bishop of Norwich – was an essential part of Sundays. As a child, I always felt the time spent in church could have been more usefully employed. Grizel, sensing my objections, would say to me, 'You've had a lovely week. Now you can spend an hour saying thank you.' She was fond of God, but dealt with him entirely on her own terms. When they eventually met I should think a good deal of finger-wagging of the 'now, look here' sort will have gone on.

In 1956 we moved up the drive from the Home Farm to Hoveton House. There was a dinner party soon afterwards, and one of my parents' friends who came along was what people today would refer to as a born-again Christian. In those days he was known as a God-botherer. He loved to get stuck into his neighbour's ribs and start banging on about God. While she was all for the general idea of converting people, Grizel felt there was a time and place for everything, and that a dinner party was not remotely a conversional occasion, so she sat him next to her to avoid the danger. But after dinner, as was the custom, the ladies left the room to powder their noses or whatever, leaving the chaps to drink their port before they all joined forces later on in the drawing room. When this moment arrived, our God-botherer found himself sitting on a sofa on the other side of the fireplace from Grizel. After a few minutes she noticed that he was giving his neighbour, a good-looking girl, a fearful going over about the Almighty. She coughed and generally registered short-range disapproval. The God-botherer, realising that he had got it wrong, stopped in mid-sentence and, leaning forward towards Grizel with his elbows on his knees, asked in a surprised voice, 'But surely, Grizel, you believe in Our Lord Jesus Christ?' Grizel narrowed her eyes, leaned back a fraction and delivered a stinging rebuke: 'Never in the drawing room after dinner.' Which was game, set and match.

Every summer for the last five years of their lives together, before my father put his cue in the rack in 1986, my parents would go for a holiday on a barge on the French canals. It was a fearfully upmarket barge, without a punt pole in sight. At six o'clock each evening they had a glass of champagne on deck, then went up to their cabin to change for dinner, which meant a dinner jacket for Tom and a long skirt for Grizel, before re-emerging to have another glass of champagne. There were always a number of Americans on board who helped make up the numbers. Grizel was suspicious of Americans. She felt that they bounced rather too much. One evening the two of them went up to change for dinner, came down suitably attired and tackled their second glasses of champagne. They had hardly begun when from stage right, a short, middle-aged American in 'perfectly ghastly rubber shoes' came bouncing across the deck to Grizel with his arms outstretched, saying in a loud voice, 'Hi, my name's Jim. What's yours?' This was too much for Grizel who took a step back, mentally at any rate, drew herself up to her full five feet six and a half inches and said in a menacingly firm voice, 'That, I am afraid, is a private matter, but you may call me Mrs Blofeld.' I think Bertie Wooster's Aunt Dahlia might well have come up with both those answers.

I have found that the older I become, the more I look back to my origins and see it all in a different perspective even from fifteen years ago. If I seem a little too critical of my parents, it is with my tongue firmly in my cheek. I feel now, more than ever, that the most surprising thing is that these things happened at all. Hoveton was terrific fun, and it would not have been so enjoyable if Tom and Grizel had been other than they were. Their strong personalities were stamped all over the place. And not only that: although they were never particularly flush with cash, they gave all three of us a wonderful education. Anthea went on to become a doctor, and John, who inherited Tom's wonderful speaking voice, became a distinguished High Court judge. Meanwhile, I scrabbled around in the press and the broadcasting boxes of the cricketing world. Then when old age was taking hold I began to tread the boards, in the hope of making a few people laugh in any theatre brave enough to take me on, although I fear I may have bored many of them to tears.

We now live in an age when much that I never even dreamt about when I was young has come about. The world of Tom and Grizel has been relegated to the stuff of fairy stories, yet at the time it was as natural as night following day. There was no other game in town for those on either side of the green baize door, and we all got on with it. As a child I had a great relationship with everyone who worked for my parents, both in the house and on the farm, except for Mrs Porcher, our cook. She was a small woman with a shrill voice, and although she was no doubt a dab hand at the kitchen stove, as far as I was concerned she never seemed to blur any issue with goodwill. She didn't exactly take on my parents, but there was sometimes a curtness to her manner that did not always bring out the best in Grizel. I remember Mrs Porcher going into the drawing room after breakfast, notepad in hand, ready for Grizel to order the food for lunch and dinner that day. Mrs Porcher always had the sense to realise that if she entered into a battle of wills with Grizel there could only be one outcome, while Grizel knew that it would be an awful bore to have to find another cook. As a result, there existed a continuous state of armed neutrality between them. When Mrs Porcher eventually returned permanently into the no doubt grateful arms of Mr Porcher, cooks came and went at a fair pace, until the redoubtable Mrs Alexander took over.

My early years must have shaped the initial hard core of me, which I hope has been smoothed down a bit by the subsequent journey through the mainly self-imposed rough seas of life. In many ways, of course, memory is selective, but there is no doubt that the family estate at Hoveton was an enchanting place in which to have been brought up. Over a great many years it had grown smaller as those in charge of it had seen fit to sell off pieces of land – mostly, I expect, to raise a bit of lolly. But the nucleus that still remained when I was young was heaven for a small boy. Two of the Norfolk Broads, Hoveton Great Broad and Hoveton Little Broad, were within its boundaries, and there were many acres of exciting marshland, with dykes and dams and all manner of birdlife, from ducks and geese to bitterns, swans, hawks and masses of smaller varieties. Grizel was passionate about the local flora and fauna, and would teach me the names of butterflies, birds, insects, trees and wildflowers. Sadly I have forgotten most of them, which would have made her very cross. Sometimes she would find a swallowtail butterfly chrysalis in the reeds on the marshes. This would be brought home and put in a cage in the drawing room, and some time later the most beautifully coloured butterfly you could imagine would emerge. Before it could damage those magical wings by fluttering against the sides of the cage, it would be released into the marshes to fend for itself. Sadly, over the years swallowtails became increasingly scarce and by now have probably completely disappeared : I should think the last one to be reared at home was sometime in the fifties.

For a time Grizel collected Siamese cats, which lived in a long wooden hut in the farmyard at the Home Farm. She won many prizes with them. The silver spoons with which we stirred our coffee after lunch all had the letters 'SCC' (Siamese Cat Club) emblazoned on their handles. She also went through a Japanese bantam stage, during which, intermingled with a fluffy collection of white Silkies, they trawled all over the farmyard, not always to Tom's delight.

Another phase of her life was devoted to Dutch rabbits. These again won prizes, and were kept in the shed that had once been the home of the Siamese cats. There was also an impressive herd of pedigree Shorthorns, which, amid great excitement, won all sorts of prizes over the years at the Royal Show. Grizel was closely involved with the breeding of the cattle, and would go down to the dairy farm almost every day. With the head cowman in tow she would have a look at whatever animals she was particularly interested in, and cast an eye over any new calves. If need be, she was more than happy to roll up her sleeves and help with a difficult birth. When I was very young she would talk for ages to Birch, who was the head cowman, and later to his successor, Pressley, whom I found more fun. I remember Grizel and Pressley constantly hatching plots to convince Tom of the necessity of buying a new bull, or a couple of heifers, or whatever. The dairy was always a fruitful playground for me. I loved watching the cows being milked, and then the milk being separated from the cream. There was one occasion when I eluded Grizel and Pressley and walked into one of the cow sheds when a heifer was in the act of being served by a bull. After I had been dragged out Pressley was embarrassed, but Grizel, who took these things in her stride, said to me, 'You'll find out more about that one day, darling, but not just yet.' This left me deeply curious, but I knew better than to question her. She had drawn a line under the subject for the time being.

Grizel, with her familiar stride, which was more a purposeful walk than a strut, was forever busying herself around the house, the garden and the farmyard. She made the life of the gardener, Walter Savage, confusing and difficult as she issued instructions over her shoulder while he struggled along in her wake. Savage, as we called him, was thin, about medium height, with a white moustache, a good First War record, and a huge and frightening wife who put the fear of God into poor old Savage. They lived in one half of the charming Dutch gabled cottage at the bottom of the Hoveton House garden. When I was a bit older, Savage would drive me and some friends in my mother's car to the Norwich speedway track, where the home team were pretty high in the national pecking order. Ove Fundin, a five-time world champion from somewhere in Scandinavia, was a name I shall never forget; nor that thrilling smell of petrol fumes and burning rubber as the riders strove to steer their brakeless bikes around corners. On other occasions Savage ferried several of us to the Yarmouth Fun Fair, where the bumper cars, the ghost train and the fish and chips were all irresistible.

When I was a child the farm, which had been whittled down over the years to about 1,300 acres, had become principally a fruit farm. There were an awful lot of people employed to tend to its needs. When I was old enough I used to help the wives of the farmworkers pick the fruit. There was the excitement of being paid sixpence by Herbert Haines for a basket of Victoria plums and a punnet of raspberries. This was a useful supplement to my pocket money. Herbert, short and indomitably cheerful, wearing a perilously placed felt hat, loved his cricket and presided over the fruit picking.

The farm manager, the slightly austere, bespectacled and white-haired Mr Grainger, tootled about the place in his rather severe-looking car. I was extremely careful of him, for I knew that anything I got up to would go straight back to Tom. Mr Grainger had a small office in the Home Farm yard which I avoided like the plague. In fact I think it was a mutual avoidance. As far as I was concerned, Mr Grainger, who lived in a small house down the drive, was always hard work, and if he had a lighter side, I never found it. My father's office was presided over by the ebullient, bouncing and eternally jolly, but not inconsiderable, figure of Miss Easter, a local lady from Salhouse who was a close ally of Nanny's. I loved it when she paid us a visit in the nursery. 'Miss Easter' was a tongue-twister for the young, and she was known affectionately by all of us, including Grizel, as 'Seasser', although Tom never bent from 'Miss Easter'. I suppose she must have had a Christian name, but I can't remember it. Sadly for us, she left Hoveton when approaching middle age, and became Mrs Charles Blaxall. He was a yeoman farmer, and they lived somewhere between Hoveton and Yarmouth. I used to go with Nanny to visit her in her new role as a farmer's wife. She remained the greatest fun, always provided goodies and was one of the real characters of my early life. I can hear her cheerful, echoing laughter even now.

Freddie Hunn, a small man with the friendliest of smiles, was in charge of the cattle feed, which was ground up and mixed in the barn across the yard from my father's office. I loved to go and help Freddie. There was a huge mixer, which was almost the height of the building. All the ingredients were thrown in at the top, mixed, and then poured into sacks at the bottom. The barn had a delicious, musty smell. Freddie's other role was to look after the cricket ground at the other end of the farmyard, through the big green gate and up the long grassy slope to Hill Piece. After his day in the barn had finished he would go up to the ground and get to work with the roller or mower or whatever else was needed. The day before a match between Hoveton and Wroxham and one of the neighbouring villages, out would come the whitener, and the creases would be marked. I found it all fascinating, and Nanny could hardly get me back to the house in time for a bath on Friday evenings.

Freddie was a great Surrey supporter, while I was passionate about Middlesex and Compton and Edrich. But Freddie always thought he had trumped my ace when he turned, as he inevitably did, to Jack Hobbs. Freddie's wife, the large, smiling Hilda Hunn, supervised the delicious cricket teas, and sometimes allowed me a second small cake in an exciting, coloured paper cup.

One of my favourite farmworkers was Lennie Hubbard, whom we all, including my father, called by his Christian name. I never discovered why or how such distinctions were made: why most of the workers on the farm were known by their surnames, while Freddie, Lennie and one or two others went by their Christian names. Lennie was tall, and had been born in the Alms Houses in Lower Street, the rather upmarket name for the lane that ran past these cottages down to the marshes. Once, a great many years earlier, that lane had been part of the main road from Norwich to Yarmouth, which had originally gone past the front of Hoveton House. During the Second World War Lennie had been taken prisoner by the Germans, but had managed to escape – perhaps it was his gallantry that had caused his Christian name to be used. Tom always enjoyed talking to Lennie, and regarded him as one of his best and most faithful employees. There was an irony in that, as Lennie told me much later, long after Tom had died, he and one or two others, for all their outward godliness, had been diehard poachers. He told me, with a broad smile, of an occasion when one day my father had suddenly appeared around the corner of a hedge and spoken to him for ten minutes. Under his greatcoat Lennie was hiding his four-ten shotgun and a recently killed cock pheasant. I dare say he never came closer to losing both his job and his Christian-name status.

Shooting was another highlight of my early life. I fired my first shot when I was nine, missing a sitting rabbit by some distance. I am afraid I was the bloodthirstiest of small boys, and I have loved the excitement and drama of shooting for as long as I can remember.

Tom used to arrange six or seven days' shooting a year with never more than seven guns. They would kill between one and two hundred pheasants and partridges in a day. As a small boy I found these days hugely exciting. Then there was the early-morning duck flighting on the Great Broad. This was always a terrific adventure, getting up in the dark and eating bread and honey and drinking Horlicks in the kitchen before setting off by car for the Great Broad boathouse soon after five o'clock in the morning. There was also the evening flighting on the marshes, when each of us stood in a small butt made of dried reeds. This was also thrilling, and of course by the time we got home night had set in.

Carter was the first gamekeeper I remember. He was a small, rather gnarled man with a lovely Norfolk voice. Apart from looking after the game and trying to keep the vermin in check, his other job each morning was to brush and press the clothes my father had worn the day before. He did this on a folding wooden table on the verandah by the back door. When he had done this, if I asked politely and he was in an obliging mood, he would come out to the croquet lawn and bowl at me for a few minutes. I had to tread carefully with Carter. I think he was the first person ever to bowl overarm to me with a proper cricket ball. Sometimes I hit him into the neighbouring stinging nettles, which ended play for the day, for his charity did not extend to doing the fielding off his own bowling. Carter was the village umpire during the summer. I'm not sure about his grasp of the laws of the game, but you didn't question his decisions – you merely moaned about them afterwards. When Carter retired he was succeeded by Watker, a brilliant clay-pigeon shot and, to me, a Biggles-like figure; and then by Godfrey, the nicest of them all. I would spend a huge amount of time with the keepers during the holidays. Once or twice I looked after Godfrey's vermin traps when he had his holiday. Sadly, neither Watker nor Godfrey had a clue how to bowl, but Nanny, who was up for most things, would bowl to me on the croquet lawn. Her underarm offerings often ended up in the nettles, and being the trouper she was, she would dive in after them, and usually got nastily stung.

It was a fantastic world in which to be brought up. Looking back on it, it was quite right that I should have been taught how to use it and respect it. I can almost feel myself forgiving Tom for those cherries. In a way it was sad when my full-time enjoyment of Hoveton came to an end. But when I was seven and a half I was sent away to boarding school at Sunningdale, almost 150 miles away, which may now seem almost like wanton cruelty, but was par for the course in those days. When I was young, all I wanted to do was to grow older, and going away to school seemed a satisfactory step in the right direction.

TWO

A Wodehousian Education

I was not unduly alarmed at the prospect of being sent away to school. John had been to Sunningdale, and had survived, although of course as he was seven years older than me, we were never at school together. Grizel had been calling me 'Blofeld' for some while before I went, for she wanted to make sure that I would be used to being called by my surname when I got to the school. For some reason I was not made to call Tom 'sir', which was how I would have to address the masters. Ordering the school uniform and all the other clothes I would need had gone on for weeks, and Nanny had sewn smart red name-tapes onto all the shirts, pants and stockings, revealing to anyone who chose to look – but principally, I suspect, the laundry – that they belonged to H.C. Blofeld. I won't say I jumped happily into the back of my father's dark-green Armstrong Siddeley in early May 1947, but I was nothing like as homesick as I was to become over the next couple of years when going back to school at the end of the holidays. I think Nanny was the person who minded it all the most, and she was probably the closest to tears amid the frantic waving as we tootled off.

The journey went on for nearly five hours before we turned left into the school drive, with rhododendrons on either side. We went up a short hill to what then appeared to me to be a huge gravelled area in front of the house, where half a dozen cars were parked. It all seemed uncomfortably large, and I think I began to quiver. I was greeted with formal handshakes by Mr and Mrs Fox, the headmaster and his wife. Mr Fox's black hair gleamed with oil, which made him smell of mildly austere flowers. He was wearing a rather severe three-piece suit, with fiercely polished black shoes, and gave me an exceedingly creased half-smile. By now I was beginning to think I had been sold an ungovernably fast one by Tom and Grizel when they had told me what a smashing place Sunningdale would be.

Tom was being pleasantly avuncular in the background while Grizel, with considerable gusto, was shooing me around the Foxes' drawing room to shake hands with everyone in sight. Having been through it all with John, she knew the leaders of the pack well enough, and briskly brushed aside an under-matron and a junior master. False bonhomie was very much the order of the day. I think we were all given a cup of tea and, who knows, a cucumber sandwich. Mrs Fox, wearing glasses and with a good deal of grey hair, did not exactly clutch me to her bosom. Her efforts to be kind did nothing to steady my nerves.

Most of the staff were present, including Matron, Miss Cryer, who had been at the school for many years and had once met Nanny when John was there. Nanny had generally given her the OK, and she made friendly noises at this some-what stilted gathering as she bustled around with tea and whatever while Grizel told me to be careful not to spill crumbs on the carpet. Mr Burrows, Mr Fox's second-in-command, was there, tall, stiffly formal, with a greyish moustache and a smile which resembled one of Carter's gin traps in repose. We were eventually to become quite good friends, but I would never have guessed it at our first meeting. Mr Tupholme,

'Tuppy' to one and all, was grinning cheerfully away and doing his best to bring a touch of jollity to the proceedings. Tuppy was an all-round good egg. Mr Sheepshanks, quite a bit younger, was also cheerful in a black-moustached, 'What-fun-it-will-all-be-oh-my-goodness-me' sort of way, and Miss Paterson put in a tight-lipped appearance just to make sure things did not get too jolly. Conversation, if it can be called that, hardly flowed. There were two or three other new boys there with their parents. I have forgotten their names although I think one was Laycock, but I well remember being introduced to one by Mrs Fox, who said in a formal voice, 'This is Blofeld.' I was grateful for Grizel's tuition.

Being the start of the summer term, there was not the influx of new boys that arrived in late September at the start of the school year. We were taken by Mrs Fox and Matron to see the lower dormitory. I was shown the bed in which I was going to sleep, and I think an under-matron may have flitted by. Grizel came with us, and kept telling me how much I would enjoy it once I got used to it. I wished I had shared her confidence. There must have been eight or ten beds, a wash stand and a bowl for each of us in a row at the foot of the beds, a po cupboard underneath, and a basket under the bed for the clothes I would take off before jumping into my pyjamas. The longer this introduction to my new quarters went on, the more I felt my enthusiasm draining. Then it was back along the passages, the walls of which were covered with school groups from prehistoric times. One new boy was shown a photograph and told, 'There's your father.' I hope it gave them both encouragement. It was not long after that that Tom and Grizel decided the time had come for them to leave. Tom certainly never specialised in emotional farewells, and Grizel did her best, giving me the briefest of pecks on the cheek, although she will have been alarmed by the thought that I might burst into tears. Then I watched, helpless, as they strode across the gravel to the car, got in, started the engine and disappeared from view. I was well and truly on my own, and I didn't like the look of it. I managed not to blub which would have been letting the side down.

I was the youngest boy in the school, and, funnily enough, found this to be a good deal more of a liability than I had expected. It seemed to bring in its wake a disdainful hostility rather than the sympathy I had hoped for. The lower dormitory passed off without too much worry, but I had problems a term or two later for as soon as I was promoted to the upper dormitory, I got on the wrong end of some nasty bullying. There was a monitor in each dormitory who slept in a bed by the door. He didn't come up until about two hours after the rest of us, which left scope for bullying. Next door to him was a little horror who I don't think I've seen since the day he left Sunningdale, although he probably went on to Eton – most of the boys did, but I don't remember him there. He forced me to do a number of things which went severely against the grain.

The worst was when I was made to go to the stairwell with my tortoiseshell-backed hairbrush, which had a piece of sticking plaster on it proclaiming 'Blofeld' in bold ink. Then, as the girl who carried the cocoa and the cups to the library for the older boys before they went to bed walked underneath, I was instructed to drop the hairbrush so that it landed on the tray, or better still, hit her on the head. Mercifully, I didn't get it right – if I had, it might have finished her off – and the brush fell with a sickening thud on the floor beside her. She was a good girl, because she didn't drop the tray or swerve or even scream, but carried steadfastly on. However, retribution was swift. I was in appalling trouble, and came head-to-head for the first time with Mr Burrows, who lived in a part study, part bedroom and part torture chamber in which there was a visible array of canes sticking out of a tall basket which he was never reluctant to use. And when he did, he put a good deal more vim into it than Mr Fox. For some strange reason, Mr Burrows did not tell me to bend over on this occasion. I have no idea what I said to him about the incident, but I didn't sneak, for that would have meant that my life in the upper dormitory and everywhere else would have been hell. Sneaking was the worst of crimes.

I am not sure why I got away with this early misdemeanour so lightly. It may have been that the powers-that-were had a fair idea of why the hairbrush incident had happened. Mr Burrows had an armour-plated exterior, but a streak of kindness underneath, even if, for the most part, he disguised it well. Anyway, if I was still able to recognise the chap who forced me to drop the hairbrush, I would even now be sorely tempted to step across the street and have a word with him. His name was Baring, and he was almost certainly one of the banking lot. I remember thinking all those years later what a splendid chap the wretched Nick Leeson must have been, and how miserably he was treated. He had no greater supporter than me. I mean, to be sent to a Singaporean gaol for performing such a notable public service . . .

I couldn't have enjoyed Sunningdale too much at the start of my five years there, because I was terribly homesick, and at the end of the holidays I had to be hauled off back to school. I howled outrageously in the car most of the way. But not everything was bad. I dipped my toes into the waters of cricket for the first time in my first term, and fell for it just like that. There were other good things too. The sausages we had for breakfast once a week – Wednesdays I think – were delicious, although the daily dose of porridge which preceded them was

29

more awful than anything I have ever eaten in my life. We were made to finish it, then or at lunch, and I have never eaten porridge since. Even the unspeakable mincemeat we were given for lunch on Fridays, which gloried in the splendid name of 'Friday Muck', was a couple of lengths better than the porridge and I have struck up a more meaningful relationship with the present-day equivalent of Friday Muck. The name was invented by my contemporary at the school Nicholas Howard-Stepney from the family which owned Horlicks. He was also responsible for Wednesday lunch's 'Pharaoh's Bricks', a cake pudding cut in Eastern European-like rectangular blocks with the merest *soupçon* of jam on the top, and 'Thames Mud', a terrifyingly solid chocolate blancmange which seemed both to wobble and frown at you. I suppose post-war food rationing hardly helped Mrs Fox when it came to creating the menu.

The cast at Sunningdale was nothing if not Wodehousian. Mr Fox, who went by the Christian names of George Dacre (PGW had a housemaster called Dacre in *Tales of St Austin's*), had signed up in 1906. Maybe there was something of the Reverend Aubrey Upjohn (Bertie Wooster's private-school headmaster) in Mr Fox, and I have no doubt that they would have hit it off like a couple of sailors on shore leave. By the time I met Mr Fox his face was inordinately lined, craggy and ancient, and would have made the Gutenberg Bible look to its laurels. To us, Mr Fox seemed older than God, and spoke in a slow, sepulchral tone that did nothing to make me think I was about to make a lifelong friend. He frightened me out of my socks, and beat me in the fourth-form classroom at the top of the stairs on the left whenever I kicked over the traces. A stern lecture would be followed by six relatively mild strokes, after which I would be told to leave. As many of the other boys as possible would have been standing outside the door to count the number of strokes. Six was the usual complement, but for something truly hideous, the count may have reached eight, making the recipient a sore-bottomed hero, but even to receive six did your street cred no harm. Mr Fox was known to us as 'Foe', and come to think of it, it was not a bad nickname, for I don't think I ever felt entirely convinced that he was on my side. He was five foot seven or eight, and his strong head of black hair was combed back and much adorned with Mr Thomas's finest unction. Mr Thomas was the school haircutter, and he came down from his HQ in Bury Street SW1 twice a term with two or three of his cohorts to cut our hair. Several masters had their hair cut too, including Foe, who was on Christian-name terms with the rotund, avuncular, noisy and highly genial Mr Thomas, who laughed a good deal as he snapped the scissors like the well-seasoned performer he was. I don't know why, but it went slightly against the grain that Mr Fox was on first-name terms with his barber. When the two of them laughed there was always something slightly conspiratorial in the air, as if they were planning a visit to a particularly shady club.

Mr Fox took the fourth form, and never encouraged jocularity, although there were times when I am sure he felt he was being the star of the party. But he always made teaching seem a solemn business, and was seldom fun and never funny. He had written a well-known green-covered history date book, which was not so much compulsive as compelled reading. It was all there, from Hengist and Horsa and Ethelred the Unready to the present day. Mr Fox was as proud of his date book as if he had made up the dates himself and given the history of this country both order and meaning. He did have another side to him – to keep themselves sane, a good many schoolmasters must lead double lives. The day the term finished at Sunningdale, the sofa in the Foxes' drawing room was pushed back, and out came the bridge tables, swiftly followed by the packs of cards and scoresheets, and then by those of his neighbours who participated. The stakes were said to be high; I imagine Foe was probably a gambler, but in a guarded rather than a reckless manner. I should think he was a pretty good player who seldom settled for three no trumps when a slam was in the air.

He was a great racing man too, and a number of important trainers sent their boys to Sunningdale. Cecil Boyd-Rochfort's twin stepsons, David and Henry Cecil, were naughty and great fun. Of course Henry went on to become a remarkable trainer in his own right, picking up a knighthood and Frankel along the way before dying horribly of cancer. Peter Cazalet, the Queen Mother's trainer, sent both his sons to Sunningdale. Edward, the elder, became a High Court judge, and as his mother, Leonora, had been PGW's stepdaughter, controls all things Wodehouse today with charm, skill and high good humour. Noel Cannon's son was also at the school. Royal Ascot week caused a good deal of activity on the private side, as Mr Fox's quarters were known. Lots of chaps were seen wandering about the place in morning coats and silk toppers, and ladies in extravagant hats were plentiful. I don't think a hat, however extravagant, would have made a significant difference to Mrs Fox, who may once have been a great beauty, but if she had been, by the time I met her she was playing from memory.

I don't know if Foe's gambling inclinations explored other avenues. I doubt that he was a casino man, unlike R.J.O. Meyer, the famous headmaster of Millfield, who when the day's duties were over would drive all the way from Somerset to a gaming club in Mayfair with a goodly portion of that term's school fees in his trouser pocket. Rumour has it that when he plonked it all on red, black almost invariably turned up. On the somewhat daunting return journey in the middle of the night

I dare say he would have found it difficult to stick to the speed limit.

To us boys there was no visible lighter side to dear old Foe, who said grace before lunch with a basso profundo solemnity and sang in chapel in a toneless voice somewhere around the baritone mark. He never made much of the high notes. His sermons always seemed to contain some less than compelling strictures; Mr Burrows was not a giggle a minute in the pulpit either and he made it all too plain what the devil had in store for us if we didn't look sharp. They both made you feel they were arm in arm with the wrath of God. Tuppy took the services in chapel, and wore a surplice as a jovial sort of holy disguise. Miss Paterson ('Patey'), who sang with a rigorous and tuneless vigour, sat two rows behind the Foxes, who were immediately behind us new boys. Mr Ling, whom we have not yet come across, and who more closely resembled a Chinese god than any Chinese god I have ever seen, did his best in the row in between. The more jolly Mrs Ling clocked in only on Sundays. They sang dutifully, while Mr Sheepshanks, 'Sheepy' to us all, played the organ and sang enthusiastically at the same time. Psalms were always harder work than the hymns, and I was glad when we had got the Magnificat and the Te Deum out of the way as well.

Mrs Fox went by the name of Nancy, which didn't really fit the bill – although Lucretia would have been a bit too severe. I can't remember Mr Fox ever looking dreamily at her and murmuring, 'Nancy.' Maybe he only did this in extremis. Anyway, she remorselessly called him 'Foxy', and they begat two sons, both Sunningdalians. By the time I came across George Dacre and Nancy, I suspect they were well past moments of high passion, and neither of them appeared particularly flighty. Mrs Fox looked a little bit like my idea of B. Wooster's Aunt Agatha, with more than a touch of Lady

Constance Keeble, Lord Emsworth's bloody-minded sister, thrown in. She gave out boiled sweets by the stairwell outside the dining room after lunch on Sundays, Tuesdays and Thursdays with gratuitous suspicion. Eight on Sundays, six on Thursdays, and a chocolate or Mars bar on Tuesdays. They were counted with great exactitude. If, on a recount, she discovered one sweet too many, it was a capital offence and you were lucky if she only took two away.

Mr Burrows was number two in the batting order after Mr Fox, and he didn't come across well. To a small boy he was alarming, and anyone could be forgiven for thinking at first that he was an all-round shit. I don't think he liked or felt comfortable with the smallest boys, and there was always a suspicion that he may have been a repressed homosexual. As far as Wodehouse was concerned, most of the time Burrows would have made Roderick Spode, alias Lord Sidcup, alias Oswald Mosley, seem a decent sort of cove. He was slim, reasonably tall and slightly bent. I think he probably had a sense of humour, but he was careful whom he showed it to. When I first came across him he was very much the Dickensian schoolmaster, but if, for whatever reason, you came into prolonged contact with him – as I did when I kept goal for the school and went on to become an unlikely captain of soccer – he was much easier. I then found a friendlier, more amenable side to him. Perhaps he was rather shy at heart, and it was only when he felt comfortable with certain boys that his outer shell fell away. I never knew what his football quali-fications were, but obviously he knew a bit about the game. Whenever we played against other schools he would be mildly unforgiving at half time as we surrounded him in a group, each sucking a quarter of a raw lemon in the hope that it might turn us into Stanley Matthews. Burrows was a serious supporter of Newcastle United, and if you mentioned Jackie

Milburn there was an outside chance that he might smile, and he would certainly look more favourably upon you. George Beaumont, a good friend of mine who was a member of the Allendale family, came from Northumberland, and was also passionate about Newcastle and Milburn, which meant that he and Mr Burrows became friends. He was a fine outside right, who ran fast and controlled the ball well. George was sadly killed in an aeroplane crash in New Zealand soon after leaving Eton.

Mr Burrows lived in a room, full of heavy dark-brown furniture, between the upper dormitory and the upper cubicles, from where he administered justice and discipline. He was a recognised and fully-paid-up beater, and a cane in his hands was much more a weapon of war than in Mr Fox's. His initials were JB – for John Berry, perhaps – and his nickname was 'Budgie'. I never remember any of his teaching colleagues slapping him on the back and calling him John, or Berry for that matter. When I joined the third form, over which he presided, I found him frighteningly unforgiving. If you were clever and were at the top of the form and gained his respect, he was a bit better. If it had not been for the soccer I would have got it in the neck.

I wonder if Mr Burrows was ever truly happy. But before we leave him, I should mention that when some of us had reached a certain age, he would allow us into his room by the upper dormitory at a quarter to seven in the evening to listen to *Dick Barton, Special Agent*. Agog, we followed the machinations of Barton, Snowy, Jock and the others as though our lives depended upon the breathtaking drama. Dick Barton was definitely not Mr Burrows' cup of tea, and he never stayed to listen. Later in life I wondered if Mr Burrows ever found an obliging woman. I doubt it. But then, did he ever want one? I imagine every private school in those days had its Mr Burrows.

Miss Paterson, or Patey, who came onto the books in 1940, was not quite polished enough to have been a contender for the Lady Constance Keeble spot, but she, like Mrs Fox, would have been a definite runner for aunt-like status. I think she and Aunt Agatha would have got along pretty well, although she had about her more than a hint of Rosa Klebb, who made James Bond's life pretty uncomfortable in *From Russia, with Love*. The debate about her Christian name continues. 'Emmeline' has its supporters, but 'Eileen' is probably just the favourite. They both fitted. She was spectacularly uncompromising, and did not tolerate nonsense in any way whatever. If she had a sense of humour, she wasn't letting on. She had the unfortunate habit of shaping her 'R's with a loop, as they appear on Harrods vans. This particularly distressed Nicholas Howard-Stepney who spoke contemptuously of 'Patey Rs'. Patey had a feminine enough shape, but with a keep-your-distance sort of face – and never to my knowledge did she have a single suitor. I think she would have discouraged passion in any form, and might not have been very good at it. She wore sensible shoes and even more sensible stockings, and spoke like a regimental sergeant-major. I can't imagine her in a warm, let alone a passionate embrace, although people who give that impression can sometimes come up against the wind. Patey was also, rather surprisingly, my first cricketing mentor. She was in charge of the third-form game, and was forever marshalling the troops. The game was played on a small piece of roughish ground somewhere between the raspberry cages and the railway line, which may give it a romantic connotation it does not deserve.

Miss Paterson must have been in her upper thirties, and there was a fair amount of her. She wobbled a good deal, both fore and aft. She loved to take part in the cricket, or at any rate she felt it was her duty to do so. I don't ever remember her batting, but she always opened the bowling. The pitch was only about fifteen yards long, if that, and while there were two sets of stumps, there were no bails. We had puny little bats, but there were no pads or gloves, and boxes were not even a gleam in anyone's eye. Patey ran in off about five paces, and bowled underarm with a certain nippiness. If she hit you on the shin, it made you yelp a bit, and she would launch herself into an extravagant, almost Shane Warne-like appeal. This was a little strange, because there was no umpire. That didn't worry her in the least, because she immediately metamorphosed herself into the umpire and gave you out. You certainly did not question her decision. She wasn't the worst bowler, and I can tell you that her swingers went both ways all right.

They were the first swingers I ever took a serious interest in. She had another interesting physical attribute: her front teeth were unstoppable. If you ran round a corner in a passage in the school and she was there, you would put your hands up in front of your face to protect yourself from the upper lot. I remember thinking some years later that if there was such an event at the Olympic Games as eating corn on the cob through a Venetian blind, Miss Paterson would have been on top of the rostrum accepting the gold medal and shaking up the champagne with the best of them.

As far as the runners and riders were concerned at Sunningdale, those were most of the bookies' favourites. But there was also a pretty good list just behind the leaders. Charlie Sheepshanks, 'Sheepy', who had clocked in from the Brigade of Guards soon after hostilities had been concluded in 1945 with a scar on his face which was evidence of close contact with the enemy, was a congenial, Bertie Wooster-like figure. His brother had been killed in the Spanish Civil War, and at Sunningdale Sheepy lived with his mother in a house in the grounds. He played the organ in chapel, or the tin tabernacle, as we knew it, and did so with a certain brio. Good-looking, black-moustached with a ready smile, a bit of a leg-spinner and greatly liked by us all, he shared Mr Fox's schoolroom where he presided over maths, genially, unpretentiously, amusingly and with indefatigable cheerfulness. He was the dearest of men, and went on to marry Mary Nickson, who was the daughter of my first housemaster at Eton. He also ran the cricket at Sunningdale, taking over from a Mr Kemp, who left soon after I arrived.

After Sheepy retired from educational activities, he and Mary moved to his family home in the village of Arthington in Wharfedale, where they would entertain the *Test Match Special* team to dinner in splendid style during the Headingley Test match. The banter between the Bishop of Ripon and Jim Swanton will not easily be forgotten. Jim regarded the bishop as an extremely close cohort of the Almighty, and tried to speak to him with a humble sanctity, while the bishop, who was only a suffragan, would leave religion at home for the evening. Sheepy was a passionate gardener and fisherman, and a great friend of Brian Johnston – they were both infectious laughers – with whom he fought innumerable battles on the tennis court. He was also a wizard on the Eton fives court. While at Sunningdale – of which he became headmaster for a time after Fox had retired – he joined forces with J.M. Peterson, an Eton housemaster whose sons were at Sunningdale, and together they won the old boys' Eton fives competition, the Kinnaird Cup, for year after year. For me, Charlie Sheepshanks was a real-life mixture of Biggles, Bulldog Drummond and Bertie Wooster.

Then there was Mr Tupholme, who came from Bournemouth or thereabouts, and was a long-standing taker of the fifth form. He was an excellent schoolmaster who made everything fun for the boys, while the more solemn members of the staff across the landing would have made the prophet Job seem a bit of a laugh. We listened to Tuppy because he had the knack of making everything fun, but interesting and important at the same time. He was in charge of rugger in the Lent term, bowled a bit in the nets during the summer, and presided genially over the swimming pool. Everyone loved him. Medium-height, plump, eternally cheerful, eyebrows that curled like Denis Healey's, he was never fierce, never shouted, and bought us Dinky Toys to order on his frequent visits to Windsor. As a boy, one always felt that Tuppy was up for anything, and we loved him. PGW would have turned him into Lord Ickenham. Another of Tuppy's sidelines was the model railway, which he organised in the Army Hut, a rather Spartan, military-looking building at the far end of the school where the school concert was held. In my first concert, which Tom and Grizel dutifully, and I suspect reluctantly, attended, I had to sing one verse of 'Cock Robin'. I doubt there has ever been a more tuneless rendering of any song since mankind first put its larynx on the stage.

I have briefly mentioned Mr Ling, who was the Venerable Bede of Sunningdale, and an awesome figure. Like Mr Fox and Mr Burrows, he had joined up with the school before the First War. He was a classical scholar, and was the principal reason why Sunningdale won so many scholarships, mainly for Eton, where most of its pupils ended up. Mr Ling was a genius as a schoolmaster. He took the sixth-form classics, and taught Greek and Latin with astonishing skill and amazing results. His most famous top scholar was Quintin Hogg, who went on to become Lord Hailsham and the Lord Chancellor, and who paid Mr Ling a most generous tribute in his autobiography, *The Door Wherein I Went*. When I first came across Mr Ling I thought he was even older than Methuselah. He was gruff, quietly and classically humorous, and his gleaming and absolute baldness positively oozed Greek and Latin verse and always looked as if he was made of jade. He was wisdom personified, and wore his rimless glasses in a way that suggested they were an essential adjunct to classical scholarship. He was also a passionate man of Suffolk. This gave us both a certain East Anglian affinity – I did not have the smallest affinity with the classics – even if he regarded Norfolk as the lesser of two equals. Lord Emsworth might have had dinner with him by mistake at the Senior Conservative Club in St James's.

Mr Ling always came hurriedly into the classroom as if he had just bumped into Socrates on the stairs and, with time running short, had had quickly to put him right about a couple of things. Having virtually lost the use of his right hand by kind permission of the Kaiser in the First War, he wrote on the blackboard and elsewhere with his left hand, and in doing so was magnificently illegible. You needed to have been on the payroll at Bletchley Park to have had the slightest chance of interpreting his offerings. He did not suffer fools gladly, and as I remember he found it jolly nearly incomprehensible that anyone could be as stupid and as unreceptive to the classics as I was. He had a good sense of humour, a pleasant chuckle, and bowled gentle slow left-arm in the nets when it came to the summer term. I don't think he ever looked much like getting anyone out, but that did not prevent him from having firm views on the forward defensive stroke.

Just occasionally I was asked to tea with Mr and Mrs Ling at their house in nearby Charters Road. Mrs Ling, who was kind in a charming, elderly way, provided more than acceptable strawberry jam and a tolerable scone or two and always loved to pull her husband's leg. Mr Ling, because of his injured hand, was not as accurate with the teapot as he had been in his heyday, and Mrs Ling was more than prepared to give him a bit of stick for this. He would laugh at his failing, and was always more fun outside the classroom than in it. He was a remarkable man, a brilliant teacher and a friend in a slightly distant, but loyal way, even if academically you were batting well down the order.

Bob (R.G.T.) Spear was young, tall and fair-haired, and taught goodness knows what for a time. He had an electrifying affair with the under-matron, Kitty Dean, whom he married. I once caught her sitting on his knee in the tiny masters' room between Mr Fox's and Mr Ling's schoolrooms, which was as near as one came in those days to hard porn. The marriage did not last, and he eked out his days as a rather penniless handicapper at Newmarket, where he died. I once or twice came across him in the Tavern at Lord's during a Test match. A long time before, he had bowled fast for Eton: Bingo Little, perhaps, although he never met his Rosie M. Banks.

There was the altogether more garrulous and clubbable Eustace Crawley, son of the immortal golfing correspondent Leonard Crawley, who wrote for the *Daily Telegraph* for many years. Leonard had also been a master at Sunningdale in the twenties, and in 1925 he was picked to tour the West Indies with the MCC. He was always greatly encouraged with his golf by Mr Fox, who was captain of Sunningdale Golf Club in 1940. This was the reason why in the winter whenever it was shut we were allowed to play French and English on the course.

Eustace must have taught something, but in those days he seemed to be Gussie Fink-Nottle to his eyebrows, and was immense fun without appearing to be devastatingly effective. This was a completely false impression, for he not only won a golf Blue at Cambridge for three years, but ended up as managing director of Jacksons of Piccadilly – Gussie F would have had no answer to that. I remember lots of floppy dark hair and a most engaging chuckle.

There was also the ever genial, tall and robust Mr Squarey, who was poached from neighbouring Lambrook. He was fun, with grey hair and glasses, and was up for everything when it came to games. He also bowled a bit in the nets, without devastating effect, but he was full of good honest cricketing theory, and always gave terrific encouragement. He was a friend.

Finally there was Matron Cryer, a veritable, and adorable, Florence Nightingale who never failed to make you feel better, and could even persuade you that the weekly dose of cod-liver oil tasted pretty good. I personally went for syrup of figs, which was a legitimate alternative and tasted much nicer. Her deputy, who later reigned for years as her successor as matron, was the indomitable Pauline, who was to become every bit as much an intrinsic part of Sunningdale as Mr Fox or any of the others. I suspect she enjoyed a bit of mischief too, and she and Roberta Wickham would have hit it off. Pauline was a great character, and before I left Sunningdale she gave me a photograph of the England side to tour Australia in 1928–29.

I may have missed one or two, but what fun it was. I lived in this milieu for five years, climbing my way up the pole under the auspices of the above-mentioned dramatis personae. I played in the cricket first eleven for four years – having moved fairly rapidly from being a leg-spinner to a wicketkeeper, and I think I could always bat a bit – and in the soccer team for two. I also played fives for the school, against Ludgrove, and we invariably lost. The only real blot was my consistent slacking on the academic side of things.

My years in the Sunningdale first eleven were fantastic fun. The star of the side was Edward Lane Fox and we not only played together in the first eleven for four years at Sunningdale, we also both played for Eton for three years. He was a wonderful all-round cricketer with the discipline I always lacked. Edward also won his colours at soccer and rugger, an impressive triple Blue. He was a remarkable games player, a cricketer who went on to play for Oxfordshire and for the Minor Counties against at least two touring sides and then became an estate agent, running his own eponymous firm with a brilliance few could have matched. He also hits a pretty mean golf ball. It would be hard to imagine a kinder, more charming and less pretentious man. He has never changed in character or in looks, and well into his seventies he is still easily identifiable as the chap sitting in the captain's seat in the 1952 Sunningdale cricket eleven photograph. Edward was a wonderful orthodox left-arm spinner who bowled with great accuracy and turned the ball sharply away from the right-hander. The representatives of Earlywood, Scaitcliffe, St George's, Lambrook, Heatherdown and a few other schools could make little of it. As a result, stumped Blofeld bowled Lane Fox was an oft-repeated dismissal.

Edward was also an excellent and solid left-hand batsman. The one school we had difficulty with was Ludgrove, who collectively played left-arm spin more than adequately. I think I am right in saying that the last time Sunningdale beat Ludgrove home and away in the same season was in 1952, which was Edward's and my last year. Sunningdale may have started a trifle gloomily for me, but success on the playing fields turned it into huge fun, and rapidly put an end to all that silly homesickness.

I was given my first-eleven colours for cricket when the team photograph was about to be taken at the end of the 1950 summer term, my second year in the side. Later that afternoon I was ferried off by Mrs Fox to St George's hospital in Windsor to have my tonsils removed. I remember Matron packing my new dark-blue cap, and when Mrs Fox unpacked my case at the hospital she thrust this cap under my pillow. When you got your colours this was the accepted modus operandi. The nursing sister was more than mildly surprised, but Mrs Fox pretty well told her to mind her own business. I never felt closer to her than I did at that moment, and I was able, with considerable pleasure, to try on the cap during the night. I had to wait until the chap with whom I shared a room, who probably wouldn't have understood, was asleep.

What an adventure Sunningdale was and a splendid way to start learning about the highs and lows of life. In the schoolroom I was never remotely a candidate for a scholarship to anywhere except Borstal, but I suppose I did just about enough work to get by, and when I came to take Common Entrance to Eton, I achieved a humble middle fourth, which was lower than was hoped, but probably higher than was feared. I was never any good at exams. That rather apprehensive five-hour journey in my father's old green Armstrong Siddeley at the start of May five years before had been well worth it. In the end Grizel had got it right, as she usually did.

THREE

The French Women's Institute

Cricket had me in its grip before I had been at Sunningdale for a year. The following June, in 1948, I found myself at Lord's with Tom and Grizel sitting on the grass in front of Q Stand eating strawberries they had brought up from Hoveton and watching the third day of the second Test against Australia. I became one of what is now a sadly diminishing band of people to have seen the great Don Bradman bat. He made 89 in Australia's second innings before being caught at shoulder-height by Bill Edrich at first slip off Alec Bedser. I can still see the catch in my mind's eye. As he departed, dwarfed by that wonderful and irresistible baggy green Australian cap, I was sad that he hadn't got a hundred, but everyone else seemed rather pleased. I distinctly remember him facing Yorkshire's Alec Coxon, a fast bowler playing in his only Test match. A number of times Coxon pitched the ball a little short, and Bradman would swivel and pull him to the straightish midwicket boundary, where we were sitting on the grass. Once I was able to touch the ball – what a moment that was.

It was not only at school that I revelled in cricket. In the Easter holidays I went to indoor coaching classes in Norwich taken by the two professionals who played for Norfolk : C.S.R. Boswell, a leg-spinner and late-middle-order batsman known to one and all as 'Bozzie', and Fred Pierpoint, a fastish bowler.

Then, in the summer holidays, Grizel would heroically drive me to all parts of Norfolk, however inaccessible, for boys' cricket matches in which I became a fierce competitor. We would set off in the morning in Grizel's beetle Renault, with a picnic basket on the back seat. Grizel was nothing if not a determined driver. Whenever she changed gear it was as if she was teaching the gearstick a lesson, and she generally treated the car as if it was a recalcitrant schoolboy. Some of the lay-bys in which we stopped for lunch became familiar haunts over the years. A hard-boiled egg, ham sandwiches and an apple were the usual menu, and it never helped things along if I dropped small bits of eggshell on the floor.

The cricket usually began at about two o'clock, and I remember many of the mums being, if anything, rather more competitive than the players. There were certain key players in the teams I played for: Jeremy Greenwood bowled very fast, Michael Broke's off-breaks took a long time to reach the batsman, Jeremy Thompson – whose father Wilfred had bowled terrifyingly fast for Norfolk and had captained the county – was another star, while Timmy Denny did his best. Henry and Dominic Harrod, sons of the famous economist Roy Harrod, had their moments, and the many Scotts all played their part, especially Edward, who bowled fast – we later played cricket together at Eton. He was a cousin of the Norfolk Scotts, although he lived in Gloucestershire, and was to become one of my greatest friends. The two Clifton Browns also contributed, and their mother scored like a demon in a felt hat.

The Norfolk Scotts lived at North Runcton, near King's Lynn. Father Archie, as tall and thin as a lamp post, was the first Old Etonian bookmaker, and his delightful and cuddly wife Ruth was a huge favourite with all of us, forever laughing and always a fount of fun. She was also great friends with the Australian cricketers of Don Bradman's generation and before.

A particular ally was the famous leg-spinner Arthur Mailey, a great character and the most delightful of men. He had been a wonderful bowler, as well as being a brilliant cartoonist. For some reason he took a great interest in my future as a cricketer, and one of my proudest possessions is a booklet he wrote in 1956 called *Cricket Humour*, with some amusing stories illustrated with his own drawings. The front cover is a lovely cartoon of Mailey himself trying to bribe the umpire with a fiver. On the first page he wrote: 'My best wishes for a successful cricket life. Saw you play at Runcton about 3 years ago and am very pleased about your progress. Arthur Mailey '56.' Later in life I put together a small collection of his original cartoons, and they are a great joy.

In between those holiday matches I would go to Lakenham cricket ground, with its handsome thatched pavilion, where Norfolk played their home games. Now I would be ticked off for spilling my picnic eggshells on the grass in one of the little wigwam-like tents which lined one side of the ground. One of them had a sign hanging on the outside which proclaimed that it belonged to T.R.C. Blofeld. Inside was a small table and some rickety deckchairs. Those days at Lakenham gave me an early glimpse of what I think I supposed heaven was all about. Norfolk never won very much, but my goodness me, it was exciting.

I always brought along my own puny bat and a ball, and sometimes I was able to persuade someone to bowl at me on the grass behind the parked cars at the back of the tents. Among them was the vermillion-faced Mr Tarr, who was the Governor of Norwich Prison and, I hope, a better governor than he was a bowler. Every so often, as I was sitting in a deckchair watching the cricket, a four would be hit in my direction and I would stop it and throw it back to the fielder. Not quite the same as fielding to Bradman, I know, but you took what came. Just occasionally there was the thrill of a six being hit towards our tent, forcing everyone to take cover in a mildly cowardly panic. My early heroes from these occasions were an eclectic bunch, including the afore-mentioned Wilfred Thompson; David Carter, military-medium; and Cedric Thistleton-Smith, who was always out unluckily – all three of whom came from west Norfolk and were thriving farmers. Lawrie Barrett, short and dark-haired, a tiger in the covers, thrilled us all a couple of times a year as a middle-order batsman and succeeded Thompson as captain. H.E. Theobald was a large man who, like his Christian name (it turned out to be Harold), remained a bit of a mystery. He was not in the first flush of youth, and nor was his batting. Then there was good old, eternally cheerful, round-faced Bozzie; we loved his spritely cunning with the ball and his enthusiastic twirl of the bat when his turn came late in the innings. He had a kind word and a smile for everyone.

Village cricket also played a big part in my life. The heroes for Hoveton and Wroxham did battle on the ground set up by those German prisoners-of-war. I had some fierce battles with Nanny, who refused to let me go and watch them when they were at work. I was determined to wear the German policeman's helmet I had been given by some returning warrior. She felt it would not have created the right impression, and unusually for her, had a word about it with Grizel – who of course agreed wholeheartedly. So my one intended thrust for the Allies was nipped in the bud.

Hoveton was captained by the ever-thoughtful opening batsman Neville Yallop, whose black hair was swept back with the help of Brylcreem. There was Fred Roy, of the huge epony-mous village store, who opened the batting with Neville and bowled slow, non-turning off-breaks; Arthur Tink, whose military-medium was full of unsuspected guile – as I dare say was his gypsy-like wife, Mona, who looked incredibly beautiful and never said anything. The vibrantly moustached, ample-figured Colonel Ingram-Johnson kept wicket and batted in an Incogniti cap. He had Indian Army and Rawalpindi coming out of every aperture. Colin Parker, a local boy who bowled at a nippy medium pace, had an attractive, befreckled red-haired sister and a father who umpired in partnership, I am sure, with the ubiquitous gamekeeping Carter. Bob Cork, a small man who I think was a blacksmith, ran around with terrific enthusiasm, but not a great deal of effect. When I was about thirteen and had been allowed to join in a fielding practice, I tried to take a high catch and the ball dislocated my right thumb. Bob was quickly to the rescue, and agonisingly yanked the wretched joint back into place.

I lived for cricket, in boys' matches, on our ground at home, and at Lakenham, and spent many of my waking hours in the summer holidays at one or other of the three. Added to which, and to Nanny's mild disapproval, I took my bat to bed with me. That, of course, was in the days when bats smelled redolently of linseed oil. I am not sure I have ever found a better smell to go to sleep with.

In the winter holidays the gamekeepers and shooting took over from cricket, and I have to confess I also took my gun to bed with me. I spent as much time as I could with Carter, Watker or Godfrey learning about trapping vermin, feeding pheasants and partridges, and looking for their nests in the Easter holidays. If a nest was in an especially vulnerable position we would pick up the eggs, which would then be hatched by a broody hen, and the chicks brought up in pens until they were ready to be put back into the wild. Carrion crows, sparrowhawks, jays, magpies, stoats, rabbits and rats all had to be eliminated where possible, and kept in proportion if not. I learned many of the tricks of the trade. What fun it was, and I was unable to put down a book my father gave me called Peter Penniless, which was about the adventures of a country boy who scraped a living by poaching and selling the fruits of his labours. Poaching was something that went on a good deal, and as I was later to learn, was perpetrated not only by the unscrupulous from neighbouring villages and Norwich, but by some, like Lennie Hubbard, as we have seen, who worked, above all suspicion, on the farm. Sometimes the ungodly would be caught and brought to justice, but more often than not they got away with it. It was all part of the excitement of growing up among the Norfolk Broads. There were poachers on the Broads too, who tried to shoot duck and to catch fish and eels. Johnson was the head marshman, and another heroic figure. One of his sons was in the RAF in the war, and once came back on leave bringing with him the first banana I had ever seen, let alone tasted. It was black and well on the way to being rotten, and tasted filthy – not that I was about to admit it.

It was from this background that I once again jumped into the back of my father's car, which had moved up a peg or two from the Armstrong Siddeley that had first taken me to Sunningdale. It was in the old 1932 Rolls that we made the journey from Hoveton to Eton on 23 September 1952 – which was not exactly the way I wanted to spend my thirteenth birthday. It was another anxious trip. I had long looked forward to going to Eton, but now that the day had arrived, I was more than a touch nervous. Twelve hundred boys, tail-coats, strange white bow ties which had to be tied with the help of a paperclip, my own room, a house of forty boys, a completely new set of rules and regulations to learn. I would have a much greater degree of freedom than I had experienced at Sunningdale, where obviously the young boys had to be kept under close and watchful guidance. Eton was a huge step nearer to the big wide world, and was both frightening and exciting because of it. 'There will be plenty of other new boys,' Grizel had said to me in a voice which suggested that that put the argument to bed once and for all.

After a journey of about four hours, not particularly helped by Grizel trying to jolly me along in between spirited bouts of backseat driving, we all trooped in through the front door of Common Lane House and shook hands with M'Tutor and Mrs M'Tutor, as they were known in the Eton vernacular, Geoffrey and Janet Nickson. Geoffrey Nickson was bald and quite small, with a beaming smile, a warm handshake, twinkling eyes and a chuckling laugh, all of which made that first frightening step so much easier than it had been at Sunningdale. He could have taught Mr Fox a thing or two, but then I was five years older, and better able to cope.

As I sat on the ottoman in my own room at Eton, with its lift-up bed hidden behind curtains, my own friendly shooting prints on the wall – I still have them today in my bedroom – and a few family photographs, I was acutely conscious that I was now on my own, in a much more grown-up society. It was a help to know that my brother John had been through it before me, in the same house, and had survived. All the new boys were in the same boat, but at that moment it was a personal, not a communal thing. When we arrived we were all tremulous little islands in a rough sea. I had had many lessons at home on how to put on a stiff collar, how to use collar studs and how to tie that alarming white bow tie – alarming until you had done it once, after which it was simple, as many apparently difficult things turn out to be. There was an official form of 'cheating', in that the white strip of the tie had a hole in the middle, through which you put the collar stud between the two ends of the stiff collar. One end of the tie was then held sideways across the collar, while the other was tucked over the top by your Adam's apple, and then thrust down inside the shirt, where it was held in position by the paperclip. This was the 'cheating' bit. The two ends were then pushed under each side of the collar – simple really – then it was nervously down to breakfast, my first outing in my tailcoat. I had well and truly begun my first half at Eton.

We new boys sat at a small table in the corner at one end of the boys' dining room, which had the somewhat mixed benefit of being presided over by 'My Dame' (M'Dame), who was a sort of high-falutin' house matron. She was called Miss Pearson, and while I must say I never found her particularly loveable, it was a less aggressive sort of unloveableness than Miss Paterson's. I suppose M'Dame had to be bossy, but she made rather a business of it. When I came down, extremely frightened, to that first breakfast I found myself being stared at by those who were not new boys in a 'Look what the cat's brought in' sort of way.

I was lucky with my housemaster, M'Tutor. Geoffrey Nickson had all the qualities of a perfect schoolmaster. He was kind; he was thoughtful; he was never in a hurry; he never panicked; he never shouted; he was unfailingly interested in everything you did; he suggested, firmly at times, rather than ordered; he had a splendid sense of humour; and he punished firmly and without relish or enjoyment. At Eton, like all masters, he was known by his initials, 'GWN'. The 'W' stood for Wigley, which was harmless enough, but gave rise to a certain amount of childish amusement. GWN was a classical scholar. He was not an Etonian himself, but you would never have guessed it. I arrived at Eton near the end of his fifteen-year spell as a housemaster, which finished at the end of the summer half in 1955. I don't think it would have been possible not to love GWN. He was always immensely approachable – a schoolmaster, and yet very much not a schoolmaster. He had a wonderfully ready, infectious and enthusiastic smile. He was always fun, whether you were a member of the library, the elite five at the top of the house, who sat at his end of the long dining-room table, or a lower boy, as we all were for at least three halves, whom he took for pupil room, known colloquially as 'P-hole', at the end of formal lessons each morning in the mildly improvised classroom outside his study. He was equally enthusiastic whether bowling his leg-tweakers in the nets or watching members of his house in whatever sporting contest they were competing in against other houses. A perfect illustration of GWN's skill as a schoolmaster came when he caught four of my friends playing bridge – cards were strictly illegal. He made them all write a Georgic which entailed copying out more than five hundred lines of Latin verse. He then asked them down to his study every Sunday afternoon to teach them to become better bridge players.

On Sundays, Mrs M'Tutor, Janet Nickson, who was the perfect complement to GWN, would read to the lower boys in her husband's study, and we had to suffer such improving literature as *Lorna Doone* in her slightly schoolmistressy voice. When we became upper boys, GWN himself read to us in pupil room. We listened spellbound to, among others, Hemingway's *The Old Man and the Sea* and J.K. Stanford's *The Twelfth*, about Colonel the Honourable George Hysteron-Proteron's exploits on a grouse moor on 12 August, the opening day of the season. GWN himself was no mean shot, and a considerable fisherman.

One of the first exams a new boy had to go through at Eton was a 'Colour Test'. There were goodness knows how many different caps, or colours, as they were known, given exclusively for prowess in sporting pursuits ranging from cricket to rowing to the field game, the wall game, fives, racquets, squash, beagling, athletics, gymnastics, tennis, soccer, rugby and many others besides. About three weeks into my first half new boys gathered in the library – in non-Eton talk, the house prefects' room – where they were asked many searching questions. A profusion of different-coloured caps were produced, and we had to identify them. We had to show that we knew the masters by their initials, that we understood the geography of the place and other Etonian lore, not least the idiosyncratic language which was peculiar to the school. The geography was extremely important, as once the Colour Test had been passed, we lower boys began our fagging career. If you were told by a member of the library to take a fag note (a written message) to a boy in, say, DJGC or FJRC, it was as well to know where you had to go. When a member of the library needed a fag, he would make a 'boy call', his yell of 'B-o-o-o-o-oy' going on for twenty seconds or so. The last lower boy to arrive got the job. Having taken middle fourth in my Common Entrance, it was my lot to be a fag for five halves.

I enjoyed my five years at Eton as much as any period of my life. As I had discovered at Sunningdale, having the luck to be reasonably successful at games was a great help. Good schoolboy games players become little tin gods, a status which provides a certain insulation against the petty struggles of school life. Of course, this doesn't happen at once. I spent my first half trying to unravel the mysteries of the field game, an Eton-devised mixture of rugger and soccer played with a round ball. There is a sort of mini scrum, known as the 'bully', and much long and skilful kicking up and down the field by the three backs, one behind the other called 'short', 'long' and 'goals'. I played at 'outside corner', on the edge of the bully, a sort of wing forward. I was never any good at the game, and didn't enjoy it much. The umpire only blew for infringements if the players appealed. 'Cornering', which meant passing, and 'sneaking', being offside, were the two most common offences, although the most enjoyable, for obvious reasons, was 'furking in the bully', which was lightly, delicately and tellingly adapted on almost every occasion. This was for what was known in less esoteric circumstances as back-heeling, as would happen in a rugger scrum. The wall game was another complicated and esoteric Eton institution. Like many Oppidans (non-Collegers), I never played it, and I still have no clue about the rules. It is best known for the annual mudbath that takes place between the Tugs (Collegers) and the Oppidans on St Andrew's Day alongside a high and extremely old brick wall in College Field, by the road to Slough.

I had a terrific time in my first half, being 'up to' Mr Tait for classics. He was known as 'Gad' Tait, for the obvious reason that his initials were GAD. Most of the beaks' (masters') nicknames were pretty unoriginal. Dear old Gad Tait was a very tall man who when he rode a bicycle wobbled so perilously and entertainingly that it was like a balancing act in a circus. He had a genius for making the learning of Latin seem interesting, entertaining and good fun, when it was palpably none of those things. By then, of course, we were well past the 'Caesar conquered Gaul' stage, which had seen Miss Paterson rise to fevered levels of ferocity in the second form at Sunningdale. At Eton we were very much free-range pupils, by comparison to what we had been at our preparatory schools. Now a good deal of our work had to be done in our spare time.

Once a week we had to construe a piece of Latin prose written by some Godawful Roman no-hoper such as Livy or Cicero. At early school, which began at 7.30 a.m. after a hasty cup of tea in the Boys' Entrance, Gad Tait, who called everyone 'Old You', would charmingly put us through our paces about whatever piece of Latin he had chosen. With equal charm he would exact retribution upon those who not done an adequate job. Also once a week, we had to learn a 'saying lesson', which involved him dictating a piece of verse which we wrote down in a flimsy blue notebook – I still have mine. It says much for Gad Tait that even today I remember most of his saying lessons. The principal one was Tennyson's 'Ulysses', which we learned in three successive weeks. Others included part of A.E. Housman's *A Shropshire Lad* and Cory's 'Heraclitus'.

There were about thirty of us in his 'div' (division), and we had to recite whatever piece of verse we had been given to learn in groups of ten. Gad Tait watched closely but effortlessly, and although ten people were speaking at once, he could tell exactly who had not learned the words properly, and distributed penalties accordingly. When, just occasionally, I had written a particularly successful piece of Latin verse or whatever, he would give me a 'show-up'. This meant that he wrote nice things at the top of my work, which I would then take to pupil room, where GWN would gratefully and happily endorse it with his initials. These were useful brownie points. Whenever Gad Tait gave anyone in M'Tutor's a show-up, GWN, who was a more than useful cartoonist, would almost inevitably draw a picture of an old ewe on the paper. When it was handed back the next day, Gad Tait always had a chuckle at this. I can't remember any of the other beaks I was 'up to' in my first half, which is a measure of Gad Tait's skill as a schoolmaster.

Soccer and fives were the two games which occupied me in my second half, the Lent half, and then it was the summer, and cricket, which I had been longing for. I spent my first two cricketing halves in Lower Sixpenny, which was for the under fifteen-year-olds, and immediately made my greatest cricketing friend at Eton. Claude Taylor (CHT) had won a cricket Blue at Oxford, for whom he had made almost the slowest-ever hundred in the University Match, and had gone on to play for Leicestershire. He was the dearest and gentlest of men, and a wonderful coach who loved the beauty of the game more than anything. Grey-haired by the time I knew him, he had the knack of being able to explain cricket, which is not an easy game, in the most uncomplicated manner. He understood the mechanics of batting so well that he was able to dissect a stroke into a series of simple movements that when put together cohesively made not only a hugely effective stroke, in attack or defence, but a thing of beauty. He loved, above all, the beauty of the game. He taught Latin, although I never had the luck to be up to him. He also played and taught the oboe, and married the sister of Ian Peebles, a delightful Scotsman who bowled leg-breaks for Oxford, Middlesex and England. Peebles was a considerable force in a City of London wine merchants, and wrote charmingly, knowledgeably and extremely amusingly about cricket for the *Sunday Times*. Before the war Peebles had shared a flat in the Temple with Henry Longhurst and Jim Swanton, whom he relentlessly called 'James'. It was a most distinguished gathering.

We began my first summer half with new-boy nets, and it was then that I caught CHT's eye for the first time. I immediately found myself playing in 'Select A', the top game in Lower Sixpenny, of which he was the master-in-charge. I had a fierce competitor for the position of wicketkeeper called Julian Curtis, a wonderful all-round games player who probably lost out to me because I just had the edge in the batting stakes. In that first year, 1953, the Keeper (captain) of Lower Sixpenny was Simon Douglas Pennant, with whom I went on to play for the school and later for Cambridge, who bowled left-arm over-the-wicket at fast-medium. Edward Lane Fox was also in the side, but now that we were playing against opponents that were better-versed in the art of playing left-arm spin, 'stumped Blofeld bowled Lane Fox' became a less frequent entry in the scorebook. It was a memorable first summer half.

My cricketing activities went on much to the detriment of my work, and I must admit that, as at Sunningdale, my greatest ambition in the learning department was simply to get by. This attitude never received Tom's blessing when my school reports, which were always of the 'must try harder' variety, were up for discussion. But as far as I was concerned, it was only cricket that mattered. If it was not Lower Sixpenny matches against other schools, it was Select A games, nets or fielding practice, and I am afraid I was the most intense competitor. The school professional at the time was Jack O'Connor, the dearest of men, who batted a time or two for England in the thirties, and played for many years for Essex. He ran the Bat Shop, just at the start of the High Street, next door to Rowland's, one of the two 'sock' shops, where we guzzled crab buns and banana splits. Jack sold sporting goods, and whenever any of us went in he would give us a smiling and enthusiastic welcome. He was to become a great friend and cricketing confidant. Buying batting gloves, wicketkeeping inners or whatever from his modest emporium always involved a jolly ten-minute gossip. Once or twice CHT brought him to the Lower Sixpenny nets to watch some of us batting. Jack always gave generous, smiling encouragement. Once when I was batting he turned his arm over; so began a lifetime of misery and mystification for me as far as leg-spin and googly bowling are concerned. I still have nightmares of an umpire signalling four byes.

The winter halves were, for me, little more than an inconveniently large gap between cricket seasons. There was nothing so gloomy as going back to school towards the end of September, when the weather was gorgeous but all, or most, of the cricket grounds were strung about with goalposts. What made it even more depressing was that my return was often just a couple of days or so before my birthday. Various wrapped presents were always tucked away in the bottom of my suitcase, but opening them alone in my room between breakfast and going to chapel was a cold-blooded exercise if ever there was one. They did, however, usually contain a couple of cricket books, which helped.

In the Lent half I tried my best to impress those who mattered with my ability on the fives court and between the goalposts on the soccer pitch, but I never quite made it on either count. Soccer was run by a wonderfully bucolic former Cambridge cricket Blue called Tolly Burnett (ACB), a relation of the novelist Ivy Compton-Burnett, who added greatly to the gaiety of nations in just about everything he did. He was large, if not portly, marvellously unpunctual, rode a bicycle as if he was, with much pomp and circumstance, leading a procession of one, or perhaps rehearsing for a part in *Dad's Army*, and walked with an avuncular swagger. I am not sure what Captain Mainwaring would have made of Tolly. He drove an exciting sports car, and took biology with considerable gusto, especially when it came to the more pertinent points of reproduction, in a div room just around the corner from Lower Chapel. If you stopped him in the street to ask a question, he would clatter to an uncertain halt and invariably say in somewhat breathless tones, 'Just a bit pushed, old boy. Just a bit pushed,' then off he'd go with a bit of a puff. What fun he was, and how we loved him. I am not sure the authorities at the school entirely agreed with us, for although he was, I believe, down to become a housemaster, the position never materialised.

Tolly captained Glamorgan during the summer holidays in 1958. The Glamorgan committee felt, as they did from time

59

to time, that Wilf Wooller, the patriarchal figure of Welsh cricket, was too old and should be replaced. In their infinite wisdom they brought in Tolly for a trial as captain for the last eight games of the season. His highest score was 17, and the dressing room came as close to mutiny as it gets. In September he was back teaching biology at Eton, and Wooller was still the official Glamorgan captain. By the time Tolly's moment of possible glory came, his girth would have prevented much mobility in the field, his batting was well past its prime, and his 'Just a bit pushed, old boy' might not have been exactly what the doctor ordered in a Glamorgan dressing room which was pure-bred Wales to its eyebrows. His charmingly irrelevant 'Up boys and at 'em' enthusiasm must have fallen on deaf ears. Tolly was more Falstaff than Flewellyn.

Back at Eton, before that little episode, he sadly, but entirely correctly, preferred Carrick-Buchanan's agility between the goalposts to my own. I did however achieve the splendid job of Keeper (captain) of the second eleven. Tolly was also the cricket master in charge of Lower Club, and sadly I never had first-hand experience of the way in which he coped with that. It would not have been boring.

Keeper of the soccer second eleven, or 'Team B', as we proudly called ourselves, was not a particularly distinguished post, but it led to my first sortie into the world of journalism, which turned out to be an unmitigated disaster. We had a considerable fixture list, which included a game against Bradfield College's second eleven at Bradfield. The *Eton College Chronicle* felt compelled to carry an account of even such insignificant encounters as this, and for some reason I was chosen to write the report. We were taken by bus to Bradfield, where we joined a mass of boys for a lunch which it would have been tempting to let go past the off-stump. Then we changed into our soccer stuff, climbed a steepish hill and found a well-used and pretty muddy football pitch. I enjoyed writing my account of the day's events, and it duly appeared in the columns of the *Chronicle*. Unfortunately, it elicited a hostile response from Bradfield, who made a complaint which promptly came to the ears of Robert Birley, Eton's large and formidable-looking, but in fact kind, rather shy and immensely able, headmaster. He was to us a remote, Genghis-Khan-like figure who hovered somewhat ominously in the background. Birley was known, unfairly in my view, as 'Red Robert'. This merely meant that he had realised somewhat earlier than most of the school's supporters the urgent need for change if a school like Eton was to survive. Many reactionary hands were thrown up in horror.

Anyway, one morning I found myself 'on the Bill', which meant that I was summoned to the headmaster's schoolroom at midday. When I arrived, more than a trifle worried, I was told in no uncertain terms that what I had written about Team B's midwinter visit to Bradfield was extremely offensive, and that I must without delay write a number of letters of apology. Apart from a general dressing down, I don't think any other penalty was exacted. I still have a copy of this most undistinguished entry into the world I was to inhabit for just about the rest of my life. I have to admit that in the circumstances it may have been a little strong in places, although it is positively mild when judged by today's standards..

The Michaelmas half in 1954 will always remain firmly in my mind, and for cricketing reasons too. England were touring Australia in the hope of hanging on to the Ashes they had won in a nerve-racking game at The Oval the previous year. There were one or two exciting newcomers in the England party, especially a fast bowler called Frank Tyson and a twenty-one-year-old called Colin Cowdrey, who was still up at Oxford. I found the whole series quite irresistible, and would tune in to the commentary from Australia under my bedclothes from about five o'clock in the morning. This was always a bit of a lottery, as the snap, crackle and pop of the atmospherics made listening a difficult business. Sometimes the line would go down altogether, and the commentary would be replaced by music from the studio in London. Those delicious Australian voices of the commentators, Johnny Moyes, Alan McGilvray and Vic Richardson, added hugely to the excitement, and John Arlott was there to add a touch of Hampshire-sounding Englishness.

First came the intense gloom at the end of November, when Len Hutton put Australia in to bat in the first Test in Brisbane, and England lost by an innings and 154 runs. Every afternoon I would rush to the corner of Keates Lane and the High Street, where the old man who sold the *Evening Standard* took up his post. I would thrust a few coppers at him, grab the paper, and turn feverishly to the back page. I had devoured what was for me the peerless, if at that time depressing, prose of Bruce Harris well before I got back to the Boys' Entrance. The second Test in Sydney began in mid-December. The anxiety was enormous, and it seemed as if the end had come when Australia led by 74 on the first innings. But all was not lost, because Peter May then made a remarkable hundred, leaving Australia with 223 to win. They failed by 38 runs with Tyson taking six wickets, bowling faster than anyone can ever have bowled before. The game had a marvellous ending, with a stupendous diving leg-side catch behind the wicket by Godfrey Evans. Phew! I lived every ball. We won the third Test, in Melbourne, but I had to wait until early in the Lent half for England to make sure of the Ashes by winning the fourth Test in Adelaide. After that, to general relief at Eton, normal service was resumed.

* * *

Another diversion that winter was being prepared for my confirmation in December. At times the process was up against pretty tough competition from events in Australia, but GWN, who prepared us for the Bishop of Lincoln, was able neatly to combine events in Australia with those in Heaven. After that heavy defeat in Brisbane I was not at all sure about the Almighty, but GWN's gentle manner and instructive way of putting things across gave meaning and relevance to the whole business of Christianity. Up until then I had felt that religion did nothing more than get in the way of things, what with endlessly having to tool off to chapel and listen to those interminable sermons. My family and one or two of my surviving godparents foregathered in College Chapel on a Saturday late in the Michaelmas half, and the Bishop of Lincoln laid his hands on our heads and turned a group of us into fully paid-up Christians. Then there was the excitement of going to my first Holy Communion the next morning, and the dreadful worry of whether or not I had got my hands the right way round when it came to the critical moment. GWN's hard work of getting us into mid-season form for the Bishop of Lincoln was underlined and taken a stage further in the Lenten Lectures the following half, given by a notable cleric, George Reindorp, who was soon to become the Bishop of Guildford. By then England were playing slightly more frivolous cricket in New Zealand with the Ashes safely beneath their belt, and the Almighty and I were back on terms. Reindorp came across as the most delightful of men and just the right sort of Christian as he explained the issues surrounding Lent in such an unfussy way that even I thought I could understand them. Anyway, it all helped fill the gap between cricket seasons.

I had been Keeper of Lower Sixpenny in my second summer half, and went on to become Keeper of Upper Sixpenny in

1955. Upper Sixpenny, for fifteen-year-olds, was being run for the first time by a likeable new beak called Ray Parry (RHP), an immense enthusiast who during the war had played as a batsman for Glamorgan. It was one of life's strange ironies that when, in my early seventies, I went through the divorce courts, my wife's solicitor was none other than RHP's son Richard. He was hellbent on delivering an innings defeat, but I think I just about saved the follow-on, if not much else.

RHP and I made great preparations for what we were sure would be a sensational season for Upper Sixpenny. But as luck would have it, David Macindoe, who ran the Eleven, and Clem Gibson, the captain of the Eleven, who actually made the decision, or at least put it into writing, summoned me to play for Upper Club, the top game in the school, from which the Eleven and the Twenty-Two (the Second Eleven) were chosen. Macindoe was another of the mildly eccentric schoolmasters Eton had a habit of producing. He had a gruff but friendly manner, a reassuring chuckle and an ever-cheerful pipe, and had opened the bowling off the wrong foot for Oxford for four years on either side of the war.

Things went well, and I donned the wicketkeeping gloves for the Eleven. I never returned to play a single game for Upper Sixpenny; nor did my old friend Edward Lane Fox, who had received a similar call to arms. At the age of fifteen it felt as near to unbelievable as it gets, especially when, early in June, I received a letter from Clem Gibson, which I still have, asking me if I would like to play against Harrow at Lord's early in July. It was not an invitation I was likely to refuse. Can you imagine? There I was, a complete cricket nut who ate, slept and drank the game, being asked to play for two days against the Old Enemy at the Holy of Holies.

Of course, I had known by then that there was a distinct possibility the invitation would come my way, for things had been going quite well behind the stumps. But there it was in black and white. No one was more pleased than dear old Claude Taylor, with whom I had kept in close contact after leaving his clutches in Lower Sixpenny. In Upper Club nets, CHT still came to help me, standing halfway down the net and throwing an endless stream of balls at me. The stroke he taught me better than any other was the on-drive, which he considered the most beautiful in the game. When I got it right he would purr with delight. He and David Macindoe had together written a splendid book called *Cricket Dialogue*, about the need to maintain the traditional etiquette and standards of the game. It may be dated, but it is still well worth reading.

I shall never forget my first Eton v. Harrow match. The anticipation had been intense, and I was given a lift from Eton to Lord's, along with Edward Lane Fox and Gus Wolfe-Murray, by Richard Burrows, a considerable middle-order batsman and a wonderful all-round games player. His father, the General, sent his Rolls-Royce – what else? – and chauffeur, and the four of us piled inside and were driven not only to Lord's, but imperiously through the Grace Gates. What a way to enter the most hallowed cricketing portals in the world for the first time as a player. No matter what those in the know talked about in College Chapel, I felt that Heaven couldn't be any better than this. I can still clearly remember the frisson of prickly excitement as we stopped to have our credentials checked. Yes, they even checked up on Rolls-Royces. Even today, every time I go in through the Grace Gates – and goodness knows how many times I have done so – I still get that same feeling. I remember carrying my puny little canvas cricket bag through the back door of the Pavilion, up the stairs and along the passage to the home dressing room, the one from which Middlesex, MCC and England ply their wares. After being given a cup of tea by the dressing-room attendant, we changed into our flannels. There were several formal-looking dark-brown leather couches around the walls and as I sat down on one to tie up my bootlaces it suddenly occurred to me that not a fortnight before, England had been playing the second Test against South Africa at Lord's. In that same dressing room, sitting more or less where I was and doing precisely the same thing, would have been Denis Compton, Peter May, Ken Barrington, Tom Graveney, Godfrey Evans, Fred Trueman and the others.

We won the contest, and were generous to let Harrow get to within 34 runs of us. As far as I was concerned, the only blemish came on the second morning. We had begun our second innings on the first evening, and needed quick runs to give us time to bowl them out again. We made a good start, but then after about an hour, wickets began to fall, and there was mild panic in the dressing room. I was batting at number eight, and no sooner had I got my pads on than there came shouts of 'You're in, you're in!' I grabbed my bat and gloves and fled down the stairs, through the Long Room, down the steps and out through the gates. I strode to the Nursery End, took guard and prepared to face Rex Neame, who bowled testing off-breaks, which he was to do later on a few occasions for Kent in between his productive efforts at the Shepherd Neame Brewery. I came two paces down the pitch to my first ball, had a swing in the vague direction of the Tavern, and my off-stump went all over the place. I retreated on the interminably long return journey to the Pavilion amid applause and yells the like of which I had never heard. In the circumstances I felt I could hardly raise my bat or take off my cap, and somewhat perplexed, I continued on my way. No one much wanted to talk to me in the dressing room, so I took off my pads and things, put on my blazer and went to join

Tom and Grizel in Q Stand, next to the Pavilion. When I arrived, Tom looked severely at me and said, 'You were a bloody fool to let him get a hat-trick.' Until then, I had had no idea it was a hat-trick – the first ever to be taken by a Harrovian in the Eton and Harrow match. Tom Pugh, who was playing that day, always says that when the hat-trick came up for discussion later, I said, 'If I'd known it was a hat-trick I would have tried harder.' You never know what to believe.

When I returned to Common Lane House in September 1955, Geoffrey Nickson had retired to North Wales, and Martin ('Bush') Forrest (MNF) had become my housemaster. It would be fair to say that we never got on. He was a charming man, but such a different type of schoolmaster to GWN that those of us who graduated from one to the other had some difficulty in getting used to the change. MNF, a large and rather heavy man, built for the scrum, was nothing if not worthy, but, at first at any rate, he lacked the quick-witted humour GWN had brought to even the trickiest of situations. I suspect MNF felt that I was the creation of his predecessor, and that as I was, at the age of fifteen, already in the Eleven, I could do with being taken down a peg or two. I found him suet pudding in comparison to the soufflé-like texture of GWN.

There is one story about Bush which illustrates my point. In the following summer half we played Marlborough at Marlborough, and won by seven or eight wickets. When we returned by bus long after lock-up, the only way into the house was through the front door. No sooner was I inside than Bush asked me how we had got on. I told him we had won, and what the scores were. He then asked me how many I had made. When I said, 'Sixty-something not out,' he looked at me for a moment in that stodgy way of his and said in a slightly mournful tone, 'Oh dear,' which was what he tended to say on almost every occasion. It hardly felt like a vote of confidence, and our relationship seldom progressed beyond a state of armed neutrality. It must have been my fault, because all of those who spent their full five years with Bush adored him. He clearly became an outstanding housemaster, and a great friend to his charges.

The 1956 cricket season at Eton was a joy. I teamed up as an opening batsman with David Barber (known as 'Daff'), and together we formed the most amusing, successful and noisiest of opening partnerships. It was unceasing ululation as we negotiated quick singles, and seldom, initially at any rate, were we of the same opinion. We played one match against Home Park, a side largely comprised of Eton beaks. One of them was a housemaster called Nigel Wykes, a most remarkable man, who had won a cricket Blue at Cambridge, was a brilliant painter of birds and flowers, and had Agatha Christie's grandson, Matthew Pritchard, a future captain of Eton, in his house. He was known as 'Tiger' Wykes, and he fancied himself as a cover point, where he was uncommonly quick with the fiercest of throws. In the course of our opening partnership, Daff pushed one ball gently into the covers and yelled, 'Come five!' We got them easily as Wykes swooped in and threw like a laser back to the stumps, where the middle-aged wicket-keeper was nowhere to be seen and four overthrows was the result. That year we played Winchester at Eton and came up against the fifteen-year-old Nawab of Pataudi, also called 'Tiger', who even at that age was in a class of his own. Like his father, he went on to captain India. He didn't make many runs that day, but the way in which he got them told the story. As luck would have it, I caught him behind in the first innings and stumped him in the second. Sadly, that year's Eton and Harrow match at Lord's was ruined by rain.

I had the luck, though, to be chosen to keep wicket for the Southern Schools against The Rest for two days at Lord's in early August. I managed to do well enough to secure the same job for the two-day game later that week, also at Lord's, against the Combined Services, which was a terrific thrill. The Combined Services were run by two redoubtable titans of the armed forces: Squadron Leader A.C. Shirreff, the captain – Napoleon himself would have envied his ever-pragmatic leadership – and his number two, Lieutenant Commander M.L.Y. Ainsworth, who had reddish hair, a forward defensive stroke with the longest no-nonsense stride I have ever seen, and a voice that would have done credit to any quarterdeck. They had under them a bunch of young men doing their National Service, most of whom had already played a fair amount of county cricket, including Mel Ryan, who had used the new ball for Yorkshire; Raman Subba Row (Surrey and then Northamptonshire), who went on to bat left-handed for England; and Stuart Leary, a South African who played cricket for Kent and football for Charlton Athletic. Then there was Geoff Millman, who kept wicket for Nottinghamshire and on a few occasions for England; Phil Sharpe of Yorkshire and England, who caught swallows in the slips; and a few others.

We batted first, and at an uncomfortably early stage in the proceedings found that we had subsided to 72 for 6, at which point I strode to the crease. Before long Messrs Subba Row and Leary were serving up a succession of most amiable leg-breaks, and when we were all out for 221, I had somehow managed to reach 104 not out. It was quite a moment, at the age of sixteen, to walk back to the Lord's Pavilion, clapped by the fielding side and with the assorted company of about six MCC members in front of the Pavilion standing to me as I came in. It all seemed like a dream, especially when I was told that only Peter May and Colin Cowdrey had scored hundreds for the Schools in this game. To make things even more perfect, if that were possible, Don Bradman saw my innings from the Committee Room, and sent his congratulations up to the dressing room. When we got back to Norfolk, I remember Grizel being particularly keen that I should not let it all go to my head. 'You're no better than anyone else, just a great deal luckier', was how it went. I played my first game for Norfolk the next day, against Nottinghamshire Second Eleven, and made 79 in the second innings.

After that, a few people thought I was going to be rather good, but they had failed to take into account my navigational ability – or lack of it. The following 7 June (1957), in my last half at Eton, when I was captain of the Eleven, I was on my way to nets on Agar's Plough after Boys' Dinner when I managed to bicycle quite forcefully into the side of a bus which was going happily along the Datchet Lane, as it was then called, between Upper Club and Agar's. I can't remember anything about it, but Edward Scott, who ended up supervising and controlling the worldwide fortunes of John Swire's with considerable skill, was just behind me. Rumour has it that I was talking to him over my shoulder as I sped across the Finch Hatton Bridge and into the bus.

The bus was apparently full of French Women's Institute ladies on their way to look around Eton, which I suppose gave the event a touch of romance, but I lay like a broken jam roll in the gutter until the ambulance arrived and carted me off to the King Edward VII Hospital in Windsor. No doubt a good deal of *zut alors*-ing went on in the Datchet Lane. One mildly amusing by-product of this story is that I still come across Old Etonians who were around at the time, all of whom were the first or second on the scene and several of whom called the ambulance. It must have been quite a party.

FOUR

Queen Charlotte and a Milk Train

After an accident like that, what next? Well, the immediate future was none too happy. As I lay in my hospital bed, prayers were said for me in both College and Lower Chapels at Eton. The power of prayer may never have been better illustrated for somehow I continued to breathe. Or maybe it was just that the Almighty couldn't face me yet. Tom and Grizel, after coming down to Eton for the Fourth of June celebrations, had high-tailed it to France and were somewhere in the Loire, but no one knew quite where. Various SOS's were sent out on the wireless urging them to return as quickly as possible. Grizel told me some time later that on that very day they were in Chartres, and after lunch they went to the cathedral. As I have already said, Grizel was a down-to-earth, on-my-own-terms, not-to-be-shaken member of the Church of England, and was ever mindful that a brace of Blofelds had long ago, or so rumour had it, been barbecued by Queen Mary. Inside the cathedral she did something she had never done before, lighting a candle in one of the side chapels and plonking it down with all the others. It was getting on for half past two, just about the exact moment at which I bicycled into the bus. This was just too much of a coincidence. Unaccountable things like this do happen. What goes on in the subconscious? Who controls these things? Was Grizel's

71

God ticking her off, through me, for lighting a candle in a Roman Catholic church? Or maybe He was telling her that she had the chance to save my life. Is that too far-fetched? Whatever the truth is, there can be no logical explanation for what happened.

Of course they came back to Eton as fast as they could, hoping against hope that they would find me alive when they got there. My brother John also rushed down, and nobly stayed for a night or two in my room at MNF's. It must have been beastly for everyone – except, that is, for me, who was blissfully unaware of anything. There cannot be anything much more boring than endlessly going to look at a body which is still breathing but resolutely refuses to come back into this world and take an interest in life. For a time I was on the danger list, which in retrospect makes it sound quite exciting, although it was not at the time for those around my bed, who soon included my sister Anthea. But there was nothing any of them could do, other than wait. Eventually, after what must have seemed an age, I stirred, and in time came to.

When I finally returned to real life I was endlessly asked how much I remembered of it all, both fore and aft as it were. The truthful answer was pretty much nothing, except for one or two unimportant things. One was strange. The day the accident happened, M'Tutor had had a guest to Boys' Dinner, a Spaniard who had come with a group to look around Eton. He sat next to MNF, and I was on his other side. Even to this day I can remember exactly what he looked like. I don't think we can have spoken much, but it is amazing how small things can stick in your mind. I do remember that my first concern in the hospital on re-entering this world was the need to get back to school, because 'I am captaining Eton against Marlborough on Saturday', a day which had long since gone. The nurses said, 'There, there, you'll soon feel better,' or something like that. Yet it was true that on Saturday, 15 June, Eton had played Marlborough on Agar's Plough. Memory is a funny thing. Various people came to see me in hospital, but my only desire was to get back on the cricket field as soon as possible.

There was a certain amount of pain, because my skull had been badly broken, and one cheekbone was squashed flat and had to be cranked up again in an operation. Cleverly, I managed to flatten it a second time while I was asleep, and it had to be done once more. I am not sure if everything went according to plan, because I still have very little feeling on the left side of my face. One or two of the nerves must have taken a turn for the worse. My large nose had a bit of a going-over too, and had to be reorganised. I was left with a whacking great scar on top of it, which was skilfully removed later on by a plastic surgeon called Stuart Harrison, who had learned his trade under the famous Archibald McIndoe in his hospital at East Grinstead. Even after that I am not sure I would ever have won a beauty contest, but I don't think I was visually much more offputting than before the accident. I think my right shoulder had to be rebroken, under anaesthetic of course, although the aftermath was painful. My skull was broken most of the way round, but not all of it, otherwise my ghost would have needed a ghost to write this. Some of it was crushed, and a certain amount of digging around had to go on to remove all the bits and pieces of bone that were floating about the place. I am not sure whether I actually remember any of this, or whether I am just repeating what I have been told. One thing I do know is that I suffered quite badly from brain bruising, which stayed with me for a number of years – there are of course those who say it is still. There were lots of other amusements to keep the doctors busy, but considering all things it wasn't too bad. I lingered in hospital for a week or two, then once again we journeyed back to Norfolk in the old Rolls, which was still one of the joys of Tom's life.

When I got back to Hoveton, there was something of the return of the prodigal son about the way in which everyone bustled around me. I didn't care for all the fuss. I felt all right, and perfectly able to get on with things on my own, without all the mollycoddling. But obviously I was not allowed to do much, and I hated the shackles that were imposed upon me. All I wanted to do was to get back on the cricket field and to look to the future, for there was nothing I could do about my accident. I also had a burning desire to return to Eton for the final week of my last half. I particularly wanted to sing one of the verses of the 'Vale', the leaving song at the school concert on the last Saturday of the half. There were four verses, and four of the best-known chaps who were leaving the school, who always included the captain of the Eleven if he was on his way, sang a verse each. I made sure this message was conveyed by Tom to Bush Forrest.

I believe, although I can't really remember it, that at some stage in those days at home I picked up a cricket bat and someone trundled in and bowled me a ball or two. Maybe Nanny made a late comeback with her right-arm unders, which were less nippy than Miss Paterson's. But there was one dreadful cricketing moment hereabouts. After my departure Edward Lane Fox took on the captaincy of the Eleven, which was lovely, as it sort of completed the circle after all the years we had played together. The two days of the Eton and Harrow match arrived, when I should have been leading Eton down the steps at Lord's, one of the very few things resulting from my knock on the head which I regret just a little. I suppose that later, there was a chance that I might have been asked to captain the Public Schools against the Combined Services, when I would have had another crack at captaining a side at

Lord's. Anyway, while Eton were taking on Harrow I was stamping around at Hoveton like a caged tiger. I was desperately keen to find out the score, and I well remember sitting in the hall after lunch on the Friday, the first day of the game, listening to the lunchtime scoreboard, which was a daily five-minute broadcast on the BBC Home Service. At the end of the county scores, the announcer said, 'And now at Lord's . . .' and gave the score, although I have long since forgotten what it was. I think it was just about the most awful moment of my life, sitting there at Hoveton knowing that I should have been at Lord's and in the thick of it, and there was nothing I could do about it. I think even Grizel was hard-pressed to entertain me that afternoon.

At first, in spite of my determination to go back to Eton for that last week, everyone shook their heads and wondered if it was sensible. I suppose that as I had been so close to snuffing it, this was hardly surprising. But all the various bits and pieces seemed to mend quickly enough, and in the end I got my way. The old Rolls was in business once more. I don't imagine anyone has ever been more delighted to return to school than I was then. Of course I found that I was Exhibit A, and from the moment I shook Bush Forrest by the hand – I don't think he said 'oh dear' – everyone stared at me, not because I was in any way disfigured, although my nose had seen better days, but in sheer disbelief that I was there at all. That week I behaved exactly as if I was an ordinary member of the school, attending the appropriate divs and joining in everything. I even played in the semi-finals of the house sides' cricket competition. Forrest's were playing Tiger Wykes's on Agar's Plough.

I can't remember if I was allowed to open the innings, but I must have batted near the top of the order. There was one perfectly ghastly moment when I was made to realise all too vividly the effect my beastly accident had had on my cricket. NGW's (Wykes's) main opening bowler was dear old Edward Scott, who I know felt in a predicament as he ran in to bowl to me. He obviously didn't want to hurt me, and was reluctant to bowl flat out. Even so, he still seemed quite brisk to me. But I coped well enough defensively, and picked up the odd run here and there. Realising that I was not as bad as he had feared, he then ran in and bowled me a short one. I had always been a good hooker – a dangerous thing to say in the modern world – and I loved to hook anything short. As soon as I saw the ball was dug in, my instinct told me to hook, but I was unable to alert my feet of the need to make the appropriate movements. It was as if they were stuck in concrete, and all I could do was flap in a ridiculous, firm-footed way at the wretched ball, and somehow fend it down. The signal system had gone, and my reflexes were in no sort of condition. I don't know how many runs I made. It can't have been that many, although I was cheered off – because of my mere presence rather than any cricketing brilliance. The fact that I could take my place in the side without making a fool of myself did me a lot of good, even if it left me with that one nagging doubt. I didn't attempt to keep wicket, which seemed too risky.

I sang my verse of the 'Vale' at the school concert, and my rendition was a tuneless rival to that verse of 'Cock Robin' in my first school concert at Sunningdale. I remember waking up on my last full day at Eton and feeling so sad that this was the last time I would be putting on the stick-up collar and tying the white bow tie – at school at any rate. I had the same feeling when I climbed into that splendid assortment of sponge-bag trousers, coloured waistcoat and floral buttonhole that members of Pop wore, and that made me look like a peacock on a day out. The old Rolls was in business again the next day as I was ferried away to Hoveton with as many of my Eton accoutrements as could be fitted into it. An era had passed, and another one was about to begin. At the time I had no idea of how precariously placed I was to face up to it.

My accident had prevented me from taking the entrance exam to King's College, Cambridge, where both Tom and my brother John had prospered notably on the academic front. The clout on the head at least saved me from failing that entrance exam, and King's, in their infinite wisdom, took me blind. It took me two years to teach them the folly of their ways. Tom had always regarded Cambridge as the pinnacle of his education, and when King's said they would take me in October that year, there was no alternative as far as he was concerned. With the advantage of hindsight, this was one decision he got wrong. He may have felt that if I had refused the invitation, it would not apply to the following year, and I might after all have had to take an exam which I would have failed by a good many lengths. Maybe, too, my outward appearance and the speed with which I had mended physically made him think that all would be well.

I did not suggest that I was not fit to go up immediately; in any case, at that time children by and large did what they were told over something like this, and I longed to get back into the mainstream of life. Nonetheless, the fact was that after 7 June I had been laid out for a long time, and the doctors had warned about brain bruising and its effects. Yet here I was, clocking in at Cambridge in the first week of October. It was hardly the moment for me to start a new life in much more of a man's world, where I was likely to struggle on several fronts. Also, my one strong point, namely cricket, had been at least partly taken away, although I was certainly not ready to admit this. I am sure that Tom and Grizel must have agonised for ages about what I should do next. Maybe they felt it would be psychologically bad for me not to be allowed to carry on as normal.

I played a few games for Norfolk in August with little success, which was another thing I should never have done. I had become a less confident chap, and it was probably a bit much to expect me to hold my own in Minor County cricket so soon after my accident, even though I was desperately keen to play.

Although I was alarmed at the prospect of starting out in a new, more grown-up world, I was happy that Cambridge was to be my lot. Plans were laid, and I was allotted rooms in a lodging house in Newnham Terrace, run by a Mr and Mrs Hughes. She was large and tough, bossy and without much humour; he was small, with a faint moustache, and was generally a rather grey character who did precisely what he was told. I had a decent-sized sitting room and a small, pokey bedroom up two flights of gloomy stairs in a house that smelled mildly but permanently of stale cooked cabbage. It was into this far from prepossessing milieu that I was dumped by Tom and Grizel, not in the old Rolls, which had been put on ice, but in a new and sleek dark-green Jaguar which Tom sometimes liked and at other times felt rather ashamed of. His friends in Norfolk mischievously pulled his leg for buying such a fast car.

They decanted me into my rooms with a few pictures, which they helped me hang, and the odd suitcase. Then it was a quick peck on the cheek and they jumped into the Jaguar and drove off to Harwich, where they boarded the ferry to spend a few days in Holland to visit some antique-dealer friends in Amsterdam.

Thus began two years in which I never felt fully at ease,

and which I did not enjoy as I should have done. National Service had not quite come to an end, and I had been heading for the Rifle Brigade, but when I had a medical the quacks all threw their hands in the air with horror when they heard the details of that encounter with the bus. Almost every other undergraduate had done National Service, and was two years older than me. I was just eighteen, and at that age two years is a lot. At school you were a trifle subservient to boys two years older than you, and at first I found it hard to realise that in spite of the age gap we were on level terms. Another sea-change was that I was expected to call my tutors and supervisors by their Christian names, which was difficult after ten years in the world of 'sir'.

I was reading history, the subject I had specialised in at Eton after scraping through eight O-levels. Those, incidentally, were the last exams I ever passed in my life. King's was an intensely academic college, and I didn't fit in on that score. My supervisor, Christopher Morris, made some allowances because I played cricket (his son Charles had played against me while he was at Marlborough), but otherwise I was some way from being his favourite pupil. I had heard he took a dimmish view of Old Etonians, but I suspect the main reason was the awfulness of my weekly essays.

I soon found that I loved the social side of life at Cambridge, which, not unhappily, took me away from King's. I became a member of the Pitt Club, which was founded in the memory of William Pitt the Younger. I would have loved to have eaten lunch and dinner there rather more often, but I was not as well off as some of my friends, and was forced to lunch and dine in College, where the standard fare still had a marked post-war flavour to it and it was much cheaper. For a number of my King's contemporaries a non-academic, Old Etonian, Pitt Club member was not quite the flavour of the month either.

Anyway, life progressed, and Christopher Morris gave me a list of lectures I should attend. I started off by going with bated breath to Mill Lane to listen to John Saltmarsh's opening discourse about Medieval European economic history. Saltmarsh himself looked discouragingly medieval. There was a good deal of facial hair in one place and another, a voice with a strong underlay of chalky, ecclesiastical tones, and if he had a sense of humour, it went way over my head. His mind was brimful of every aspect of the medieval condition, but sparkling stuff it was not. For about ten minutes I took feverish, indecipherable notes, but I was soon wondering what on earth I was doing there, being lectured to on a subject about which I knew nothing and cared even less. I saw a pretty bleak future for me with Medieval European history. I was too young, too naïve and too unsure of myself to be seriously rebellious, so I sat through a fair number of these sessions. I listened as attentively as I could to the offerings of a good many other lecturers too, who as far as I was concerned were also dreadful bores. It was not all bad though, for there was one don at King's called Hibbert, with an agreeably unsolemn way of putting things across, who made American history come off the shelf at you. But that was about it.

I didn't have a car of my own, or indeed a driving licence for much of my first year, but I found myself getting lifts up to London from various chums for deb dances, although I was not certain how or why the invitations kept turning up. I fell in love with just about every girl I met at these dances, but sadly I was no competition for the swaggering chaps who were three or four years older than me and had just come out of some famous regiment or other. I did get one or two of the crumbs that fell from the rich men's tables, but that was about it. Generally speaking, of course, one's expectations from sorties such as these at that time, even from the crumbs, were not anything like as high as they would have been a few years later, when the joys of what was to become a hugely permissive society were chucked into the mix.

As the summer of 1958 approached, I felt both excited and anxious. Cricket was very much on my mind, but so was the memory of that short one from Edward Scott. I went to Fenner's early in April for net practice with the main candidates for a place in the university side that year, which included a formidable body of old Blues. The magisterial figure of Ted Dexter, the captain, towered over everything. He was tall and good-looking, but an aloof figure to those of us who were not his special friends. Watching him bat in the nets was extraordinary, and I needed no more than that to tell me I was entering a completely new cricketing world. There was Ossie Wheatley, tall and blond and a wonderful fast-medium seam bowler who went on to Warwickshire and Glamorgan; Michael James, always approachable and friendly and a fine striker of the ball, who in 1956 had scored a hundred as a freshman against the touring Australians; and Ian Pieris from Colombo, who bowled at a sharp and mean medium pace and was more than useful in the lower middle order, if a man of few words, to newcomers at any rate. He was to become an influential figure in the development of Sri Lankan cricket, and was always extremely hospitable whenever cricket took me there. Another old Blue was Ian McLachlan from Adelaide, the oldest son of a huge landowning family in South Australia, who in later years would take care of this visiting Pom with a nonchalant and generous ease. The most genial of men, and an opening batsman who like Dexter was at Jesus College, he was once twelfth man for Australia, but never made it beyond that. In the 1990s he would be a member of Malcolm Fraser's Australian government, and he is still very much the patriarch of Adelaide and South Australia. Then came the also-rans, of whom I was one.

The two pros who came up to Cambridge to coach that year were the redoubtable Tom Graveney, ever elegant and charming, just like his batting, who made me feel very much at ease, and 'Dusty' Rhodes, the leg-spinner from Derbyshire who went on one England tour to the subcontinent, but never played a Test match. He was a small man, with a vermillion face which was not only the product of many days spent in the sun, and the ready humour I have always associated with wrist-spinners. Like Tom he was a good coach, and there were many happy hours spent just across neighbouring Parker's Piece in the bar of the Prince Regent, where the two of them were billeted.

Perhaps the most important figure of all at Fenner's was the groundsman-cum-coach-cum-general-bottle-washer who quite simply ran the place, the incomparable and ever-helpful Cyril Coote. He was a man of many parts, and to describe him as the groundsman, as many did, missed the point by miles. At first, the most noticeable thing about him was his pronounced limp, for he had been born with one leg significantly shorter than the other. No one could have made lighter of such a handicap as his limping stride took him all over the place, brimming with enthusiasm and encouragement. He turned himself into a considerable batsman, and opened the batting for Cambridgeshire for many years in the Minor County Championship, although my friends from the Norfolk side of that vintage remembered him more for his adhesiveness than his fluent strokeplay. No one I have ever met understood the mechanics of batting better than Cyril, and it was remarkable how clever he was at correcting faults in the nets. He was almost invariably right in his assessment of the characters of the players he coached, to whom he varied his approach accordingly. Half an hour in the nets with Cyril was worth a week with many others. He also had the reputation of being one of the best shots in Cambridgeshire, and any bird that had the luck to get past him once knew better than to try again. In addition to all this, he was a wonderful groundsman, and produced the superb batting pitches which in the fifties were the hallmark of Fenner's. He was cheerful, extremely determined and uncompromisingly robust in all his opinions. There were no grey areas with Cyril.

I played a few matches for the university in my first year, without getting into the side. The delightful and charming Chris Howland filled the wicketkeeping spot. He was undoubtedly better than I was after that stupid accident, but I still have the feeling that if I had missed that wretched bus, it might have been the other way round. My reactions were a mess, and my keeping suffered more than my batting. It was only for one brief spell, on a tour of Barbados with Jim Swanton's Arabs in 1967, that my wicketkeeping ever fully came back to me, but it was too late, for I had by then become a cricket watcher and writer, and had little time to play. I suppose all through my life I have suffered occasional pangs of what might have been, if only . . . But there was no future in that line of thought, and I was always anxious to get on with the present, even if that did sometimes mean flying by the seat of my pants.

My first-class career had an unusual start. May 1958 was an important month for me, what with exams, the cricket and keeping a watchful eye on the social scene in London, with deb dances and all that. My particular love at that time – and gosh, she was beautiful – had asked me as her partner to the tour de force of the London season, Queen Charlotte's Birthday Ball. This was an invitation it was impossible to refuse, although as it happened I was well out of my depth by then, not that I knew it, and it wouldn't have made the least difference whether I had gone or not. As luck would have it, two days before the party, the team for the university's forthcoming game against Kent went up in the window of Ryder & Amies the outfitters on King's Parade. The match began the day after Queen Charlotte's, and of course sod's law decreed that my name should have been down on the team sheet. Showing all the optimism – or maybe the insecurity and bloody stupidity – of youth, I attempted to fulfil both functions, which remains one of the craziest decisions that even I have ever made.

I caught the train up to London, and changed into a white tie and tails at my brother John's mews cottage. But as soon as I turned up at the appropriate house and met the rest of the party, which was full of dashing cavalry officers and a fair sprinkling from the Brigade of Guards, I realised that any hopes I might have had in the direction of the beautiful deb had disappeared weeks ago. Anyway, off we all went to the Grosvenor House in Park Lane, where we danced a good deal of the night away. Eventually I bade farewell to all concerned and legged it to Liverpool Street station to catch the milk train back to Cambridge before taking on the might of Kent that same morning. As luck would have it, the first person I ran into on the platform was Ian McLachlan, who was being rested for the Kent game and who had also been to Queen Charlotte's. As he was a good friend of Ted Dexter's, the news of my nocturnal progress soon got about. Sod's law again.

I took a taxi back to my lodgings, and after the briefest of lie-downs before a hurried bowl of Corn Flakes, I pedalled my way to Fenner's in the hope of greater success than I had achieved at Grosvenor House. Dexter and Colin Cowdrey tossed, and we were batting, which was not quite the way I had planned things. Shortly before half past eleven, therefore, I was making my way, horribly nervously, to the crease as one of the openers. I don't think I took the first ball, but very soon I was down at the business end preparing to face Alan

Brown, a tall, blond fast bowler. I managed somehow to survive my first ball. The second was short, and lifted on me. I followed it up in front of my face, and it hit the splice of the bat and dollied up to give forward short leg the easiest catch in the history of cricket. I shuffled miserably off to the pavilion, and as I passed Cowdrey at first slip he said, 'Bad luck,' in the kindest of voices. It was no help. In the space of approximately fifteen hours I had played two and lost two. So much for youthful optimism. I would always have lost at Grosvenor House, but who knows, I might have made a better fist of things at Fenner's. Some time later, I wondered if I might have hooked that ball if it had not been for my bang on the head. I made one in the second innings. What a start.

I opened again in the next game, against Lancashire, and somehow managed to put on 78 with Dexter for the second wicket. I spent my time at the non-striker's end jumping out of the way of his thunderous straight drives, and at the other end playing and missing or edging the ball just short of the slips. Eventually, having made 41, I missed a low full toss from off-spinner Roy Tattersall which hit the outside of my leg-stump. Lancashire were captained by Cyril Washbrook, and their attack consisted of Brian Statham and Ken Higgs with the new ball, while the spin was provided by Tattersall and the left-armer Malcolm Hilton, who as a beginner in 1948 had famously dismissed Bradman. I faced a few overs from Statham, bowling almost off the wrong foot, and I don't think he sent down a single ball I could leave alone. His accuracy was of course legendary, and at that time he and Fred Trueman formed one of England's greatest pairs of opening bowlers.

A week or two later I was out first ball to the examiners, but as this was only a college exam and not part one of the tripos or anything particularly serious, King's looked benevolently upon me, and I was not shown the door. After that I wiled away the summer working on the first floor of Simpson's in Piccadilly. There was one moment of excitement, which proved to be a false dawn. The university were on tour, playing various counties before the University Match, and I received an SOS to go to Guildford and keep wicket against Surrey. I was mean-spirited enough to hope that Chris Howland had perhaps broken a finger, but when I clocked in at the Hog's Back hotel I discovered that he was merely having a game off. So four days later I was asking Simpsons for my job back and it was Daks trousers and cashmere jackets all over again. I never quite got the hang of the measuring tape, but I was not too bad at the chat, which just about got me by.

I played a bit of cricket for Norfolk, without much success, before beginning my second year at Cambridge. Towards the end of the summer term I had arranged to move lodgings to a house at 3 St Clement's Gardens, which was run by an elderly landlady called Agnes Smith, who must have been the best of her sort in the whole of Cambridge. Her cooked breakfasts were magnificent, her kindness, enthusiasm and humour simply remarkable, and she had a wonderful, chuckling laugh. One of my companions there was Christopher Mallaby, who went on to reach spectacular heights in the diplomatic profession: his last posting was as our man at the amazing embassy in Paris. Another benefit of St Clement's Gardens, which didn't altogether please my bank manager, was that it was just around the corner from the Pitt Club.

My second year was much more fun than my first, especially as far as the social whirl was concerned. As a result my overdraft increased inexorably, which irritated Tom, who found it difficult to understand how I could not live within the slender means he allowed me. We had a number of lively conversations on this subject. Academically, little had changed.

My distaste for lectures grew worse, and alas, I did not work hard enough to get by. I did a bit better against the examiners, surviving almost a complete over and scoring what was known as 'a Special', which meant guilty unless there were extenuating circumstances. King's made it clear that if I returned for a third year I would not be allowed to play cricket until after the exams, which didn't seem much of a bargain to me. I turned it down, and had a sorrowful letter from John Raven, the college's dark, angular, friendly, bespectacled head tutor, saying that perhaps it was time I moved on to the next stage in life – without attempting to specify what that might be.

By then, however, I had had one piece of great good luck. Cambridge was not as good a side in 1959 as it had been the year before, and I just managed to squeak in as one of the last two choices. I was probably the worst opening batsman to play for either Cambridge or Oxford since at least the Boer, and probably the Crimean, War. It was the most exciting experience though, and in a funny way the best education I could possibly have got when you consider what I was going to be doing for most of the rest of my life.

My two greatest memories of the cricket came when the home season at Fenner's had ended. We went on tour, and late in June we arrived at Trent Bridge to play Nottinghamshire in a Saturday–Monday–Tuesday game; there was no play on Sunday in those days. Nottinghamshire were captained by Reg Simpson, who had opened the batting many times for England, and was a fine player of fast bowling. In order to try to drum up some interest in a game which was otherwise pretty small beer, Reg had got hold of Keith Miller, the great Australian all-rounder, to come and play as a guest star. He had retired three years earlier, and was now writing about the game for the *Daily Express*. He would prove to be one of the greatest men

I ever met in the world of cricket, and we remained good friends until he died.

This must have been Keith's last or last-but-one first-class match. We batted first, and he opened the bowling, slipping in some quickish, almost humorous, leg-breaks in the first over. I faced a couple of them. He then made a hundred in Nottinghamshire's first innings, thanks partly to the fact that I dropped him off a skier at deep midwicket when he was on 65. There was nothing remotely solemn about his approach or his strokeplay. He hit the ball murderously hard, and talked happily away to everyone throughout his innings. More than forty years later I came across a completed scorecard from this game, and when I asked Keith to sign it, he scrawled across it without any prompting, 'Well dropped, Henry.'

But the best part of Keith's foray to Nottinghamshire happened off the field. He brought with him a former Miss Victoria called Beverley Prowse, and until I set eyes on her I had not realised that God made them that good. She sat in the ladies' stand at straight deep midwicket for three days, and put us all off our stroke(s). Of course, she was the reason I dropped that skier. On the first evening Keith was a few not out at the close of play, and therefore had to be at the crease, booted and spurred, at half past eleven on the Monday morning. About twenty minutes before the start of play, Reg Simpson came into our dressing room, which was below the home dressing room, and asked if we had seen Keith. We had not. A couple of minutes later there was a crash against the door, which burst open, revealing a somewhat breathless Keith. 'Come on, boys,' he said. 'I can't get all the way up there. Lend me some kit.' We did our best to fit him out, and I had the luck to help him off with his shirt. His back made a deep impression on me, and I could only deduce that Miss Prowse had long and powerful fingernails. I'd never seen such a sight.

It was all part of life's rich learning curve. It didn't affect Keith in the least, and he went on to make that splendid hundred. Years later I asked him if he had remembered to slip a packet of emery boards into Miss Prowse's Christmas stocking that year. He smiled, and looked mildly sheepish.

Ten days later we played MCC at Lord's, in the game before the University Match. Denis Compton, who had retired from serious cricket year or two earlier, turned out for MCC in what must have been just about his last first-class match. In their first innings he made a quite brilliant 71. Despite his having had a kneecap removed in 1956, his footwork was remarkable, his improvisation astonishing. He is the only batsman I have ever seen who appeared to be able to hit every ball to any part of the ground he wished. His bat really was a magic wand.

I was so lucky to play against two such Adonises as Miller and Compton. Every girl in England and Australia was in love with one of them, and many with both. If it had not been for their joint efforts, I have no doubt that Brylcreem would have gone out of business. By then, of course, I knew that I would not be returning to Cambridge for my third year. But what memories I had to take 'on to the next stage in life'. Tom and Grizel didn't have the faintest idea what they were going to do with me, so they enlisted the help of Uncle Mark.

FIVE

Mad Dogs and Honeymoons

Grizel and her younger brother Mark were the joint products of my maternal grandparents, Kit and Jill Turner. My grandfather was a smallish man whom, if you were sensible, you treated with the greatest care. He had white hair when I knew him, and he spoke in a rasping voice, as if he was firing machine-gun bullets at all and sundry. He was easily irritated, and I remember him having no obvious love for children beyond what passed for duty. Before the war he had worked in the House of Commons where he became Deputy Clerk. He was, by all accounts, a difficult man to work with and did not make friends easily. This is probably why he never got the top job. He was also for time Clerk of the Pells at the Exchequer. Jill, who was close to Grizel, was a dear, but died of leukaemia while I was at Sunningdale. Mrs Fox told me the news, and made me sit down there and then and write letters to Grizel and to my grandfather, whose grief was prolonged, dreadful, and perhaps a trifle stage-managed. Kit loved Switzerland, and every day he received a copy of a Swiss newspaper written in German, a language he spoke fluently. He gave everyone in the family a crumpled pound note in a brown envelope for Christmas, although I think I probably started off with a ten-bob note which I am sure was just as crumpled. He even gave Uncle Mark, who had made a lot of money in the City, a pound note along with everyone else.

After Jill had died I never much enjoyed the visits to 'Greenhedges' in Sheringham's Augusta Road, which was about as ghastly as it sounds. We would go over for lunch, and the food was some way from being haute cuisine. Mrs Fenn, the diminutive, bespectacled, straggly-haired, middle-aged cook, was an eccentric character. She spoke with a deep voice in the broadest of Norfolk accents, and had only a rudimentary knowledge of cooking, although she did make excellent marmalade. When I was very young I would have lunch in the kitchen with Nanny and Mrs Fenn. Afterwards I would be taken off to swim in the North Sea, which I loathed because it was always appallingly cold. I would put on my swimming trunks in the family bathing hut, which stank of stale seaweed and salt water. To get to the beach I had to walk down a huge bank of painful pebbles in my bare feet, which made the prospect of shuffling slowly out into the sea, getting colder as each step took me an inch or two deeper, seem even more appalling, but I was shamed into it. Sheringham put me off swimming for life, just as Sunningdale made sure that I never again ate porridge. The only time I enjoyed it at all was when, with the help of Nanny, who holding up her skirt was an inveterate paddler, I was allowed to catch shrimps. Pushing the shrimping net along in the sand where the water was about eighteen inches deep, I always netted a few, which were taken triumphantly back to Hoveton and boiled for tea. The North Sea also produced a good haul of cockles and winkles. Winkles were great fun, mainly because I used one of Nanny's hatpins to winkle them out of those curious twisted shells. They were delicious, as long as you didn't get a mouthful of sand at the same time.

My grandparents would always come over to Hoveton for lunch on Christmas Day, in their austere black saloon car with

Kit at the helm. They arrived soon after we had got back from church, and we waited with bated breath for those crumpled one-pound notes. Kit, who just managed to reach his nineties, drove almost until the end with steady 35mph purpose. About twice a year he went to stay in Huntingdonshire with Aunt Saffron, my grandmother's much younger sister, who was a great ally of Grizel's. The old boy drove himself there and back. Once, well into the 1950s, he was asked why he always drove in the middle of the road. He dismissed the silly question with a brusque 'In order to avoid the nails from the tramps' boots.' You could see where Grizel got some of it from.

During the Second War Uncle Mark had been one of the more important brains in the Department of Economic Warfare, for which he had been knighted. He was a delightful man, with an open, smiling, enthusiastic face, and I don't think I ever saw him disgruntled about anything. Both he and Grizel were extremely bright, but their lives followed completely different paths. Grizel had thrown herself into being the country squire's wife, while Mark had negotiated the City of London with remarkable success. Tom and Grizel were of the old school who felt that making money was intrinsically rather vulgar, and that while City slickers might be tolerated, their habits and customs should be viewed with a somewhat jaundiced eye. Uncle Mark drove a Bentley, which I think Tom and Grizel may have felt was a touch flashy. We always had fun when we came up to London, going to his house in Edwardes Square, and later on to the Grove in Highgate Village. Mark's wife Peggy was great value too. A continuous smoker, she drank whisky, coughed and laughed raucously, and always entered into the spirit of everything. Like Uncle Mark, she was an inveterate bridge player.

With my spell at Cambridge being cut short, and my future career looking decidedly uncertain, Tom and Grizel turned to

Uncle Mark as an act of last resort. Of course, he delivered. I was signed up for three years, starting in late September 1959, as a trainee in the merchant bank Robert Benson Lonsdale, of which he was a director. So began the most boring period of my life. Uncle Mark had done his best, but there was no way I would ever have made the grade as a merchant banker, or have wanted to. For two years I tooled off five days a week to Aldermanbury Square, where the headquarters of RBL were located, before I was shoved off to Fenchurch Street after RBL had merged with Kleinworts in 1961. I can honestly say that I never came within several furlongs of doing anything within those two years that remotely quickened the pulse. I had a room in a flat in Egerton Gardens in Knightsbridge, and the early-morning walk to Knightsbridge Underground station, the change of lines at Holborn and the ten-minute walk to Aldermanbury Square still haunt me. I wore a stiff collar and a three-piece suit, carried a rolled umbrella, and topped it off with a bowler hat. I must have looked the most preposterous of oafs. I suppose that if I had kept my hand out of the till (which I did), and they had found me some backwater where I could do no harm, I might have made lots of money, with a bonus or two thrown in, who knows? But it wasn't for me. Living like that for five days a week in order to enjoy the other two seemed the wrong way round, and a lousy way to spend my life.

I started at the immense salary of £365 a year, and I would like to be able to say that I was worth every penny of it. On my first morning I walked up the stairs to the fourth floor and reported at nine o'clock to Mr Paine, the General Manager, who couldn't have lived up to his name better. He was tall, bespectacled, and had the irritating manner of an over-fussy schoolmaster without the semblance of a sense of humour. After a short introductory talk, he took me down to the General Office on the third floor. We walked the length of a long room full of slaves sitting at their desks and working their fingers to the bone, to an office at the far end, where I was introduced to the generally benevolent and red-faced Mr Lewis, who presided over the General Office, peering down at all and sundry through a glass wall. When Mr Paine had gone, Mr Lewis talked to me briefly about cricket, which made me feel that at least some of his heart was in the right place. He then walked me back down the General Office to a desk at which a large man with a moustache who must have been in his late forties was leaning over a huge ledger with his pen at the ready. This was Mr Sutherland.

After we had been introduced, he was told that he was going to have to teach me the tricks of his particular trade. A small chair was found, and, keen and eager as I was at that stage, I perched myself enquiringly alongside Mr Sutherland, who looked a little bit like an amiable but overweight and slightly myopic porpoise. He was friendly in a distant, who-is-this-interloper sort of way, and began to tell me the purpose of his life in the General Office. It was not exactly a thrill a minute. The bank had a number of private clients, most of whom had rather more than a bob or two. Whenever they wanted or were persuaded to buy or sell some stocks and shares, the details of these transactions eventually found their way to Mr Sutherland, who entered them with due care and diligence and a deeply furrowed brow into the vast ledgers under his care. I did my best to register enthusiasm and excitement when someone's holding of the Lonsdale Investment Trust was increased from 384,000 shares to 421,000, but I'm sorry to say it didn't give me much of a buzz. I watched Mr Sutherland's progress for the rest of a morning which was interrupted only by the appearance of an aproned lady who gave me a cup of tea. Later I had the excitement of receiving four weeks' supply of Luncheon Vouchers, which were worth the huge sum of half a crown

(12.5 new pence) each. It was heady stuff, all right. Mr Sutherland appeared to regard me as an amusing, if inconvenient, diversion with which he was prepared to put up from time to time – as long as it did not go on for too long.

When Mr Lewis was satisfied that I was at one with the highways and byways of the clients' ledgers, he moved my chair to the other side of Mr Sutherland's desk, so that I could bring my genius to bear on the contract notes which flooded in from various stockbrokers. There was rather more get-up-and-go to this. I sat next to the ever-cheerful, tousle-haired Mr Langley, and I really thought I was going places when he suggested I should call him Derek. Mr Sutherland was an unbending stickler for stuffiness and tradition, and I never discovered if he had a Christian name, let alone what it was. Derek Langley was himself not averse to the odd flutter on the markets, although while clients bought shares by the bucketful, he was a more modest performer. I too found the fascination of making a profit impossible to resist, and before long I would be ringing his pet broker and buying fifty shares of this or a hundred of something else. I was all right when I listened to his advice, but when I had ideas of my own they usually came unstuck, but not too seriously.

I had not been with Derek for long when I had an extra-ordinary piece of luck, which came from the most unlikely source, and did my image in the General Office no end of good. I went up to Norfolk one weekend, and Grizel told me that Gwen, her local hairdresser on the top road in Hoveton, had heard through a friend that the shares of a company called Jugra Land & Carey were an absolute snip. Jugra and his friend Carey owned rubber plantations in Borneo, or somewhere like that, and were due to be taken over; or so the story went. I arrived in the General Office the following Monday morning in a state of rare excitement, and bought a batch of 150 Jugra Land & Carey at not much more than a pound a share. I couldn't afford any more. Derek, who had never heard of the company, smiled sympathetically and nodded understandingly when I told my story. But, lo and behold, the price soon began to rise, and it was not long before my mentor plunged in after me. It began to look as if we were on to a pretty good thing, although it would have been lovely to have known when the takeover was going to happen. I had learned from Derek that if I bought shares at the start of an account, as it was called, which lasted for two weeks, and sold them before the end of this same account, I did not have to pay for the shares or the full broker's commission. The profit, or loss, would then come thudding into my account at RBL's. It was tempting, but a bit risky, and I can't remember whether I took that particular tack with Jugra Land & Carey. The shares moved slowly, but happily in the right direction, and one morning I arrived in the office to be greeted by a smiling Derek, who showed me a piece in the *Financial Times* which said that Jugra Land & Carey had been taken over. In a modest way, I had cleaned up. My stock rose enormously in the office after that, but sadly this success made me think that making a profit from the stock market was an easy business. I discovered painfully over the next few weeks that it was not. Nonetheless, thank you, Gwen.

After Derek Langley, my chair and my skills were moved by Mr Lewis to a tricky position alongside Mr Mitchell, a spirited character, although I cannot remember the particular function he fulfilled. Mr Mitchell had a loud voice and strong opinions, and was a mad-keen racing bicyclist. Although I doubt he ever made the Tour de France, I am sure he won lots of local prizes, eating up the tarmac in Kent where he lived. I was never entirely relaxed with Mr Mitchell, who was more than a little disturbed by the presence of trainees like me. Sometimes he could be great fun, but at others his irritation got the better of him, especially when, as usually happened, my arithmetic was way out and I entered the wrong figures in the wrong column.

Perhaps the most important figure in the General Office was the cashier, whose desk was just outside Mr Lewis's office. Timmy Ellis was just about the nicest man I have ever met. He had a full face, which was usually smiling, the gentlest of voices, and he was always concerned about my and everyone else's wellbeing. He even managed to make it a pleasurable encounter when I tried to draw some money from him and there was not enough in my account. There are not nearly enough Timmy Ellises in this world.

Outside the office, my life was pretty hectic. At one of those deb dances during the first of my two years at Cambridge I had met an extremely pretty girl called Joanna Hebeler, and we fell for each other. Like me, she had a Germanic-sounding name: one of her forebears had been the Prussian ambassador to London early in Queen Victoria's reign. The Hebelers lived in north Sussex, where Joanna's father Roland had a small farm. He was passionate about cars – before the war he had been a racing driver, and he knew every inch of the course at Brooklands, where he had driven Lagondas. Every year, on the day of the London-to-Brighton vintage-car rally, the whole family would drive to a section of dual carriageway on the A23 near Hurstpierpoint, parking on the grass in the wide central reservation, and watch the old cars struggle up the hill, with most of the drivers wearing deerstalkers and looking like Kenneth More and John Gregson in that wonderful old film *Genevieve*. Roland was furious if anyone ever referred to the cars as 'old crocks'. Once or twice I went with him to watch motor racing at Goodwood, in the splendid days of Stirling

Moss and Mike Hawthorn. Roland was a great one for cleaning his car at the weekend, and would spend hours in dungarees washing and polishing. He even shamed me into trying to clean mine, although it was something I never caught on to.

I often went to parties in the evenings, doing my best to keep up with the lovely Joanna, who was in London learning to arrange flowers at Constance Spry up by Lord's. Hangovers came and went rapidly enough, and at that age it was easy to get by without much sleep.

I didn't have a great deal of time in which to ponder over the dramatic change that had come into my life so suddenly, but looking back now, I am amazed I didn't rebel sooner. I think the truth of it was that I had no money, and therefore felt unable to take a risk in the face of what would have been fierce parental opposition. I soldiered wetly on, in the vague hope that something might turn up. Another reason I was uncomfortable in the City was that in this, the era of the long lunch, I wasn't well enough off to be able to join my friends from Eton and Cambridge more than occasionally for one of these; and in any case, trainees were only allowed a strict hour for lunch.

I still wonder how much that brain bruising had changed or affected me. I can't believe that in my pre-accident form I would have simply done what I was told like this without any protest. The whole business of stocks and shares, money, loans, research into companies, private investment and the rest left me stone cold, but I went along with it because I had no idea what else I could do. The only thing I had ever been any good at in my life so far had been cricket; as that had now been taken away from me, and I badly needed something to take its place. I shoved my head into the sand and tried to make the best of things as they were. I was also determined to marry Joanna, and in my financial state I didn't see how I could do this unless I stayed where I was and made a go of it. My one crumb of comfort was that all around me in the City were successful people who had begun their life there like me, and look at them now. All I could do was grit my teeth and hope.

After the General Office I toured the building, but still nothing gripped me, and people in authority at Robert Benson Lonsdale were not exactly going around saying, 'You want to watch this Blofeld. He'll go far.' Foreign exchange did nothing for me, and the research department, under the auspices of a gloomy-looking Scot called Alastair Craig, a director of the bank, was much the same although there was a delightful chap in charge of it called Harry Conroy, who was always cheerful – except when dealing with the Hoover pension fund – and who loved a good story. George Duthie, his number two, was a much jollier Scot than Craig, and, I believe, a formidable researcher (whatever that may have meant). The place was full of Scots, for the chairman of RBL was Philip McPherson, who walked about the place with a certain grey-haired detachment and had played rugger for Scotland. There were Sassenachs too: the genial and chatty Rex Benson, who had been chairman of the Benson side of things, and Leo Lonsdale, a rather more staid figure who had led the Lonsdale charge, and who had the most formidable of wives, called Blanche.

Next it was on to the investment department, which was on the fourth floor, where decisions were made about which stocks and shares to buy and sell. The chap in charge here was a Mr Passmore. With clients he was gold-medal oleaginous, but to me he was an irritating know-all. He couldn't stand me, and I am bound to say it never occurred to me to put him on my Christmas-card list either.

It was about this time that RBL and Kleinworts joined forces. The powers-that-were in Aldermanbury Square were evidently so fed up with me that I was sent off as a trainee guinea-pig to Fenchurch Street, where the Kleinworts HQ was situated. I started on the banking side of things, where I found that the huge amounts of money, and the interest rates that accompanied them, made the General Office at Aldermanbury Square seem positively life-enhancing. My working existence had progressed rapidly from the painful to the agonising.

By then I had been to Royal Ascot for the first time, in the splendiferous box of Sir Eric Bowater, the paper magnate, who was Joanna's godfather. During the two days I had plonked a certain amount of money on the horses ridden by Lester Piggott, who obliged as he usually did at Ascot. I also acquired an account at Ladbrokes. After my initial success I thought this was the easy way to prosperity, but Lester Piggott, like Jugra Land & Carey before him, proved deceptive. While I was working in Fenchurch Street I spent much time in a bookie's by the Monument tearing up betting slips in great frustration. It was around now that Mr Barnett, my bank manager at Barclays in Aldermanbury Square, called me into his office one lunchtime and said to me, quite perkily really, 'I have been looking at your account, and you have a decision to make, because you cannot afford fast women and slow horses.'

Joanna and I were now constantly together, and decided, although we were both very young, that we should tootle down the aisle together. We duly did so on 15 April 1961. Although I was a mere penniless trainee in the City, I think everyone, not least my new parents-in-law, saw riches coming my way a little later on. I wish I had shared their confidence.

Joanna and I were given the perfect start to married life. For many years Tom and Grizel had gone each summer for a holiday to Florence, where they had met an American couple with whom they became the greatest of friends. Despite Grizel's general suspicion of Americans, some got under her radar, usually because they possessed huge quantities of doubloons and pieces of eight. Pat and Edith Kerrigan fulfilled this requirement. He was the senior partner in what was known in Wall Street as 'the thundering herd', otherwise Merrill Lynch, Pierce, Fenner & Beane. Joanna and I met them with Tom and Grizel in London at the end of one of their joint visits to Florence, and within moments Pat had come up with the idea of giving us an astonishing honeymoon as a wedding present.

The day after we were married we flew to New York, where we stayed for two nights at the Mayflower House Hotel on East 66th Street. Pat had then arranged for us to fly down to Montego Bay, on Jamaica's north coast, and stay for two weeks in the principal suite at the Jamaica Inn in Ocho Rios. As if that was not enough, we then returned to the Mayflower House for a week before flying back to London. It was amazing. Not long after we first arrived in New York, Pat handed me a substantial brown envelope and said, 'You Britishers are pretty mean when it comes to tipping in places like Jamaica. I don't want that to happen with you.' Who said good news seldom arrives in a brown envelope? We set off for Montego Bay and Ocho Rios in even better spirits than before. I tipped vigorously when we got there, but perhaps not quite as vigorously as Pat had hoped.

The taxi taking us from Montego Bay airport to the Jamaica Inn in the late evening ground to a halt halfway through the two-hour journey with a broken big end. This caused momentary alarm, which was soon relieved when another taxi pulled up and we all crammed in with some other passengers and were delivered, late and exhausted, to our amazing hotel.

The Jamaica Inn was built on three sides of a rectangle, with the beach forming the fourth side. The principal suite was at the end of one of the arms stretching out towards the sea, and the luxury was unbelievable at our age. We were told that to fit us in the Jamaica Inn had almost literally had to prise a famous actor and actress apart (sadly not Richard Burton and Elizabeth Taylor, whose thighs had not begun smacking together with any regularity by that time). Most of the other guests were Americans from the Deep South, and there was one late-middle-aged couple with whom we dined on two or three nights. They came from Tallahassee, and when they pronounced the word in their lovely Southern drawl it went on for about three minutes. The first evening we joined them for dinner, the husband was keen to know what my father did. I told him he owned an estate in Norfolk, and that he farmed and ran a business and one or two other things. Then, to round it off, I said, 'Oh yes, and he owns a couple of Broads.' The response came back immediately, 'Why gee, I sure would like to meet your father.' In my innocence I had been paying homage to Hoveton Great Broad and Hoveton Little Broad, but before the evening was out I realised there was a different interpretation of the word 'broad' in the US of A. When I told this story to Tom, he chuckled; it would be hard to imagine anyone less likely to have a couple of the American kind of broads tucked away on the side – and I'm not entirely sure he got the point.

We had been in Jamaica for two days when we went to lunch with Ian Fleming at his house, Goldeneye, near the neighbouring banana port of Oracabessa. The dock workers loaded bananas into boats all night, and went home as soon as the first rays of dawn appeared. Oracabessa was where that lovely calypso 'Day-O' ('The Banana Boat Song'), famously sung by Harry Belafonte, first appeared: 'Daylight come and me wan' go home . . .' There was quite a party to lunch, and while we were having a drink beforehand, Ian, whom I had met a few times in Boodle's, a club my father had shoehorned me into when I started my illustrious career in the City, told me about the origins of Ernst Stavro Blofeld. He's the chap who strokes the white pussy in the movies, and who made his first appearance in the eighth James Bond novel, *Thunderball*. Ian had been at school with my father, and the story he told me was that when he started writing *Thunderball* one night after dinner at his home in London, he wanted an evil name. He couldn't think of one, and went to bed scratching his head. He didn't have any luck in the morning either, so at about midday he took a taxi to Boodle's, sank gratefully into a leather armchair and proceeded to go through the membership list in alphabetical order, looking for a suitably sinister name. He had reached the Bs when he was pulled up short by a couple of Blofelds, my father and brother. In his own words, 'I slammed the book shut, gave a yelp of delight, ordered a pint of champagne, and never looked back.'

It was all good fun, although I think Grizel always regarded Ernst Stavro as part of the castle not normally shown to visitors. One of the guests that day was The Master, Noël Coward. Looking immaculate in white trousers with impeccable creases, and with a smile which was both suave and ever so slightly wrinkled, he sat in the middle of one side of the table, and didn't seem to draw breath for about four and a half hours. I was fortunate to be sitting near him him while he assassinated more characters in the acting profession than I knew existed. It was bitchiness personified, and absolute magic, and he never laughed at his own jokes. When the time came to think about leaving, he asked me if Joanna and I would like to have dinner with him one evening at his little house along the coast. 'Don't worry,' he said. 'I will be in touch. You have better things to do on your honeymoon than worry about a dirty old man like me.'

The next morning the telephone rang in our room, and when I answered an unmistakeable voice said, 'Can I speak to

Henry Blofeld?' I said that this was me, and he said, 'This is Noël Coward. I don't know if you remember, but we met at Ian Fleming's place for lunch yesterday' – which either meant that he thought I had advanced Alzheimer's, or it was a delightful piece of mischief. He asked us to dinner two days later, and that evening a car arrived to take us to Firefly Hill Road, just back from Port Maria, where he had built himself a house. There was one bedroom, and all the usual offices. The only room of any substance was the dining room, which had a table and lots of chairs, and also the Bechstein grand on which he told us he had composed most of his music. Outside there was a lawn with a small swimming pool and a grassy verge on which the great man liked to sit drinking infernally strong rum punches as he looked through the haze at the Blue Mountains in the direction of Kingston.

There were six of us for dinner, which was cooked and served by a delightful, rather large Jamaican lady who lived in the small house by the entrance to the short drive. An actress friend of Noël's was there, and two other chaps who were clearly very much part of his life and Noël endlessly brought them into everything. From what I heard later, they didn't so much take guard outside off-stump as somewhere between fourth slip and gully. We had a good dinner, with some excellent fish, and Noël spoke throughout. Afterwards, having lit a cigarette which he smoked through the obligatory holder, without warning Noël pushed back his chair, put cigarette and holder down on a gold ashtray on the piano, then sat at the keyboard and played and sang 'Mad Dogs and Englishmen', 'Don't Put Your Daughter on the Stage, Mrs Worthington' and 'The Stately Homes of England'. Looking back, I think it was just about the greatest moment of my life. Noël's nuances and inflections were extraordinary. To be almost within touching distance of him, listening to that unique voice and watching his fingers on the keyboard, was an extraordinary experience.

When we returned to New York, Pat Kerrigan gave me another brown envelope and told us to buy whatever we wanted – but then we found that he and Edith always came with us and paid for everything. We were taken to all the fashion houses, to theatres, and to restaurants. When we returned to London I found that I had made an indecently large profit on my honeymoon. There was one small incident which I have not forgotten. One day Pat took me to Wall Street, and while we were having lunch I told him how fed up I was working in the City, and asked if there was any way he could find me something to do in New York, which seemed to me to be the most exciting place in the world. He told me quite sternly that what I had to do was get my feet under the desk and really work hard at what I was doing. Then an opportunity in New York or elsewhere might crop up.

After my return from this remarkable honeymoon I realised that it was madness for me to go on working in the City. But what could I do instead? I stuck it out at RBL for another interminable year. At first Joanna and I lived in a small house in Chelsea which had its own asparagus bed. We acquired a taste for dry martinis, and I tried to teach her to play bridge, a game she never really took to. Nonetheless, she came up with an amusing and unusual way of remembering the order of the suits: 'Silly Henry Dreams Cricket' accounted for spades, hearts, diamonds and clubs.

Five days a week I went off to work in the City. Most week-ends we went down to the country to see our respective parents, intermingled with cricket matches in the summer and shooting parties in the winter. This well-ordered life suited Joanna, but because of my dislike of my job, I was less certain that it was the answer. Something had to give.

It was when I found myself trying to cope with the intricacies of lending and borrowing money in Fenchurch Street with Kleinworts that I finally realised I could take it no more. A year had gone by since our return from honeymoon, and I was at my wits' end. I had thought long and hard about what else I might do, but had come up with nothing.

Then, one evening early in May 1962, when Joanna was staying with her mother and father, I had dinner on my own at an Italian restaurant, an old family favourite in the Brompton Road called La Speranza. As I was tucking in, it occurred to me again that the only thing I had ever been any good at was cricket. A couple of my friends were writing about the game for newspapers, and I thought, why the hell shouldn't I do likewise? It would be fun, and it would bring me back to cricket. I didn't let the fact that my academic record suggested I was pretty well incapable of producing a sentence that had a subject, a verb and an object worry me too much.

I didn't remotely consider the financial implications of what I was thinking, but the idea took me over, and I wrote to one or two people, and spoke to a few more, about my chances of writing about the game. Their answers were invariably disappointing: effectively, everyone told me I would have to go and work for a provincial newspaper and get some experience otherwise no national paper would even look at me.

By this time I had become a member of the Arabs, a nomadic cricket club founded before the war by E.W. (Jim) Swanton, the well-known cricket correspondent of the *Daily Telegraph*. One Monday evening the Arabs had a cocktail party at the old Hyde Park Hotel in Knightsbridge. I went along, and met Johnny Woodcock for the first time. Johnny had been the cricket correspondent of *The Times* since 1954, and was to continue until he retired in 1987. I wonder if anyone has ever written better about the game? That evening we talked

106

for quite a while. He asked me what I was doing, and I told him I was in the City and how much I hated it. He asked me what I wanted to do. I replied that I would like to write about cricket. He shook his head, gave one of those disarming smiles of his, and said, 'I wouldn't do that if I were you.' Which was not exactly what I wanted to hear from the great man. He said that he feared there was no way he would be able to help me, but that if anything did crop up he had my address and would bear me in mind.

The next day I went to Fenchurch Street for another unsuccessful session at the bookmaker's, and returned home to Chelsea as soon as I felt my absence would not be too keenly felt in the office. As I came in through the front door I noticed that one of those vivid yellow envelopes in which telegrams were delivered in those days was lying on the mat. I tore it open, for although I had no idea what to expect, those yellow envelopes always promised drama. The typed words stuck onto the piece of paper told me to ring a telephone number in Hampshire, and the message was signed 'Woodcock'. I dialled the number immediately, and Johnny asked me if I would like to cover the Kent v. Somerset match at the Bat and Ball ground at Gravesend over the next two days, as one of the usual cricket writers at *The Times* was ill. They needed someone to stand in for him. I couldn't believe my luck. Of course I jumped at it, and Johnny told me to go straight round to the *Times* offices at Printing House Square to meet the sports editor, John Hennessy, and collect a press ticket for the match. Hennessy, a solid, reserved man, not much given to smiling, did not seem entirely convinced that I was the chap he needed. Nevertheless, he introduced me to Laurie Wayman, who I still believe to be the best copy-taker in the world, and who I would have to ring from Gravesend the next day to find out how much they wanted me to write.

In the morning I rang my office and told them that I was ill. I imagine they heaved a huge and collective sigh of relief. Joanna and I set off for Gravesend in my Triumph Herald, which had been given to me by Tom after he had sold a field by the Hoveton church. We arrived at the ground, where my precious press ticket gained admittance for me and the Triumph Herald, but I had to pay full whack for Joanna. I found the press box, a smallish tent on the far side of the ground, and immediately encountered two other journalists. One was the *Evening Standard*'s avuncular Dick Hollands, who had a figure which suggested he did himself pretty well, a sports car he must have found it difficult to squeeze into, and a lovely, large, cuddly wife who sometimes came to the matches with him. Dick and I would work together for many years.

The other chap was an austere-looking man in his forties with fair hair, called Peter Johnson. I can't remember who he was working for, but he was extremely disturbed by my presence, and in no time at all had asked me if I was a member of the National Union of Journalists. When I confessed that I was not, he began to mutter dark threats about chaps who turned up to write and didn't have the correct credentials. I said he had better get in touch with *The Times*. He was the sort of chap Brian Johnston would have described as 'only a fairly nice man', which was his severest rebuke. I would meet Peter Johnson a few times in the future, and he was always belly-aching along these lines. He ended up for a while as the editor of the *Cricketer* magazine.

The day progressed. I took copious notes, and at four o'clock, as instructed, I rang Laurie Wayman at *The Times* to ask how many words they wanted me to write. He said '450' in a gentle but uncompromising voice, and told me that they wanted my copy by seven o'clock. At that moment 450 words made *War and Peace* feel like a piddling little pamphlet, and

I panicked, inwardly at any rate. I pulled out my writing pad and got down to it, for some reason in green ink. Eventually, about half an hour after the close of play, I had cobbled together approximately 450 words, with the help of much scratching out. I read them through most uneasily, for they amounted to something considerably less than a literary masterpiece. Joanna and I drove out of the ground, and we stopped at the first telephone box. Thinking, 'Here goes,' I put through a reverse-charge call to *The Times*, and was soon dictating my piece to Laurie Wayman, who took it down with amazing speed. I was painfully aware that it sounded too awful for words, and every single phrase I dictated seemed to hang accusingly in the air. He did not comment, but merely thanked me and asked me to call back in an hour's time to check if there were any queries. So far, so good.

Joanna and I had decided to spend the night in Gravesend, but we found that all three of the hotels there were full, so we turned our attention to nearby Rochester. We eventually tracked down a double room in what was a trifle optimistically called the Grand Hotel, in the High Street. The bedroom was minute, with the smallest double bed I have ever slept in, and the bathroom down the corridor. I called *The Times* again, and was deeply relieved when Laurie Wayman told me, without too much conviction, that my stuff was OK. Joanna and I ate something that passed only loosely for dinner in the restaurant downstairs, then returned to our garret.

Sleeping in Rochester was, in those days, a bit of an adventure. There was a cathedral and a number of other churches near the centre of the town, as well as a number of large commercial buildings. The one thing they all had in common was a clock which chimed relentlessly through the night, on the hour, at a quarter past the hour, at half past the hour and at a quarter to the hour. The result was a constant cacophony of chiming clocks, because none of them were synchronised, and sleep was almost impossible. To make matters worse, they began to deliver the milk, rather noisily, at a quarter to five, and soon afterwards some spirited late-to-bed locals began to toot their horns.

At about six o'clock I decided that the only thing to do was to get up and go in search of a copy of *The Times*, to see what they had done with my piece. I got dressed, went downstairs, and was about to go out of the front door when the night porter blocked my passage. He clearly thought I was attempting to scarper without paying my bill. I assured him that I had left my wife upstairs as surety, but he didn't think that was funny. However, I ducked under his arm and found a news-agent almost opposite the hotel. The proprietor greeted me warmly, and I asked him for *The Times*. Looking crestfallen, he said with a shake of the head, 'I'm afraid, sir, I've already sold it.' Which was not a promising start. Up at the far end of the High Street, I found what I was looking for. I turned frantically to the sports pages, and was amazed to discover that they had printed just about every word I had written. I returned to the Grand Hotel with a spring in my step.

Before Joanna and I went back to the ground for the second day's play, I rang my office again and told them I was still unwell. They suggested I see a doctor, and I told them I thought that was an excellent idea. *The Times* asked for another 450 words, and once again they printed almost all that I had written.

The next morning I was back in Fenchurch Street, trying not to look too pleased with myself. The following Sunday *The Times* rang me and asked me if I would go down to Portsmouth on the Wednesday and write about the first two days of Hampshire's game against Warwickshire. Of course I said 'Yippee!' and rang the office on Wednesday morning to say the doctor had not been as successful as I had hoped. I wrote my reports for those two days, and they printed the lot. I was so emboldened by my success that on the Sunday I rang Laurie Wayman and asked him if there was any work for me the following week. He told me there were four days.

The next morning, I rang the dreaded Mr Paine, and we had an interesting conversation. I told him that I had left Kleinwort Benson's employment, and hoped they would manage to get along without me. He asked me what on earth I meant, and I said simply that I was not coming in again. In a shocked, schoolmasterly voice, he told me severely that I couldn't do that. I said something to the effect of 'Just watch me,' and that was that. So ended one of the potentially great merchant-banking careers of the twentieth century.

When I told Tom and Grizel the news about my departure from the world of finance for intermittent freelance work as a journalist, I received a resounding vote of no confidence. They muttered deprecatingly about penny-a-liners, and what would Reggie and Christo think, and that sort of thing. I am not sure that Joanna was entirely happy either, but for me the sheer relief of not having to go to the City any more was too wonderful for words.

As a postscript to this saga, I must say that Uncle Mark, whose escutcheon I had pretty well blotted at Kleinwort Benson, was the only one in my entire family who supported me. I well remember him saying to me, 'If this is what you really want to do, go and do it, and no one will be happier than me.' I dare say he was pretty grateful to have got me away from Kleinwort Benson, where I must have been a colossal embarrassment.

SIX

Slum Dogs and Maharajahs

I relegated the bowler hat to the window-ledge at the back of my car, unrolled the umbrella with gusto, and put the waist-coats and stiff collars into cold storage. For the rest of that summer of 1962 I drove gleefully to county cricket grounds on behalf of *The Times*, usually two or four days a week, according to their whim. For some reason for which I have still not discovered the answer, British newspapers in those days were smaller on Fridays than on other weekdays, and went to bed rather earlier, which meant shorter pieces and earlier copy. *The Times* loftily disdained such hectic last-minute scrambles, and simply didn't bother to ask me and the other writers to serve up their clichés on Fridays. (It was the famous and delightful Ian Wooldridge who gave me an early and shrewd piece of advice on that score when he said, 'Never turn your nose up at a good cliché.' Without them many of us would have been lost, but he less than most.)

As well as *The Times*, I also wrote a few pieces on Saturdays for the *Observer*. The Sports Editor there was the redoubtable Clifford Makins, one of the great characters of Fleet Street and just about the only other man I have known to have a truly Arlottian thirst. It was therefore appropriate that it was Clifford who introduced me for the first time to John Arlott, who also wrote for the *Observer*. Before moving to Fleet Street,

Clifford had been editor of the *Eagle* magazine, which we all devoured at school, demonstrating that he was a man of many parts.

In those days the *Observer's* offices were in Tudor Street, close to Blackfriars Bridge. The building was obviously designed by an architect with a great affection for keyhole surgery. It was a rabbit warren, with narrow, dusty passages and small, winding staircases which, I suppose, must have appealed to those with a literary sense of adventure, as you never quite knew what you would come across at the top of them. Halfway up one I found a tiny, ramshackle office which housed the desks belonging to Clifford himself and to his main writer, reporter, columnist or whatever, Hugh McIlvanney, a meaningful Scotsman to his Kilmarnockian eyeballs, who was the most formidable of rising stars in the ranks of sporting journalists. To this day, with the *Sunday Times*, he remains at the pinnacle of his profession, although, understandably given his age, in a slightly less productive way. Hugh was at his best in the Muhammad Ali days, when he wrote some truly memorable pieces.

Clifford was the most innovative of sports editors, if a trifle before his time, and was always coming up with new ideas. He was a good friend of my Cambridge contemporary, now the England cricket captain, Ted Dexter, who was another *Observer* writer, and together they wrote two sporting whodunnits, *Testkill* and *The Deadly Putter*. They were both great fun, if not exactly pension-providing material. Clifford was up for anything, and maybe he was a thriller writer manqué, but on this evidence he lacked the killer Agatha Christie-like touch.

He was seldom among the early arrivals in the office, although on Friday and Saturday mornings, when publication was approaching, he was there or thereabouts. He had a warm sense of humour, was always interested in what you had been up to, and was unfailingly cheerful, indicating that he was able to throw off the effects of the night before with unusual ease. He also made you feel that the interminable period between ten o'clock and midday was a boring distraction which had to be elbowed aside before he could begin his purposeful walk up the hill to Fleet Street and El Vino's. If mobile telephones had been on the agenda then, El Vino's profits would have soared, as it would have become a more or less permanent office for Clifford and many of his chums.

The most interesting among these was the large, garrulous, charming and generous opera critic of the *Guardian*, Philip Hope-Wallace. He presided over a table with four chairs halfway down the left-hand wall in the room which opened out beyond the bar. There is still a gold plaque on the chair in which he sat with such distinction, like a medieval potentate holding court and freely dispensing justice, in vintage liquid form.

Philip was a kinsman of the Dukes of Devonshire, although I was never quite sure how that worked. He was an avuncular, elderly bachelor whose ample form and countless chins spoke of a hugely enjoyed life of impressive self-indulgence. He would, in an intimate sense I think, have taken guard some distance outside the off-stump. You only sat at his table by personal invitation, and even when I was taken into El Vino's by Clifford, who was a member of the inner sanctum and a close friend and conspirator, I would never have dared to take a seat there unless Philip himself had asked me to. Once or twice an unknown intruder who did not know the form tried to sit in an empty chair at his table, and Philip would see them off with a few firm words which left them in no doubt that they should make alternative arrangements as quickly as possible. A formal 'Can I help you?' came into it.

One day when I was walking with Clifford from Tudor

Street to El Vino's, he said he thought Philip would be back from his holiday. Sure enough, there he was, sitting in his usual chair, brooding happily over a bottle of claret and greeting all and sundry with great and noisy enthusiasm. He had been with some friends to the Greek islands, where they had rented a boat and sailed all over the place. He told us, hugely enjoying the memory of the moment, that they had arrived early one morning at the island of Lesbos. As he and his friends were standing in the prow of their boat while they tied up at the jetty, Philip noticed a group of builders on the dockside who were chatting together and drinking from steaming mugs. He spread his hands towards the group, turned to his chums and said with a flourish, 'There they all are, Lesbians to a man.' With ever-increasing relish he told the story to each new arrival, each time embroidering it just a little bit more. It always ended with huge guffaws of laughter from the great man himself, and a call for another bottle to be summoned to his presence. Philip's table always attracted a large number of bibulous intellectuals: among those I met there were the jazz musician George Melly and the writer Kingsley Amis. I don't think I did much more than say hello to both before Clifford shooed me away; for as far as that august table was concerned, I was still wearing 'L' plates.

Another formidable Fleet Street character I was to meet with Clifford, but only briefly and this time in his office, was Chris Brasher, a predecessor of Clifford's as Sports Editor, who had been one of the pace-setters for Roger Bannister's four-minute mile at Oxford's Iffley Road Track in 1954. He had finished first in the 3,000 metres steeplechase at the Melbourne Olympics in 1956, but was then disqualified for bumping into a fellow runner. The next day, on appeal, the disqualification was overturned and he was able to gather in the gold medal. I am not sure what his exact role at the *Observer* was when I met him, but presumably he was in some sort of overlord capacity. He had the reputation of being a bit of a tyrant, and I remember him coming into Clifford's office and firing off a volley of suggestions, which were more like deafening instructions. He found time to give me a curtish nod, but he didn't strike me as a man you wanted to cross. Brasher was later the moving force in the setting up of the London Marathon.

I loved this new world in which I found myself, although there was one colossal drawback: the pay. Each day's cricket I covered for *The Times* earned me the princely sum of five guineas. Every month I would receive a large envelope containing a cheque and a sheet of paper on which the details of each piece I had produced during the preceding month were written down in longhand, in a lovely classical script. I then had to stick a postage stamp on the invoice, sign my name across it, and return it to the financial department of *The Times* to show that I had received the money. It was a delightfully antiquated procedure which took one back to an archaic world where guineas were the order of the day. I had no complaint with any of that; the only problem was the amount on the cheque, which of course included my expenses, a department in which *The Times* showed a marked lack of largesse. The sum total was sadly and consistently inadequate, even though it was topped up a modicum by the monthly cheque from the *Observer*, which, in a dashing, avant garde manner, dealt in pounds, shillings and pence.

Nevertheless, I still felt that I was on the right track. It was wonderful to be doing something I really enjoyed, and which, so far, had not proved too difficult for me. Anyway, being a professional journalist did my self-esteem no harm, and I felt incredibly grateful to have escaped the shackles the City of London had put round me, even if the lack of shekels was a trifle dispiriting.

Inevitably, however, this created an atmosphere of some uncertainty on the domestic front, and we needed all the parental financial assistance we could get. Grizel said to me more than once, 'Darling, when are you going to get yourself a proper job?' and meant it. That winter I found myself writing about such esoteric things as public-school soccer matches for *The Times*, but it was an exceedingly icy winter, and games were constantly being cancelled, which my bank manager found less than encouraging. Clifford Makins used me too, in a similar capacity, and once or twice I found myself in the gallery of a racquets court writing about two and a half paragraphs on some epic contest between two public schools. I once went to Haileybury for a racquets match, and wrote something that deeply upset R.J.O. Meyer, an old Haileyburian who was the famous founder and first headmaster of Millfield School in Somerset – I have already mentioned his love of the gaming tables. I had, according to him, been rude and patronising about his old school, and he remonstrated forcibly with me in a string of letters. I always hoped that one day I would meet him, but alas it never happened.

During the summer of 1962 I had met a fair number of other cricket writers at various county cricket grounds. One of these was Christopher Ford, who wrote about cricket and rugger for the *Guardian*, and was a sort of patron saint of Rosslyn Park rugger club. Christopher was quite tall, with crimpy dark hair, a deep voice, a strict sense of humour which generally stopped well short of a belly laugh, and neat and precise handwriting. When he was working at a cricket match he was a scrupulous taker of notes, and something of a dab hand at statistics. He lived with his mother and his two Siamese cats in a mansion block in the New King's Road, by Putney Bridge. He and I got along well enough, and later on I would drive him home at night if we were both working late at the *Guardian* and left the office after public transport had gone to bed.

In about March 1963 Christopher rang and asked if I would be interested in a permanent job throughout the following summer, as the holiday relief on the *Guardian* sports desk. This offer from *The Guardian* was a life-saver as well as a wonderful coincidence. It came only a day or two after Joanna had given the most thrilling news of all: she was having a baby. After the frenetic initial excitement which we spent listening to advise, checking the doctor had not made a mistake, tracking down the right gynaecologist, trying to map out D-Day which was still about seven months away and, I should think, talking about prams and cots and schools and names and a thousand other things, we had to face an uncomfortable truth. How we could really afford all that was about to happen? It was in this context that Christopher Ford and his telephone became the stuff of which miracles were made.

A day or two later I made my way round to Gray's Inn Road where the *Guardian* had taken over a couple of floors in the *Sunday Times*' building, to meet David Gray, the Sports Editor. Christopher must have given a reasonably good account of me, for David, tousled brown hair and smiling, with a wide and open face, was geniality itself. Yes, he said, he wanted me, but not at any price. The figures he mentioned were modest and Joanna's mother had already signed a trendy and upmarket gynaecologist called Roger de Vere. When I heard David's figure, my first thought was, 'Well, I expect a lot of De Vere's other customers pay him on time. I hope he'll wait for me.' We were still going to need an awful lot of presents of white babies' socks, shoes and the rest. When I got home I am afraid I was economical with the truth when the first inevitable question was asked which was a resounding

'How much are they going to pay you?' After revealing the meagre amount he was going to pay me, David Gray had followed with news which was even less encouraging: I was not going to have the glorious summer watching cricket that I had anticipated, I was going to be corralled at the sports' desk in the office, learning to sub-edit, and would have to arrive at four o'clock in the afternoon and sometimes stay until after midnight. I wasn't sure how that one would sell at home, but still, like going to boarding school at the age of seven and a half, it seemed a step in the right direction. David promised me that I would be let out to watch the odd cricket match, but not all that often. Anyway, it was permanent employment for a bit, and it was agreed that I would start towards the end of April.

David was not only the Sports Editor of the *Guardian*, he was also the lawn tennis correspondent, and a considerable figure within the world of tennis – he was later to leave journalism and become the Secretary and Chief Executive of the All England Club at Wimbledon. He was kind, understanding, and as accommodating as he could possibly be. He presided over a sports desk which was fun, although in a permanent state of semi-conflict with the Manchester office, which until a few years previously had been the head office. Now that the *Guardian* had become a national paper, the head office had moved to London. Disgruntled northern voices down the telephone from Manchester, who were not enjoying the unhappy fact that they had been relegated to the branch office, were a constant fact of life, and gave us more than the odd smile. Another fact of life was the paper's refusal to have anything to do with horse-racing, the gambling side of which presumably offended the puritanical instincts of its founders. Once during that summer a small piece of news from the turf somehow found its way into the paper, under the heading of

119

'Equestrianism'. The editorial office gave the sports desk a firm 'Don't let it happen again' warning.

David Gray had an interesting body of men beneath him. There was John Samuel, recently arrived from the *Observer*, where he had been the Sports Editor before Clifford Makins; he bore an eternal grudge against Chris Brasher, who had given him the heave-ho. Lean and wiry, with a sharpish voice which burst from time to time into loud and extravagant laughter, John had lively opinions about almost everything, and was not given to self-doubt. He was, however, not unreasonably a bit unsure about a young chap who had just arrived from Eton and Cambridge, and who for much of the time must have been more than a mild irritant. John would take over as Sports Editor when David Gray became permanently attached to Wimbledon, and he made an excellent job of it too.

Then there was Charles Harvey, who was well into his sixties and had spent most of his journalistic life on the sports desk of the *Daily Mail*. He was a delightful man with a round face, a small moustache which bristled meaningfully when he was upset, a lovely chuckle, a stately presence and a figure to match. He lived in deepest Hampshire, and was always worried about what his wife, who kept him constantly on his toes, might think on any given subject. He was irretrievably set in his ways, always using a fountain pen, and was a stickler for what I was discovering to be the complicated business of sub-editing. My contribution under Charles's watchful eye consisted mostly of underlining capital letters twice, putting a ring around full stops, marking the start of new paragraphs, and trying, usually unsuccessfully, to compose headlines. Then there was the business of rewriting stories when the chap on the front line had problems with either his facts or his grammar, or had not done the story justice for some reason

– but this was a job reserved for steadier, more experienced hands than mine. I was under Charles's tutelage for a while, and if I ever dared to disobey his iron rules, or to challenge his views about English grammar, or the art of sub-editing, it was at my peril. He could, however, be delightfully friendly in an old-school sort of way. Each evening at around eight o'clock, when the sports pages for the first edition had been put to bed, we had a break for about forty minutes during which we would disappear into one of the local pubs for a pint or two. He was then the jolliest of companions.

I didn't make a fortune out of my new job, but at least money was coming in regularly, even if it did not put much of a spring into my bank manager's step. My particular responsibility was to look after the cricket scoreboard. When the county scores came in from the Exchange Telegraph I had to compile them and send them up to the compositors with the appropriate instructions. Then, upstairs on the stone where the metal was put into the page, there was the daily jigsaw puzzle of trying to make a perfect square or rectangle of all the scores. Of course it never worked out exactly, and each day a number of four- or five-line fillers in small print had to be fitted into the gaps in the interests of geometrical precision. These exciting little titbits would come in through the afternoon, and would be sent upstairs to the compositors with the appropriate instructions. Soon after I started in the office, Charles Harvey suggested that I should try my hand at subbing one of these fillers. I soon learned an interesting grammatical lesson. The first one I laid my hands on stated that 'F.S. Trueman, the Yorkshire and England fast bowler, has recovered from injury and is available for Yorkshire's next match, against Derbyshire.' I did all that I thought was required of me, and passed it to Charles for his approval. I received a sharp and accusatory look as he picked up his pen, made one devastating alteration and thrust the piece back at me. It now read, 'F.S. Trueman, a Yorkshire and England fast bowler . . .' Charles reminded me with a touch of asperity that there had been other Yorkshire and England fast bowlers. It may seem pedantic, but he was of course correct. It is a good illustration of the mores of sub-editing in those distant days, which were firmly upheld by Charles Harvey.

Joanna's tummy was beginning to make slow progress in the right direction. Tom, my father, sold a field or something and another bedroom was put onto our house, a nursery was designated and bottom drawers were filling up like nobody's business. If we had quadruplets there was still going to be plenty left over. The only blot was that I was working in the late aftenoon until getting on for midnight which didn't really help. What a pity life doesn't allow you to press a fast forward to give a glimpse of where it all goes eventually. I have to say that I was still as determined as I had ever been to get on with my life as it was now evolving, if not more so.

One evening after I had returned from one of my three-day breaks for freedom to watch a county match, David Gray and I went over to the pub after the first edition had gone. Over a glass, he made a suggestion which was to remove whatever infinitesimally small doubts I might have had about continuing my newspaper life. The following winter, in 1963–64, the England cricket side was scheduled to tour India and play five Test matches. David told me that the paper's cricket correspondent, Denys Rowbotham, would not be going on the tour. He suggested that, as a freelance, I should try to collect two or three other papers who would like me to cover the tour for them, and that if I succeeded I could add the *Guardian* to my list. By the time we got back to the office to look after the next two editions I had made up my mind that I was going to India that winter, come hell or high water. By the time I returned to my car to drive back to Chelsea I had begun to see one or two snags. The idea was unlikely to sell at all well on the home front. How could any young wife with a newborn child be happy about being left alone for so long, especially since it was avoidable? And yet I knew I had to do it. I imaginged my mother-law's face when all was revealed, to say nothing of the likely outpourings from Tom and Grizel. I was right. It didn't go big although everyone realised that it was a step in the right direction. There was a grudging acceptance which will not have been helped by my ill-suppressed enthusiasm.

The next day I rang Clifford Makins to ask him if he would consider using me to cover the tour for the *Observer*. He thought it was a good idea, as long as Alan Ross, his number-one cricket writer and the editor of the *London Magazine*, did not want to go, which he suspected was highly probable. So far so good. As the summer wore on I was given more games to watch, and I got to know all the main cricket writers. I made guarded enquiries about the likelihood of papers sending one of their own journalists to India, and found that most were likely to. But I then found help from an unlikely source. E.M. (Lyn) Wellings, the main cricket writer for the *London Evening News*, was an awkward customer who piled up enemies rather faster than friends – not that I knew that then, as he was always friendly enough to me. He enjoyed upsetting what he considered to be the cricketing establishment, and was never afraid to take the unpopular, minority view of almost any subject. People tended to be wary of him, and controversy was his constant companion. Tall and thin, with swept-back black hair, glasses, a pretty healthy scowl and a distinctly combative manner, he would then have been in his mid-fifties.

At a county match we were both covering, I mentioned to

him that I was hoping to go to India that winter. He said he thought it was an excellent idea, and that he might be able to help. A week or two later he told me he was almost certain the *Daily Sketch* would be happy to have me write for them. I couldn't believe my luck, although I did see a potential snag. I may have been getting a pass mark writing for broadsheets like *The Times*, the *Observer* and the *Guardian*, but I had no idea of what would be required by a popular tabloid – the so-called 'red tops' were to come years later – and was doubtful if I would be able to give them the sort of stuff they wanted. Wellings assured me that it would be child's play. The *Evening News* and the *Sketch* were stablemates, and he would almost certainly have been asked to cover the tour for both papers. By recommending me, he realised he would save himself a lot of trouble.

There was another hidden motive for his generosity too. He told me a little later that he owned a small travel business in the West End of London, which was run by his wife, and that she would of course make all my travel arrangements. At the time I thought this was a splendid idea. I didn't realise then that Wellings always liked, when he could, to keep apart from the other journalists, staying in different hotels and taking different flights. All my colleagues were taken care of by the saintly George Wareham, who would look after me brilliantly for many years after that, and whom Wellings despised.

None of that particularly concerned me at that moment, as I was so excited about the prospect of touring the subcontinent with the England side. I obviously didn't have an agent at that stage of my career, and being such a new kid on the block I was hardly in a position to negotiate my terms and conditions. David Gray told me what the *Guardian* could afford to pay me, which wasn't a great deal. Clifford Makins didn't go overboard either, and Lyn Wellings negotiated a pretty modest fee from the *Sketch*. I didn't attempt to argue with any of them, and anyway the *Sketch*'s contribution would enable me to cover my likely expenses with a little, but not much, left over. Even so, it was another hard sell on the home front.

My temporary job with the *Guardian* ended with the domestic cricket season, but the paper continued to employ me as a freelance journalist, which meant that I wrote about professional football for the first time. I didn't find this anything like as much fun as cricket. I had to scurry about by car, train and taxi, turn up in time for evening kick-offs at half past seven, and then spend the night in a series of pretty average hotels. At the end of the game I only had a few minutes before I had to be on the telephone dictating my copy, and it was often panic stations.

Sometimes it was difficult to get hold of a telephone. On occasions I had to flee down the street to a telephone box I had spotted before the game, keeping my fingers crossed that some lovelorn loon would not be pouring his heart out off his long run to his girlfriend. One Saturday afternoon I was sent down to the Goldstone Ground in Hove, where Brighton and Hove Albion were playing an FA Cup tie which I was to write about for that Monday's *Guardian*. The narrow, cramped press box was presided over by one of Fleet Street's most turbulent sports writers. David Williams had spent most of his journalistic life writing about football on behalf of the now-extinct *Daily Herald*. His face was puce, and he knew his way around a bottle of whisky as well as anyone I have ever met. He was now working for the *Brighton Argus*, sitting in the corner of the box by the door, and was in charge of the two telephones, which made it important to keep on the right side of him. If you wanted to use a telephone to get in touch with your office, you had to ask his permission. If this was granted, he would then bill your paper for the use of the telephone.

That day Clement Freud had come down to write about the game for the *Observer*. During the second half of the match, Williams, as was his wont, left the box to go in search of a glass of whisky. In his absence, Freud picked up the receiver of one of the telephones, got through to his copy-takers, and began to dictate his piece. He was midway through it when Williams returned with a full glass, the brimming contents of which suggested at least a quadruple. He stiffened when he saw Freud using one of his telephones without permission, put his glass down on the desk and slammed his hand on the telephone, cutting Freud off. Freud was not easily ruffled, despite the volley of abuse Williams was directing at him. He stood up and quietly picked up the glass of whisky and poured its entire contents over Williams' head. The fall-out echoed around the press box, and indeed the ground, for several minutes.

I had first met Clement Freud in 1957, when I became a member of the Royal Court Theatre Club, which he ran, above the Royal Court theatre in Sloane Square. As part of the cabaret he would tell stories that were only one up from shaggy dogs, yet his timing and his slow, lugubrious voice made them uproariously funny. One evening, soon after I had joined the club, I took along the love of my life. As the night grew later and the music slower we danced together cheek-to-cheek in what I would like to think was a most unextravagant and inconsequential manner. Suddenly I felt the proprietor's hand upon my shoulder, and was informed in that unmistakeable voice that if I did not observe the decent proprieties when I was in his club, he would have no option but to tear up my membership card. Freud was strong beer for some people, among them Geoffrey Green, who wrote sublimely for *The Times* about football and tennis. They encountered each other in the press boxes at football matches, and Green, an extraordinarily amusing and unconventional character himself, composed a mildly censorious jingle about Freud which tripped off the tongue as 'Freud is afraid he's a fraud'.

Clement's brother Lucian would no doubt have agreed. The brethren did not speak for many years. The reason for this, according to someone who knew them, and who swore to me that it was a true story, was that as young men they were both extremely competitive. One day they were walking in Hyde Park when one of them took off his jacket and said to the other, 'I'll race you to that tree over there.' They went through the usual one, two, three, go. Clement, or 'Clay', as he was known, set off at a great lick. Lucian did not move, and shouted, 'Stop that man! He's stolen my wallet!' Clay was chased and brought to ground by some bystanders. The constabulary arrived, and he was led away while brother Lucian picked up his coat and walked off.

Suki Blofeld was born early in the morning of 1 September 1964, and was christened Suzanna Clare.

At the first signs on the last evening of August that Joanna was close to being under starter's orders, my mother-in-law and I made sure that, as soon as possible, she was safely ensconced in the Westminster Hospital. In those days husbands were not encouraged to have a ringside pew at such events, so after a short chat with Roger de Vere, her extremely upmarket gynaecologist, who had a most impressive track record, we wished her the best of luck and hightailed it to La Speranza, on the corner of the Brompton Road and Beauchamp Place, where, in a high state of excitement, we had an extremely good dinner. We washed it down with something red, talked at length about possible names for the baby, and drank everyone's health. Afterwards we drove back home to Chelsea, and rang the hospital. We were assured that everything was going according to plan, although Joanna had not yet fully entered the production line. We said we would ring again first thing in the morning. Looking back now, it all seems rather detached, almost callous. But that was the way these things were done in those days.

I rang the hospital at about half past seven the following the morning, to be told I was the proud father of a bouncing baby daughter, and that both she and Joanna were in mid-season form. It was a thrilling moment, and in no time at all mother-in-law and husband were speeding towards the hospital. In a matter of moments I was holding a little bundle, with nurses and goodness knows who else bustling anxiously around in case I should drop the most important catch of my life.

I think I was the driving force behind the name 'Suki', but the thinking behind babies' names in those days was not exactly progressive. There was of course an Eastern connotation to Suki, and I was roundly outvoted by the assembled company of advisers, who took the strictest of views over the desirability of a Christian name having a Christian aspect. 'Suzanna' came to the rescue, although I only ever remember it being used when, as a small girl, Suki had done something naughty. In a way it was as if a sharp 'Suzanna' became part of the punishment. For me, she was always Suki, and very soon, as is the way with these things, she came to be her name; it seemed unthinkable that she could ever have been anything else. Sadly, I was not to see very much of her when she was growing up, but she has become the most wonderful and loving friend. We get on famously, and I love her, and her splendid husband Olly, to pieces.

*   *   *

Meanwhile, the Indian tour was getting closer, and I was finding the prospect tremendously exciting. I was convinced that going to the subcontinent and writing about the Test series would change my fortunes, although I don't think I ever stopped to try to work out how or why this would happen. I suppose I may have thought that some paper or other would find my outpourings so fascinating that I would be snapped up immediately on my return.

Lyn Wellings informed me that prohibition prevailed in India at that time. If I was going to be able to get a drink while I was there, I would have to take a letter from my doctor, stating that I was an alcoholic, to the Indian High Commission in London, where they would stamp something in my passport which declared that I was an alcoholic. In most serious Indian hotels there was a 'permit room' in which alcohol could be served to those who had this stamp. I showed reasonably impressive form in this direction even in those days, and neither my doctor nor the chap in the Indian High Commission showed the slightest hesitancy when asked to do the decent thing.

Christmas was a bit iffy on the home front, because I was leaving on New Year's Eve, which cast a shadow over things. I should have been careful not to appear too indecently excited, but I am sure I didn't hide my emotions as well as I should have done. I flew out from Heathrow by Comet, which was mildly interesting, because they had acquired a reputation for falling out of the sky. I was a pretty nervous flyer at that time, and was quietly terrified when the wretched thing encountered a severe bout of turbulence and began to bounce around all over the place.

My first experience of India, an early-morning taxi ride from the old Santa Cruz airport into Bombay, was disgusting, fascinating, deeply disturbing, irresistible and a great many other things, all at the same time. The journey was accompanied by every sort of lavatorial smell known to mankind. When the taxi ground to a halt in the almost continuous traffic jam of extraordinary proportions, beggars, usually missing an assortment of limbs and in the most dreadful state, descended from all directions to rap at the windows in the hope of some money. Some of them were small children, who I was later to learn would almost certainly have been deliberately maimed to make them more successful beggars. There were wandering, mooching cows almost everywhere, auto and manual rickshaws, and an incessant cacophony of car horns. The entire population of India seemed to be milling around in and on the sides of the road, and in the endless alleys which led off into the most subhuman living conditions I had ever seen. A few bamboo sticks and some torn hessian covering, with an open drain alongside, provided accommodation for countless millions, with about ten people to a shack. That first drive into Bombay was one of the most extraordinary and unforgettable moments of my life.

I was heading for the Ritz Hotel, which was in the smarter, more orderly part of Bombay, which included Nariman Point, the Gateway of India and the famous Taj Mahal Hotel. As we got nearer to it, the visible living conditions on either side of the road began to improve. At that time the interior of the Bombay Ritz had a musty, dark, Victorian flavour. My small room had curtains that weighed a ton and looked as if they had not been properly opened since they were closed when news arrived of Queen Victoria's death. The bathroom might have been a listed building on its own. Every time I turned a tap on there were exciting squeaks and gurgles and a hesitant and noisy supply of rusty water. The bed was hard and uncomfortable, and I had great difficulty in persuading the management to produce some more coat hangers.

I had a bath, shaved and changed my clothes and went downstairs, planning to go for a walk. But when I reached the end of the hotel's short drive and saw the countless thousands of people beyond, I returned to the hotel and occupied myself with a selection of local English-language papers. At lunchtime, in the Ritz's charming dining room with much greenery around the walls, I had the first of the many delicious curries I was to eat over the next few weeks. This was the start of a great adventure in a country I would grow to love and enjoy as much as any I have visited.

It turned out to be an infinitely boring Test series, with all five matches being hopelessly drawn. India were captained by 'Tiger' Pataudi, who I had played against in the Eton v. Winchester match in 1956. In 1961 he had lost an eye in a car crash in Brighton when he was captain of Oxford, but he recovered well enough to play forty-six Test matches for India, scoring six hundreds, including an unbeaten double century in the fourth Test of this series, in Delhi. Mike (MJK) Smith captained England rather than Colin Cowdrey, whose forearm had been broken while he was facing Wes Hall in poor light in a remarkable Test against the West Indies at Lord's the previous summer. All four results were possible when the last over began. Cowdrey came out to bat with his arm in plaster, stood at the non-striker's end for a couple of balls, and the match was drawn. Neither Smith nor Pataudi was a particularly adventurous captain, and the bowling on both sides was not strong enough to cope with a succession of flat pitches. A state of inglorious stalemate was never likely to be challenged.

The first Test in Madras was memorable only for one of the most remarkable bowling performances in Test cricket. In England's first innings Bapu Nadkarni, a slow left-arm spinner of phenomenal accuracy, bowled thirty-two overs, twenty-seven of which were maidens, with the other five producing only five singles. His full figures read 32–27–5–0, and they included twenty-one consecutive maiden overs, which is still a world record. The admirable Nadkarni hardly gave the game an irresistible tempo. The best chance of a result came in Bombay in the second Test, when the visitors' forces were seriously depleted, and I actually got within spitting distance of playing for England. Ken Barrington had broken a finger in an intervening game in Hyderabad; John Edrich, Phil Sharpe and John Mortimore had tummy troubles; Mickey Stewart, the vice-captain, was in hospital with a bad go of dysentery; and one or two others were very much walking wounded.

David Clark, who was manager of the team, held the usual press conference on the afternoon before the match, at which he never mentioned a word about the desperate shortage of players. When it had finished, he asked me if I would stay behind. He took me aside and said to me, 'We've only ten fit men for tomorrow's Test, and you and I, Henry, are the only others here to have played first-class cricket. As you're twenty years younger than me, you may have to play. Try and get to bed before midnight.' I promised that I would try really hard, and then added, 'There is one other thing. I know Colin Cowdrey and Peter Parfitt are flying out as reinforcements, but if I get fifty or more in either innings, I'm damned if I'm standing down for the third Test in Calcutta.' David looked at me for a moment, smiled, and said, 'If you don't mind, I think we'll jump that particular hurdle when we come to it.'

I did go to bed well before midnight, but with such astonishing excitement hanging over my head, sleep was pretty well out of the question. As I lay there I thought of my days in the City, and wondered if Mr Sutherland was still soldiering gallantly on with all those massive ledgers. I got up at the crack of dawn, and after an early breakfast made my way to the Brabourne Stadium, the home of the Cricket Club of India. This was years before the Wankhede Stadium was even a twinkle in the Wankhede eye. Alas, my hopes were laid to rest pretty quickly when David Clark came up to me and, striving to look suitably regretful, told me that Mickey Stewart had risen from his hospital bed and was making his way to the ground.

It was exciting even to have got that close to playing in a Test match, although I think I was as much relieved as sad. I was disappointed that my chance of wearing that lovely touring sweater with the MCC colours had disappeared. If I had managed to get my hands on one, I think I would still be sleeping in it. My patriotism didn't extend to offering to be twelfth man; that job was given to one of the Indian squad who was not selected to play in the match. The twelfth man is always expected to be a useful fielder, but this particular chap hardly had the name for this exacting task. He was a delightful man and a very good off-spinner, and as it happened a fine fielder, even if his name of Kripal Singh suggested otherwise.

A splendidly eclectic bunch of journalists, representing just about every angle that Fleet Street could come up with, was covering the tour. I always felt that Johnny Woodcock, my guide and mentor, was the first among equals. I've written a certain amount about 'Wooders', as he is universally known, and I sometimes wonder if anyone has ever written better about the game. I am sure that no one could ever have laid claim to be a better reporter and recorder of a day's cricket. He was an acute watcher of play, and missed nothing. If we were at the same match, I would always turn anxiously to Wooders' piece in *The Times* the next morning, and invariably he would have seen and written about at least a couple of things that I had failed to spot. He also had a rare ability to be able to write about a deeply important issue, either on the field of play or in the committee room, and immediately put it into a long-term perspective.

Wooders was short, but what he lacked in inches he more than made up for with his charm, his sense of humour, his mildly dirty, chuckling laugh, and his sheer courage: he has a dodgy pair of hips, which must have been replaced at least a dozen times between them. They have led him on countless occasions to terrifying falls, and many times onto the operating table. He was often in great pain, but never let anyone know. His love of a glass of the right stuff has always been impressive, as have his generosity and his ability to get on with everyone. Alan Gibson, a brilliant writer and commentator, aptly described Wooders in *The Times* as 'the Sage of Longparish'. I have never had a better friend.

There was Michael Melford, whom Brian Johnston quickly turned into 'Mellers'. He was the dearest of men, but he was never too well, and when I knew him he looked as though a businesslike gust of wind might blow him over. His father was the actor Austin Melford, and Mellers himself won an athletics Blue at Oxford, where he was a hurdler. He had a lovely turn of phrase, and the most endearing and gentle sense of humour, which I came across for the first time on this tour. One morning during the first Test in Madras he turned up for breakfast looking more than usually pale and unwell. He made an unsteady progress to our table, where Wooders asked him if things were as bad as they looked. After a moment's hesitation, Mellers smiled weakly and said that during the night he had been to the lavatory no fewer than seventeen times, then added, 'But I am not claiming a world record, because I was wind-assisted.'

Mellers wrote beautifully about the game in the *Daily*

Telegraph, where he was second in command to E.W. (Jim) Swanton, who had not wanted to cover this tour because he was taking a touring side of own to the Far East and India soon after the England side went home in February. My travel agent, Lyn Wellings, was there for the *Evening News*, and as always he moved around with panther-like tread, his mysteries to perform. He was, as ever, a time-bomb, and the point of explosion usually seemed imminent. Wellings was responsible for perhaps the most remarkable incident of the tour, when he erupted in inimitable fashion on the first morning of the fourth Test at Delhi's Feroz Shah Kotla stadium. This ground had originally belonged to the Maharaj Kumar of Vizianagram, who had captained India when they came to England in 1936. He had given the ground to Indian cricket, and although he was now getting on a bit, he was still a member of the All-India Radio commentary team, in a 'What do you think, Vizzie?' kind of way between overs, and also wrote for one of the Indian papers.

Vizzie, who was portly and a trifle pompous, moved about the place with an entourage of retainers, supporters, friends or whatever. In between his commentary duties he liked to come and sit in the back row of the open-air press box, which had desks arranged on each step of the terracing. The three desks in the back row all had Vizzie's name on them; as he was a one-time owner of the ground, it would have seemed unreasonable to complain about this.

Wellings took a different view. He arrived early at the ground, and decided he wanted to sit in the top row, all the seats in which had been assigned to Vizzie. With considerable enjoyment and no little vigour, he removed Vizzie's name from each in turn, and sat down at one of them. Because I was staying in the same hotel, I had accompanied Wellings to the ground, and took up my designated position near the bottom of the box, in spite of his exhortations that I should elevate myself and sit beside him.

After a few minutes I heard raised voices up at the back. Vizzie and his chums had arrived and, finding Wellings in one of their seats, told him he would have to move. Wellings' reply considerably raised the decibel count, and when I looked around much furious gesticulating was going on. It was not long before Vizzie himself began to bubble, and insult followed insult. The exciting climax arrived when Wellings got to his feet, picked up his typewriter, twirled half round to gain a bit of momentum, and let it go. His aim was good, although the target could hardly have been missed, for the typewriter hit the ample tummy of the Maharaj Kumar of Vizianagram plumb in the middle. I thought there was going to be a scuffle, but with the minimum of grace Wellings, muttering with hostile intent but realising he had gone too far, collected his typewriter and moved off to his allotted seat lower down in the box.

It had been entertaining stuff while it lasted, but matters did not rest there. News of the assault was passed on, presumably by Vizzie or one of his cohorts, and reached the ears of the British High Commissioner, Sir Paul Gore-Booth. My presence at the scene of the crime had been noted, and when I returned to my hotel that evening I received a note from the High Commission saying that His Excellency was anxious to see me for breakfast in his residence on the rest day. I think the MCC were somewhat anxious too, and there was later talk that Wellings might be expelled from the club.

I went to breakfast as bidden, and His Excellency was delightful, as were the other senior members of his staff who were present. I told him what I had seen, and I had the impression that he was anxious to let it all blow over – which is what happened. The coffee and scrambled eggs were delicious,

No hint of the dramas to come. Grizel and HCB, aged about one and a bit, in the garden at the Home Farm. All seems to be going according to plan.

Top left: When I was young, Tom was a dab hand with a pipe. *Top right:* Grizel at about the same time. An early showing of the gimlet eye.

Above: The Home Farm. I was born in the top left bedroom. The cricket ground was through the farm yard.

Above: Tom with mildly improbable hat, pipe, gun and the Maharajah of Jaipur, ready for a day's shooting on Jai's moor in Scotland.

Left: Nanny Framingham was the saint she looked and I adored her. She came to my family when Anthea was born in 1929.

Above: Not quite Brideshead, but preparing for a May Ball at Cambridge in the Twenties. Tom, dashing with cigarette, is sitting by the spare wheel.

Left: The old 1932 Rolls at the Home Farm with Anthea in stately pose and HCB showing off in the driver's seat.

Below: Ronnie Aird, Secretary of MCC, presents me with the first ever Young Cricketer of the Year award in the Lord's Tavern in 1956.

Above: Letter from Buns Cartwright, the patron saint of the Eton Ramblers, telling me none other than Don Bradman had watched my hundred from the Committee Room at Lord's in 1956.

Right: Tom and Grizel on the tennis court in the garden at the Home Farm. Maddeningly, Grizel had a way of getting everything back over the net.

Left: The Sunningdale School side in 1952 with Edward Lane Fox as the ever shrewd captain. I am on his right.

Right: The Eton Eleven four years later. I am sitting on the right and ELF is on the left.

Above: An historical moment. At Eton, the Dry Bob tug-o'-war team out pulled it over the Wet Bobs for the first time in living memory. ELF, the suave manager, on the right.

Above: Hoveton House, finished in 1666, from the field in front known as The Lawn. The sheep are grazing on what was once the village cricket ground.

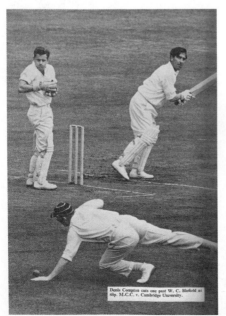

Left: All my dreams come true: me fielding in the gully (unsuccessfully) to my all-time hero, Denis Compton, in his final first-class match at Lord's: MCC v Cambridge in 1959.

Below: A rare leave-alone outside off stump when opening for Norfolk at Lakenham with its lovely thatched pavilion.

Denis Compton cuts one past W. C. Blofield at slip. M.C.C. v. Cambridge University.

Above: Tom and Grizel doing duty at a local wedding in our church at Hoveton St John.

Right: In his last few years Tom looked like a pleasantly avuncular pirate with an eye patch over a detached retina.

Above: In the right corner the aforementioned Raj Kumar of Vizianagram with retainer. Vizzie had given the ground to Indian cricket and predictably won the bout with a technical knockout.

Left: India 1963/64. In the left corner my obstreperous travel agent, friend and colleague, Lyn Wellings, who threw his typewriter at the Raj Kumar before the start of the Delhi Test in 1963/64.

Above: On the outfield before the start at the Brabourne Stadium, January 1964. I am on the left at the back alongside Crawford White and SK Gurunathan (a local journalist). In front is Clive Taylor (sprawling) and Ian Todd.

and having been educated at the same establishment, we discussed it for a while before it was time for him to get on with his day. It would be overstating the case to say that a major diplomatic crisis had been narrowly avoided, but it was an interesting little skirmish nonetheless.

London's *Evening Standard* was represented by the wonderfully idiosyncratic John Clarke, who went around in a trilby hat which made him look more like Inspector Maigret than Inspector Maigret. John was delightfully amusing, and a man with a series of unshakeable fixed habits. During the first Test in Madras, I went down for breakfast one morning and found him sitting on his own holding a newspaper in one hand and a cup of coffee with the other. I pulled out the chair opposite and with a 'May I join you', made to sit down. He looked up sharply, said, 'I am afraid I breakfast on my own,' and turned back to his paper. I shuffled off to another table, feeling somewhat chastened.

The next game was in Hyderabad, against a state side. One evening I returned from the cricket and, clutching my appropriately stamped passport, made my way to the permit room, past two highly suspicious chaps in khaki who were sitting by the door and positively bristling with weaponry. My passport was closely scrutinised before they reluctantly allowed me to proceed. I was mildly surprised not to be given a severe talking-to about the dangers of alcohol. John was sitting at a corner of the bar reading a newspaper and smoking a pipe while he drank a sizeable glass of beer. I went up to him and made some frivolous remark, then attempted to sit down on a neighbouring stool. 'I always have my first pint of the evening on my own with the paper and my pipe,' he said. Once again I shuffled off feeling like an errant schoolboy.

Crawford White toiled away relentlessly on behalf of the *Daily Express*. A tall and striking Lancastrian whose hair was beginning to go dashingly grey, he was always good-humoured, to me at any rate: typically, he referred to Bombay as 'Bombers'. He was an inveterate hummer, especially when composing his pieces. As a journalist he was perhaps a little insecure, and was always obsessed by what his competitors on the other papers might be writing, fearful that he might be scooped. He loved a pretty girl, and was always courtesy itself. The only time he showed edginess or unease was in the morning after he had received a late-night cable from his sports editor which told him either that his copy had not come through or that he had indeed been scooped.

Ian Wooldridge was there for the *Daily Mail*, having been a surprise selection for the tour to Australia the previous winter, when he had in effect unseated the long-serving Alex Bannister. Ian was a brilliant journalist who for years, until his death in 2007, wrote the best weekly sporting column in Fleet Street. What fun he was. He took on life in capital letters, and whoever he came into contact with, whether it happened to be Alex Ferguson, Idi Amin (with whom he was once photographed in boxing pose), or anyone else. We had a strong mutual interest in good red wine, and always laughed together endlessly whenever we met. This Indian tour was the first time I had seen him at work, and I never met anyone who took greater trouble over the piece he was writing, however big or small, important or trivial. And that advice of his, 'Never turn your nose up at a good cliché,' often comes echoing back. Woolers was generous to a fault, a great character and another true friend.

Clive Taylor, another freelance who was in the party, was a journalist of great skill, whether writing for broadsheet or tabloid. He understood the game well, and you couldn't have wished for a nicer man. He was quietly spoken, but always ready to enjoy a joke and to come back with one of his own.

Most unhappily, he died at the early age of fifty in 1977, having been taken ill during the Centenary Test between England and Australia at the Melbourne Cricket Ground that February. The diagnosis was botched: he was treated for jaundice, and died of peritonitis after the most agonising of flights back to England. His brilliance as a journalist lay in his ability to write a story for the *Daily Mirror* as it was in its pre-red-top days which would have stood up just as well, word-for-word, in the *Daily Telegraph*. Clive was a great and understated man.

This was also Ian Todd's first tour. He had a delightfully fresh-faced charm and a ready laugh. He was almost as young as I was, but a far shrewder and more experienced performer, a master tabloid journalist in the making. He knew exactly what he was doing and what he was after, and went about his business with the minimum of fuss. He was later to make his name on the *Sun* at the time when the battle of the red tops really flared up, and would spend his life going 'head-to-head' with Chris Lander of the *Mirror*, although they were the best of friends.

By the time I left India to return home I knew there was no other life for me. I had enjoyed the writing, and while I had just about got a pass mark with the *Guardian* and the *Observer*, the *Daily Sketch* couldn't possibly have given me more than one and a half out of ten – and that would have been mostly for going to the right country. I don't think I could ever have turned myself into a successful tabloid journalist.

I had visited the amazing Taj Mahal, and gone duck-shooting in the jheels (marshes) around Delhi, a day which was organised by Tiger Pataudi, who owned the land, and included my fellow Norfolk man Peter Parfitt. I met some beautiful young girls from Bollywood, established a lifelong love for curry and all spicy food, and learned just as swiftly to loathe Black Knight whisky, India's own version of the famous drink. Nor was I happy with much of the local beer. It contained a powerful amount of glycerine, which had a most discouraging effect upon my tummy. I did however manage to bump into a fair amount of real Scotch whisky, which may have been the reason I somehow steered clear of a serious tummy upset.

I stayed in the Great Eastern Hotel in Calcutta, visited Firpo's, the famous nightclub in the same city, and went to the polo and the races on the maidan in Alipore. In Bombay I drank a dispiriting lime-and-soda in a huge bar in the Taj Mahal Hotel which had been rendered ghost-like by prohibition, although the Taj is now once again one of the great hotels of the world. I write this having just stayed there with Valeria for ten days during England's tour of India in November 2012. There was so much else too. Those six weeks in India were truly mesmerising, and I was sorry to see them end, as I had acquired a real taste for it all.

SEVEN

A Lie at the Blue Mountain End

When I returned from India, my journalistic career continued with reasonable success, although it was being asked to finance a lifestyle that was some way out of its reach. Now that I was a married man and a father, I fear that there were some who thought it was horribly self-indulgent of me not to throw journalism in, and find a job which would lend rather more of a hand towards paying the bills. Grizel wasn't the only one to be muttering things, and not so much under her breath either, about me getting a proper job. In addition to the money question, the anti-social hours which my sub-editing duties at the *Guardian* inevitably involved made dinner engagements, at home or away, out of the question. I was also often away from home, sometimes for three or four days at a time, watching county cricket. But if the increasingly vocal lack of support did anything, it was to make me even more determined to prove them all wrong, and to plough on until I had done so.

I had been playing Minor County cricket for Norfolk since 1956, although my journalistic commitments meant that I now had to give this up, as I couldn't take the time off to play. In 1964 Norfolk finished high enough in the table to qualify for a place in the following year's Gillette Cup. We were drawn to play Hampshire on a Saturday in May at the old Northlands

Road ground in Southampton, and I was asked to play. Bill Edrich was born in Norfolk and began his career in the county side. When he retired from the first-class game, he came back to captain us in the Minor County Championship and he and Colin Ingleby-Mackenzie now went out to toss. Bill guessed wrong, and we fielded. Roy Marshall, who had opened the batting for the West Indies, gave them a typically thunderous start, but we managed to restrict them to 295 for 7 in their sixty overs. In the dressing room between innings Bill assured us that we would win in a canter, but unfortunately it didn't work out quite like that. I went in first, and we fought valiantly, if unproductively, against Derek Shackleton, Butch White and Bob Cottam, all of whom at one time or another bowled for England. 'Shack' bowled ten overs for 20 runs; I did once drive him to the straight boundary, which he took on the chin. My most glorious moment came when I square-cut Butch White for four. I don't think that worried him unduly either. It rained that evening, and the game could not be finished. Of course we did not play on Sundays in those days, so we all had to turn up again on the Monday morning. We had not lost too many wickets, but the problem was that we couldn't score any runs. Then Colin Ingleby-Mackenzie had the inspired idea of turning to Peter Sainsbury's left-arm spin, whereupon we made the Gadarene swine look like selling platers. He took seven wickets for almost nothing; I was stumped by many a mile trying to force things along. But I had made 60, which was fun. I rang the *Guardian* when the game was over, and David Gray suggested I write a piece about the whole experience. I churned out seven hundred words, which appeared next day under the headline 'Leg Slip to Marshall'. After my two days in the sun I returned to my sub-editing duties in Gray's Inn Road, which I have to say was a bit of a letdown.

There was one highly diverting moment when we were in

the field, which was surely unique in the entire history of the game. One of our most doughty batsmen was the Reverend A.E.H. Rutter, who answered to the name of 'Claude'. His batting style was upright, with an occasional skittish stroke thrown in. He was tall, bespectacled, very jolly, and when he spoke he always managed to sound as if he was mindful of his duties in the pulpit, even if he was calling you for a quick single at the time. When he ran, his gait had a distinctly ecclesiastical flavour to it. I have to say I always felt his calling and running between the wickets showed that his Christianity had its blind spots. But it was in the field, in the covers, that he made his small contribution to history. A ball was driven firmly in his direction, and with a flurry of arms and legs he did well to get to it. Then it all went wrong. He lost his balance, and there was a terrifying twirl as Claude became airborne. His chin, or thereabouts, must have hit the ground first, because the next thing we knew was that he had dislocated his jaw. Later on, of course, we had a tremendous laugh at his expense. It must have been extremely painful, and surely made him a spent force in the pulpit for some weeks to come.

Employment was more infrequent during the winter, although I was prepared to take anything on. There was one day when the *Guardian* sent me off somewhere near Watford to watch a county rugger match, followed that same evening by Stamford Bridge, where Chelsea were entertaining a northern side. Unfortunately, I wrote in the piece about the rugger match that straight from the kick-off, Hertfordshire took the ball into their opponents' penalty area, when of course I meant into their opponents' twenty-five, as it was in those pre-metric days. The sub-editor either failed to spot it or smilingly let it go through. That was the end of my rugby-reporting career.

I somehow managed to avoid Chelsea taking the ball into their opponents' twenty-five later that evening.

After a year or two I became the *Guardian*'s sort of unofficial Midlands football correspondent, and spent many weekday evenings and Saturday afternoons in and around Birmingham exploring the delights of such grounds as the Hawthorns, Villa Park, St Andrew's, Molineux and Highfield Road. There was also one truly memorable visit to the Victoria Ground in Stoke, on the occasion of Stanley Matthews' final league match for Stoke City. He was fifty years old, and dribbled the ball down the right wing with beguiling footwork which mesmerised a Fulham defence that included full back George Cohen, who was later to become a member of England's World Cup-winning side in 1966. Matthews didn't score a goal, but he laid one on and had a hand in another. Although I was once sent to watch Scotland play Italy at Ibrox, this game at Stoke was easily my greatest footballing moment. It was incredible to see a legend working his magic, and at the age of fifty as well. It could never happen today, for wingers as such are all-but extinct, and Matthews, with his delicate footwork, would have had his legs scythed instantly from under him. Stanley Matthews and Wayne Rooney would have been not so much chalk and cheese as Fred Astaire and an athletic bulldozer.

I couldn't wait to go on another overseas tour. Although my visit to India had not produced any dramatic increase in my financial status, it had introduced me to a way of life I found irresistible. In 1964–65 England went to South Africa, but I could find no takers for my services. The same happened the year after, when England toured Australia, and so I continued to rattle my way around the football grounds of the Midlands. In the summer of 1967 I found myself writing about cricket for the *Sunday Express*, who paid me a fraction more than the *Observer*. I was never certain why Leslie Vanter, the stocky, voluble, black-moustached and moderately dictatorial sports editor who loved a good story – the naughtier the better – decided he wanted my services. I greatly enjoyed the experience, and my visits to the Express Group's shining black headquarters in Fleet Street, which was, if anything, even closer than the *Observer* to El Vino's. Like all the staff at the *Sunday Express*, Vanter was mightily apprehensive about the formidable John Junor, the paper's all-powerful editor, who would never brook anything that looked remotely like dissent, and was probably a stinker in any coinage. He was a tyrant and a bully in the way that poachers turned gamekeepers can easily become.

On a few occasions when I was visiting Vanter and his delightful, understated and highly competent deputy Gus Hines, Junor, a combative Glaswegian who had been befriended by the proprietor of the paper, Lord Beaverbrook, would walk through the office. Instantly, the atmosphere would chill, and when he returned to his own quarters the huge sense of relief was abundantly clear. I had met Junor a year or two before, at a drinks party given by a friend of Joanna's parents in north Sussex when he was friendly in a remote, looking-over-your-shoulder sort of way. On one of my visits to the sports department he burst upon the scene, grabbed my hand and thanked me profusely for all I had done for the paper. I felt very important, although I was mildly surprised that my contributions, which seldom amounted to more than about eight modest paragraphs on the inside back page, should have impressed the great man as much as they apparently had. I mumbled modestly, and when he walked away I felt I had been anointed. As soon as Junor was back behind closed doors in his own office, Vanter swiftly put me back in my place. He told me that Junor had mistaken me for James Mossop, who at that time was a relatively new recruit, based in Manchester, from where he wrote long, telling and controversial pieces, mostly about football. I shuffled off a broken man, and I still wonder if anyone ever dared to tell Junor of his mistake.

Every year the staff of the *Sunday Express* played a gloriously unlikely game of cricket against the diocese of Oxford, who were captained with charming eccentricity by the vicar of Blewbury, Hugh Pickles. He had once been chaplain at Worksop College, where he never let us forget that he had a hand in coaching the young Phil Sharpe, who later caught swallows in the slips for Yorkshire and England, and much later for Norfolk, besides scoring plenty of runs. Hugh was passionate about the game, and could often be found on county grounds, especially at New Road in Worcester, in the company of his small, Jack-Russell-inspired mongrel called Justice. I think he would have placed Justice marginally ahead of the Almighty in his own personal pecking order. When Justice departed this life Hugh anxiously rang up an ecclesiastical friend to ask about the church's current thinking about animals in the hereafter. I don't think he received a reply that fully satisfied him. His form in the pulpit, from which he dispensed prehistoric views about almost everything, was never less than amusing, although inconsistent. He was tall, with sloping shoulders, and his clothes, thickly covered with Justice's hair, invariably needed an urgent appointment with a dry cleaner, and maybe an estimate first. On the one occasion I turned out for the *Sunday Express* I was probably bowled by a rural dean on a day out, or maybe a day off.

The winter of 1966–67 produced a wonderful piece of luck, for which I really have to thank Joanna, who dipped her hand deep into her purse. Jim Swanton's Arabs were going to tour Barbados for a month in early 1967. Jim and his wife Ann had built themselves a charming house, Coralita, beside one of the fairways of the old nine-hole golf course at Sandy Lane, and Jim, as was to be expected, had become a somewhat magisterial figure in the island, with Ann giving him admirable support. He received important help in organising the tour from Peter Short, who ran Barbados cricket for years, and also managed some West Indies teams overseas. He was charming and great fun, with the most impressive moustache in the business outside an H.M. Bateman cartoon. I was keen to go on the tour, but obviously I would have to pay my own way. Thanks to Joanna's generosity, we both signed up.

The side was captained by Colin Ingleby-Mackenzie, and we were a spirited body of men. I remember our aeroplane at Heathrow being delayed by a few minutes to give our captain time to arrive from the gambling club in Berkeley Square in which he had spent the night hoping to make enough money to pay for the tour. He slept well on the flight, and when we arrived at what was then called Seawell Airport in Barbados he was asked, in front of television cameras, what he thought of his side. In light-hearted tones he said, 'We have no weaknesses except the manager,' a comment which was quoted in one of the papers the next day. It produced only the briefest of smiles from Jim when we drew it to his attention. It was at Seawell Airport that I had my first ever rum punch thrust into my hand; I knew at once that we would establish the warmest of personal relationships.

They were an amazing three weeks. We stayed at the Paradise Beach Hotel, which then seemed aptly named, but on future visits to Barbados grew less paradisical and more touristical. On the way to the nets on our first morning, Jim insisted that we called in at the lodge at Government House to sign the book in which visitors officially announced their arrival in the island. Noblesse still very much obliged. A central character of the tour was Jim's driver, Gibbons, a small man with a mischievous grin below a modest but purposeful moustache, and an endearing habit of saying 'That I do believe' if you said something to him with which he agreed. He wore a homburg hat which he unfailingly and intriguingly took off from behind. He was a religious man, and was a trifle confused by one of our players, the Earl of Cottenham. Whenever he was questioned about the likely arrival time of the Earl, whom Gibbons felt it was his right to propel around the island, he would take his hat off and say with great solemnity, 'The Lord is coming.'

Matches had been arranged against a number of local club sides – one of which, Pickwick, played at Kensington Oval where the West Indies played Test cricket – and some schools, including Lodge, the Eton of Barbados, where there was a cane field along one boundary. Recovering a ball that been hit for six meant organising an expedition. Our final match was against Everton Weekes's XI at Kensington. After a sharp storm the uncovered pitch was next to unplayable, and Danny Piachaud, our off-spinner who played for Oxford, Northamptonshire and Sri Lanka, almost made the ball talk. The great Everton, with whom I was to commentate many times in later years, was then past forty, but he came in and, with footwork you would not believe, made 70 of the most extraordinary runs I have ever seen, let alone kept wicket to. His innings reminded me of Denis Compton's 71 at Lord's. Surprisingly, with the important assistance of a local fast bowler, Keith Walters, we beat Everton's eleven, which included three other former Test players: the charmingly urbane Peter Lashley, a left-handed batsman, who had played in the famous tied Test in Brisbane in 1960–61; the small, fair-haired wicketkeeper

David Allan; and the tall, upright opening batsman Robin Bynoe. It was all an unforgettable experience.

When I got back from the West Indies, the *Sunday Express* laid claim to my by-line, and the *Daily Telegraph* had, therefore, to be content to use my first two names, Henry Calthorpe. I was happy with this, as the Calthorpe family were distant relations, which meant that the Honourable F.S.G. Calthorpe, who captained MCC on its first ever tour to the Caribbean in 1929–30, was a kinsman of a remote sort. It was the Calthorpe family who in 1885 had leased the ground at Edgbaston to Warwickshire County Cricket Club. A long time ago a male Blofeld married a Miss Calthorpe, who was the last surviving member of a branch of the Calthorpe family. Ever since, male Blofelds on that important visit to the font were dished out with Calthorpe as one of their Christian names. When my nephews' sons were born, however, it was felt that enough was enough, and Calthorpe was allowed to go past the off-stump, as it were. I don't blame them in the least, although I have always thought there is something rather splendid about being a part of that sort of tradition, and in a way it is sad to see it go. I suppose only old fuddy-duddies like me object.

Meanwhile, life in 1968 went on much as it had done before. By the time I had returned from the West Indies, the joy of touring was flowing pretty rapidly throughout my veins. I was at a point of no return. If I needed any confirmation that I was on the right track this was it. Come what may, I was going to see it out.

The following winter, 1968–69, I went to Australia to watch the West Indies being severely trounced, which was another enthralling adventure. This visit was to begin a close relationship with Antipodean cricket, and from the late seventies to the nineties I would cover every series played in Australia. Each year in early February I would also fly across the Tasman Sea and spend getting on for two months in New Zealand, where I watched cricket mostly on behalf of Television New Zealand. What adventures they were.

For all that, the most significant event for me in 1968 happened in June, at a county match at Lord's. I was chatting away about nothing in particular to John Thicknesse, who had succeed John Clarke at the *Evening Standard*, when he suddenly said, 'Why don't you see if you could commentate on the game?' I had never thought about this before, and it took a moment or two for the idea to sink in. Of course, I quickly realised it would be a splendid idea if it came off, and I asked him how I should go about it. He suggested that I write to the Head of Outside Broadcasts (OBs) at BBC radio and ask him if they would be prepared to give me a trial commentary, to see if I had a suitable voice and the ability to describe what was going on.

The Head of OBs at that time was Robert Hudson, who was an outstanding broadcaster in his own right, and BBC radio's lynchpin when it came to state or royal occasions. He had made his name as a rugger commentator, and had later turned to cricket. I had never met him, although I had listened many times to his charmingly understated voice. I duly wrote to him, and was surprised to receive an answer within a few days saying that he would be delighted to give me a trial. A few days later he got in touch again to ask if I would be able to go along to The Oval for a midweek county game in July, on which Brian Johnston would be commentating for listeners to the old Home Service.

In those days three county matches would be covered by the BBC: one in London, another in the West Country, and a third in the North. The idea was that when Brian had finished his ten-minute spell in the morning and had handed over to, say, Alan Gibson in Bristol, I would go into the box and do twenty minutes of commentary, which would be recorded down the line in Broadcasting House. I sat beside Brian's scorer, the old Middlesex wicketkeeper Fred Price. Needless to say, I was incredibly nervous, but when, to get things under way, Brian said into the microphone, 'We'll now go over to Henry Blofeld,' I found that the words came quite fluently out of my mouth. Brian had thoughtfully gone to sit in the stand outside the box, so as not to make me feel too intimidated. I rattled on for twenty minutes, and then had another go in the afternoon when Brian had finished his next piece. I remember feeling as if I was in a vacuum when it was over and not at all sure if I had got anywhere near a pass mark. I was afraid I hadn't been much good – but at least I had tried it, which was something.

There was nothing I could do then but wait anxiously for further contact from Robert Hudson. It must have been about a week before another BBC envelope arrived and I tore it open, fearful of what I might find inside. It was a letter of one paragraph asking me to come to Broadcasting House at a quarter to five the following Thursday afternoon to discuss the recordings from The Oval. It was signed by Henry Riddell, who was the Assistant Head of Outside Broadcasts (Sound).

On the appointed day I put on a suit and was at Broadcasting House in plenty of time. I can still remember each moment as if it was yesterday. I gave my name to one of the girls at the huge semi-circular front desk, then waited for ten minutes before an attractive, smiling girl arrived and ushered me through a labyrinth of corridors and up in a lift. Eventually we arrived at her small office, perched outside a door which presumably led to a bigger office. I waited there while she went through the door and spoke to her boss. She soon returned, followed by a large man who must have been around sixty and was wearing a dinner jacket. He asked me to come into his office, and then gestured towards an upright chair in front of his desk. I sat down, I should think more than a trifle awkwardly, for I was excited and nervous. It never occurred to me that he was unlikely to have summoned me to his office just to tell me that I was a lost cause. I was still a little surprised to find him in a dinner jacket in the middle of the afternoon, but he explained that he lived in Brighton, and liked to dine at his club in Pall Mall before catching the last train home; in those days dining at your club meant wearing a dinner jacket. I wondered if he shared that last train with members of the Crazy Gang, Bud Flanagan et al., who also lived in Brighton and went back there each night after their wonderfully funny shows. My father, Tom, had loved the Crazy Gang, and each year the family descended upon the Victoria Palace theatre to see their new show. Even now I can remember the splendidly avant garde humour, or so it seemed then, which only the Crazy Gang could get away with.

Henry Riddell had spent most of his life with the BBC, beginning his career there in the days of Lord Reith. He told me in a quiet voice that he wanted me to listen to my two recordings before we talked about them. He then flicked a switch, and suddenly I filled the room. This was the first time I had ever heard a recording of my own voice. I did not enjoy it, and have never done so since. I am not sure that it's possible to hear your own voice as it sounds to others, and I always think I sound like a pompous prat. When we finally got through it, I was acutely aware that there were any number of things I could have described a great deal better.

Henry Riddell leaned forward, and began to tell me, slowly and quietly, about the whole business of commentary. He spoke about the pace of delivery, the need to keep up to date and not to let the game get ahead of you. He stressed the importance of always talking in the present tense, because in every over there are six sacred moments at which the ball is bowled, and anything can happen. The commentator has to be ready for any eventuality, and it is important to create an air of suspense at the critical moment. At last he said, 'We like it.' It was not a sort of royal 'we', more an attempt to imply departmental solidarity. 'You try and paint the picture,' he added.

Feeling greatly encouraged, I asked him what he meant by that. He pointed to a painting on the wall opposite his desk. It was of some horses. 'When people look at that picture,' he began, 'they mostly concentrate on the horses. But if it wasn't for the grass under their feet, the trees at their side, the sky above, and then the mount and the frame, it wouldn't be a complete picture. As a wireless broadcaster, you have to be the eyes of the listener. You must position yourself on the ground very precisely, so that he knows exactly where you are sitting. He needs to know where the pavilion is, where the various stands are, and the general setting of the ground. His imagination will then take over, and he'll be able to see the action in his mind and form his own pictures of what's going on while you're talking. If you only tell him about the cricket, he won't get this sense of position so easily, as you won't be giving him the full picture. He'll be in a partial vacuum. Tell the listener what you can see and where you can see it: whether it's to your right or your left, close or far away, and so on.' He didn't encourage me to talk about pigeons and buses and all the other things I have since brought into my commentaries, but I think they may have had their origins in what Henry Riddell said to me that day about painting the picture. 'There are also times,' he went on, 'when the cricket can be repetitive and dull, with nothing much happening. Then, if you paint the picture, it will lighten things for the listener.'

He added one or two other points about the medium of broadcasting, and ways of putting across cricketing technicalities. After about an hour of this, he said quietly, 'Yes, we think you have a good idea of what's needed, and we're going to add your name to the list of BBC cricket commentators.' I simply couldn't believe my ears. He then added as a rather sorrowful caveat, 'But I'm afraid there may not be too many opportunities.' I hardly took that in, and have seldom been more excited than I was when I left Broadcasting House that evening and ended up, as usual, in La Speranza, probably with my last ten-pound note.

This conversation, which took place in early August 1968, left me full of hope. But, as I say, I had not taken his caveat to heart, and by the end of the 1971 season the telephone had still not rung. That winter, 1971–72, I once again made my way to the Caribbean, to watch New Zealand's first ever tour to the West Indies. I had had my work cut out to persuade two or three sports editors that it would be an interesting series. New Zealand were not the strongest of sides, and were unlikely to cause many ripples in the Caribbean.

The tour began in Jamaica, and early in February 1972 I found myself, not for the first time, at the old Courtleigh Manor Hotel in north Kingston. It was two days before the opening game of the tour, Jamaica v. New Zealand at Sabina Park, and just before eight o'clock in the evening I was sitting by myself and studying the menu at a small table in the hotel's less than stately dining room when a New Zealand voice said over my shoulder, 'May I join you?' I looked round to see a chap of medium height with fair, crimped hair and eyes that didn't give much away. 'Of course,' I said, and grasped his

154

outstretched hand. He introduced himself as Alan Richards of the New Zealand Broadcasting Corporation. We had never met, and I'm sure he didn't have a clue who I was. I recognised his name, though, as I had heard his commentary when New Zealand had played England. As still happens today, the visiting country's main broadcaster sends over its principal commentator with the team. His job is to broadcast back to his audience at home, and he also joins the local commentary team. That was the role Alan Richards was to fulfil on this tour.

In each West Indian territory there were two competing radio stations: the government station and also a commercial broadcaster, most of which in those days were owned and run by the English company Rediffusion. During a Test series in the Caribbean both networks gave the cricket blanket coverage. The visiting commentator invariably joined the government-owned station in each island, while the commercial channel also liked to have someone from the visiting country on its airwaves.

I could see that Alan was worried, although he was not a man given to letting his hair down, either on the air or off it. Curiously, his main love in life was football – perhaps that was where he indulged himself outrageously – although he always seemed to me a man of restraint, except when describing lbw decisions with which he did not agree. He had arrived in the Caribbean only one day before me, and had spent the day of my arrival at Sabina Park watching the New Zealanders practise. My more modest role in cricket came to light during our conversation, and when I had finished explaining who I was he leaned across the table and said, 'Have you ever done any commentary?' Something went off in my head, and I sensed a chance. 'Oh yes,' I replied. 'I've done lots over the last year or two. County level, mostly,' I added self-deprecatingly. He pushed his chair back a fraction and said, 'You know, you may be just the man I want. You see, I'm in an awkward situation. Before I left New Zealand, the Caribbean Broadcasting Union [the government-owned network] approached Radio New Zealand and asked if they would allow me to join their commentary team while I was here. My bosses naturally agreed. I was watching our blokes in the nets this morning when this chap came up to me and asked if I was Alan Richards. I said I was, and he said that was great, because "you commentate with us". Knowing of the arrangement that had been made, I said I was his man. He told me the commentary box was above the sightscreen at the Blue Mountain end of the ground, and that they'd like me to be there at 10.15 the day after tomorrow for the start of play for the game against Jamaica. We shook hands, he bought me a Coke, and I didn't think any more about it. Then, after lunch, I was sitting in the front of the pavilion when another man comes up to me and asks if I'm Alan Richards, and we go through the whole thing again, although this time we were positioned above the other sightscreen. I told him I'd already been made aware of everything, and that I'd see him in the box before the start of play. Later, talking to a couple of locals in the pavilion, I heard that there are two networks on the island, and that they'll both be commentating all day from boxes over the sightscreen, but at opposite ends of the ground. I realised then that I'd agreed to commentate simultaneously for two different stations. That's why I badly need your help.'

The next morning at Sabina Park, Alan introduced me to the suave Winston Ridgarde, who ran sport and probably the whole of RJR, Radio Jamaica. He was a charming man, and was suitably impressed by my fictitious credentials to sign me up to commentate for RJR on Jamaica v. New Zealand. If all went well, he said, he would also want me in the RJR box for the second game of the tour, when New Zealand played the President of the West Indies Board's XI at Jarrett Park in Montego Bay, and maybe for the First Test too. I could hardly believe my luck, although I soon began to wonder if I had bitten off rather more than I could chew. Having listened to cricket commentary on radio for as long as I could remember, as well as doing those trial tapes for the BBC, I thought I had a pretty good idea of what to do. But now that I was actually about to do it, I was not so sure. I met the rest of the commentary team that night. Among them was Jackie Hendriks, a Jamaican who had kept wicket for the West Indies with great distinction in the latter part of the Wes Hall–Charlie Griffith era, when those two formidable fast bowlers reigned supreme. Jackie was a good commentator, who brought with him the most infectious of chuckles, and was always full of good humour. Then there was our scorer, the unforgettable Laurie Foster, an enormous man with an appetite to match and a sparkling sense of humour. He always enjoyed the rather poor jokes we made about how he had to squeeze sideways into our open-air commentary box above the sightscreen at the Blue Mountain end of Sabina Park.

I must have just about got away with it in the Jamaica game, because not only was I signed up for the other two matches in Jamaica, but Winston Ridgarde went so far as to alert RJR's sister stations around the Caribbean to my presence. The visit to Montego Bay on the north coast provided a hugely different, more expensive, tourist-orientated but very enjoyable view of Jamaica. Then I returned to Kingston via the Blue Mountain Inn and its unrivalled Banana Flambé for the first Test, which was a remarkable game and spoke volumes for the tenacity of New Zealand's cricketers as they fought through for a draw. This match saw the debut of the Jamaican batsman Lawrence

Rowe. He made 214 in the West Indies' first innings, and 100 not out in the second. It was remarkable that a young man in his first Test was able to make batting look so easy, and he remains the only player to have made two hundreds, including a double century, in his first Test match. Sadly, he never quite lived up to this extraordinary start. Glenn Turner then batted for nearly ten hours while carrying his bat for 223 not out in the New Zealand first innings. At the end the Kiwis did rather more than hang on, with four second innings wickets left.

We moved on to Trinidad for the second Test, by way of Antigua, where in the game against the Leeward Islands I saw Viv Richards bat for the first time. He was only nineteen, but he gave a massive hint of all that was to follow. For that game I shared a rather diverse commentary box with the conservatively minded Lester Bird, who was later to succeed his father, Vere Bird, as prime minister of Antigua, and Tim Hector, a politician with distinctly communistic rumblings and inclinations which he was not reluctant to reveal.

For the second Test at the lovely Queen's Park Oval in Trinidad I joined forces in the Radio Trinidad commentary box with one of the most eccentric of all commentators, Ralph ('Raffie') Knowles. A white Trinidadian, tall, thin and once fair-haired, he was Trinidad to his bootlaces. His broad accent, which delivered words in (I think) English, at a speed that made a machine gun look like a catapult, was impossible for a visitor to understand. Raffie had once played hockey for the island, and he loved horses – of which he owned a few – and pretty young girls equally, and in any order you like. The fierce Mrs Knowles was, perhaps understandably, less than keen about the latter. He had the most idiosyncratic of commentary styles, which, among other things, consisted of screaming 'He's on his way!' at least ten times in quick succession whenever a batsman was out. He was a terrific enthusiast, but with a slender knowledge of the technical aspects of the game. Also in the box was a man who became a good friend, and whom I admired as much as anyone I have ever commentated with, Gerry Gomez. He had been a more than useful all-rounder for the West Indies at the time of Weekes, Worrell and Walcott, and was the fairest of commentators. He owned a sporting business in Port-of-Spain called Sport and Games, which was known locally as Sport and Gomes.

I couldn't commentate on the third Test in Barbados, because the trade union covering such things there put their foot down for some bureaucratic reason I never understood, and declared that it would have been against their rules if I had taken to the airwaves. As a result I was confined to the press box for the draw at Kensington Oval, which, but for a couple of dropped catches, New Zealand would have won.

The next port of call was Guyana, where the fourth Test was played at Bourda, a lovely small colonial cockpit for cricket with mounted police in full and colourful attire, on both sides of each sightscreen throughout the match. There I joined Radio Demerara, whose sporting chief was another remarkable character, B.L. Crombie. A large man, he spoke with a strong Guyanese accent and produced a gravelly, excitable and, for me, utterly incomprehensible sound which frequently rose to an earsplitting crescendo. He had an English wife, and drove around Georgetown in an elderly but eternally faithful Morris Minor, which he seemed to care for at least as much as he did for her. We were joined in the box by Clyde Walcott, who for part of his life had switched his loyalties from Barbados to Guyana. B.L. was much miffed when the West Indies narrowly failed to win the Test, with Glenn Turner making his second double century of the series. The fifth and final Test in Port-of-Spain was also drawn. This tour was a triumph for New Zealand, who in their wildest dreams would not have expected to come away from the Caribbean with a drawn series.

So, I returned to England at the end of April 1972 a fully fledged Test match commentator, having been able to cut my teeth in circumstances in which I probably committed the most horrendous howlers that mostly went unnoticed. I have no idea whether word had got around or if it was just a coincidence, but waiting for me at home in London was a letter from Robert Hudson, asking if I would be able to go to Chelmsford late in May to cover Essex's game against Warwickshire for BBC Radio 2's Saturday-afternoon sports programme *Sport on Two*. I could not answer the letter quickly enough, and duly turned up at the County Ground with stopwatch (the most crucial piece of equipment), notebook and pen. The commentary box was at the river end of a ground which was then a good deal bleaker than it is today. Little more than a wooden hutch, it was perched on the top of a green BBC van, and entry was gained by means of a rickety ladder. When I had completed my perilous ascent to the box, I found a bearded figure seated inside, with reams of paper in front of him and a couple of briefcases bulging with books as well as his picnic lunch. He introduced himself to me as Bill Frindall. At the time the whole arrangement seemed the last word in exciting modern technology, but looking back now, it makes me think that Heath Robinson might well have had a hand in it all.

The game began, and I watched intently. The programme started at lunchtime, and with headphones on and stopwatch at the ready, I was occasionally told by the producer that they were coming over to me soon for forty-five seconds, or even thirty; just occasionally I had the luxury of a whole minute. Within these extremely tight boundaries I had to try to tell listeners what had been going on. It took me a while to get used to reporting cricket in this awkwardly constricted way, but I soon realised that the most important thing was to stick exactly to the time I had been asked for. The programme probably had reporters at four county matches. If we were all asked to do forty-five seconds, and the first three each went on for a full minute, there would be no time left for the fourth report. The people in the studio at Broadcasting House were much more worried about the timing than the content, as long as one didn't make a complete hash of it. By no stretch of the imagination could this be called commentary, although there were times later that summer when I would be actually asked to commentate for an over or two before handing back to the studio.

Under the Bearded Wonder's watchful eye, I managed to do roughly what I was told on that first day at Chelmsford, and I left the ground hoping it had gone well enough for me to be asked again. Imagine my surprise, therefore, when the following week I got another letter from Robert Hudson, asking if I would be free to commentate on the second and third one-day internationals against Australia at Lord's and Edgbaston in late August and early September. This was the first one-day international series ever to have been played anywhere in the world. I could hardly believe my luck.

As those two days drew closer, I found myself growing more and more apprehensive. I was about to share a commentary box with the likes of John Arlott, Brian Johnston, Alan McGilvray, Freddie Brown, Norman Yardley, Jack Fingleton, and even the formidable Jim Swanton, who provided measured and brilliant summaries at the end of each day's play. These were people I had grown up listening to in the nursery at Hoveton, and for me they had acquired a god-like status. Suddenly, if only for two days, I was going to be one of them.

I was as nervous about the illustrious company I was going to keep as I was about doing the commentary itself. I had scarcely met McGilvray, Brown or Yardley, and apart from Swanton, I had not done much more than touch base with any of the others. I would have raced back to the commentary box in Trinidad without the slightest qualm, but that series in the West Indies now seemed a million years away.

I felt very much the new boy as I walked into the commentary box for the first time on that first morning at Lord's, but I was warmly greeted by the slightly overbearing Michael Tuke-Hastings, the producer, who was to retire at the end of that season and make way for Peter Baxter. Tuke-Hastings, a large man with fair hair and glasses, raised strong feelings in others. He and John Arlott would never have sent each other Christmas cards, although by a strange coincidence they were to end their days as near neighbours on the tiny island of Alderney where they still didn't speak. There was something dictatorial about Tuke-Hastings' manner that did not appeal to everyone. He also produced *Forces' Chance*, a quiz programme that was broadcast from the various parts of the world in which British troops were stationed. On one of the trips for that show he found himself introduced as 'Michael, Duke of Hastings', and showed a marked reluctance to put the record straight.

Everyone else in the box was also extremely welcoming, but it hardly calmed my nerves. After what seemed an age, the game began, and eventually my first twenty-minute spell at the microphone came around. I can't remember who handed over to me, but somehow I got through it, although it was a bit like going in to bat at Lord's for the first time: once I had spoken my first sentence, and in effect had gone through the gate and out onto the grass, I felt much more at home. No one was friendlier than the two summarisers,

Freddie Brown and Norman Yardley, both of whom had captained England when I was still in short trousers. They did their very best to make me feel at ease, and when I asked them questions on air neither of them made me feel I was an idiot. I well remember the pomp and ceremony that, as I was soon to learn, always greeted Jim Swanton's arrival in the box in preparation for his close-of-play summary. He always did this brilliantly, even if he did at times sound like a medieval monarch addressing his courtiers.

England batted first, and made 236 for 9, at that time the highest score that had ever been made in a fifty-five-over contest – although admittedly this was only the third one-day international to have been played. How times have changed: today a score of 400 would not be unknown in a fifty-five-over innings. But Australia broke the new record and won the match, levelling the series, for England had won the first at Old Trafford.

I somehow managed to get through my first day on *Test Match Special* without committing any sins that were too appalling. We moved on to Edgbaston for the third game, which England won amid great excitement by two wickets after being set 180 to win. I thought that day went reasonably well for me too, but at the end I was given a fearful dressing-down by Jim Swanton after he had done his close-of-play summary. During the day there had been a discussion between Alan Gibson – this was the only time I ever commentated with him – and the former Australian opening batsman Jack Fingleton, about the reasons why a cricket ball swings in the air. Gibson quoted a letter from a distinguished professor of aerodynamics, but in the end the discussion was inconclusive. Shortly after it had finished, Gibson handed over to me, and I started by saying that whatever the reason for the ball swinging, there was no doubt that it did so, as I had discovered many times when facing the new ball.

After the close of play Swanton came up to me and said, in the fiercest of voices, 'How dare you talk about your own insignificant cricket as a new, young commentator surrounded in the box by former Test cricketers.' I was amazed by his words, as in no way had I been trying to show off. But of course I took them to heart, for it was as if Moses or Edward the Confessor had wagged a finger at me. For a long time after that I never so much as mentioned on air that I had ever played cricket.

This blip apart, I thought I had acquitted myself reasonably enough. Of course I hoped I would be called into action the following year, when New Zealand and the West Indies would both be playing three Tests in England. But while the telephone summoned me for more stopwatch-orientated county cricket, I never got a touch as far as the Test matches were concerned. I was beginning to think that maybe I hadn't done that well in those two one-day games after all, although I realised there was not much room for new commentators such as me, because John Arlott and Brian Johnston were automatic selections for every Test, and then there was the visiting commentator – in 1973, Alan Richards accompanied New Zealand, and Tony Cozier came over with the West Indies – which meant that if any other commentator was to have a chance, four commentators would have to be used. That year Alan Gibson filled the fourth spot on three occasions and Neil Durden-Smith, with whom I had never commentated, on two, while Christopher Martin-Jenkins had done his first Test in the last game of the summer, against the West Indies at Lord's. In football parlance, I was still on the bench.

So it was a great relief when, in the spring of 1974, Peter Baxter got in touch and asked me to do the first Test against India at Old Trafford. Although I had done those two one-day internationals, I was still pretty nervous, but for a slightly different reason. It was becoming a tradition for the commentators to carry on talking about anything and everything when bad light or rain stopped play. This was to become a much-loved feature of the programme. There had been a wet start to that summer, and being played in Manchester, it seemed pretty likely that the first Test would be affected by rain. I was not at all sure that I would be any good at contributing to the banter that went on when there was no cricket.

John Arlott, Brian Johnston and CMJ were my fellow commentators. In those days, when we were at Old Trafford, the *TMS* team stayed at an early motel called the Swan at Bucklow Hill, on the road to Manchester, a mile or two south of Altrincham. The rooms were in a modern redbrick chunk built around a severe, custodial courtyard, and while the Swan did a job of a sort, its highest ambition would have been to avoid relegation. On our first evening there I had a good glimpse of John Arlott's vibrant oenological leanings. Five of us had dinner together, and John was – metaphorically at any rate – at the head of the table. We had been sitting down for nearly ten minutes, and if at that moment we had had anything in our glasses, and the toast had been to absent friends, it would have been coupled with the name of the wine waiter. When he eventually turned up, John gave him a warning shot across the bows in those exaggerated Hampshire tones: 'To start with, we'll have five of the red and three of the white.' The wine waiter, having no idea who he was talking to, replied, 'You mean glasses, sir?' John was quick to correct that ridiculous assumption: 'Don't be absurd. Bottles, of course.'

The others wished me good luck as we went to our rooms at the end of the evening. I don't think I slept a wink, and felt pretty ropey the next day, most of which I spent scanning the clouds. It did rain, but by sheer chance I never had to help out in the breaks of play, and I stumbled through my commentary spells.

The next day, however, there was no escape. It started coming down like stair rods towards the end of the lunch interval. Johnners got things under way at ten past two, when play should have restarted, in his usual brilliant way. He was amusing, relevant, idiotic and extremely funny, all at the same time. I was down to take over at half past two, and at 2.29 I tiptoed nervously into the back of the smallest commentary box I have ever been in, a wooden affair tucked into the corner of the scoreboard at the Stretford end of the ground. It must have been designed by an architect who had once visited Calcutta, seen the Black Hole and admired it. I hoped no one would notice me, but of course Johnners did, and within seconds I was sitting in his chair. By then I had thought of a few things to say, and looking out at the pouring rain, I set off. I was eloquent, fluent, lucid, funny, pertinent, and I thought rather good. I went on for twelve and three quarter minutes before I ran out of steam and looked to my right, where one or even two of my colleagues should have been sitting, in the hope that they would lend a hand. There was no one there! Help! I had another quick look just to confirm my aloneness, and spotted a piece of paper beside me, with a handwritten note in Johnners' scrawl. I read it quickly: 'Keep going until 6.30, and don't forget to hand back to the studio,' was the bleak news. I could think of absolutely nothing to say, and when I tried, I stuttered and stammered. It was agony and went on for about two minutes – it seemed like two hours – before the door was flung open and they all came tumbling back in, bursting with not so suppressed laughter. I realised later that what Johnners had really been saying was: 'You're playing a team game. Don't forget it.' Which I don't think I ever did again, except for one shameful afternoon in Bulawayo

166

twenty-five or so years later. Apart from that, I don't think the day went too badly, but for those few moments I feared my career as a Test match commentator was over almost before it had begun.

The rain allowed a total of approximately three days' cricket, which was ample for England to beat a weak Indian side. This was Geoffrey Boycott's last Test match before he declined to play for England for the next three years. He was undone by Abid Ali at a brisk military-medium in the first innings, and in the second by Eknath Solkar, who took the new ball with his slow left-arm dobbers. That was it for me in 1974 as far as Test cricket was concerned, but with a Test in England beneath my belt I felt that I had arrived, even though my grip may have been a good deal less than a stranglehold. Apart from that one Test, my summer was spent watching county cricket for the *Guardian*, the *Sunday Express* and, intermittently, for the BBC. I couldn't see how things could get much better. I was at the start of the course I was to pursue with considerable vigour for most of the rest of my life.

EIGHT

Mugabe at the Pavilion End

I have often been asked which cricketing country is the most enjoyable to tour, and I can honestly say that I don't have a preference.

As you will know by now, much as I have always loved the game of cricket, I first entered the press box primarily as a means of escaping the clutches of the City of London. It was jumping into the deep end, for I had no idea if I could write, and by pure luck I found I could. The same went later for commentary. By some fluke I was able to do it. But, as you may already have gathered, I was captivated, perhaps more than anything, by the excitement and variety this way of life seemed to offer. Looking back now, I feel very grateful for the enormous enjoyment I have had from my many years spent watching, writing and commentating about cricket. It has been a life which has been rather like that picture of Henry Riddell's: the cricket may have been the central theme, the prime object of it all, but if it had not been for all those other fascinating adventures on the periphery, the game itself would not have been anything like such fun. The many countries I have visited, the great number of delightful and amusing characters I have come across, the superb restaurants, the delicious food, the formidable wines together with the gut-wrenching plonk, the hotels and clubs in which I have stayed, all the many hysterical and ridiculous adventures along the way. Then, of course, there is the cricket: extraordinary tours, great matches, remarkable individual performances, the controversies that constantly surround the game, from Kerry Packer to Kevin Pietersen, the commentary boxes and their inmates, the press boxes and the scribes inside them, and all the many wonderful stories that have been a part of each and all the good friends I have made. Finally, there are the bit-part characters who may have passed through only briefly, but long enough to leave a footprint even so.

I have, above all, enjoyed watching cricket overseas, and every tour I have covered has been an irresistible adventure. I suppose in some ways I have never grown up, because I still find airports the most exciting of places, in spite of the interminable and exasperating modern security procedures. The taxi journey to Heathrow quickens the pulse, and when the aeroplane leaves the ground – still an anxious moment – there is no turning back. That first glass of champagne, given to you before take-off if you have the luck to turn left on the aeroplane, or even the glass of water in Economy if you don't, has a special taste to it.

Of all the countries I have visited, India has to be the first among equals, if only by an inch or two. On my first trip to the subcontinent, in 1963–64, it was nothing like as sanitised and luxurious for the visitor as it is today, and it was all the better for it. If I had not seen India as it was then, I do not think I could say that I had experienced the true character of the country as it had been for such ages. Each day threw up something new, extraordinary and stimulating, even if that visit coincided with just about the most boring series I have ever watched, with all five Tests being drawn. There is even a sort of perverse logic in the fact that, amid all this debutant's wondrous excitement, the cricketing feat I remember most from that series was slow left-arm spinner Bapu Nadkarni's extraordinary world record of twenty-one consecutive maiden overs in the first Test in Madras. Those six weeks fairly raced by, and made a deep impression on me which was only enhanced on future visits. India is so many things: from the Taj Mahal in Agra to Mother Teresa, Tollygunge and the Calcutta nightclub Firpo's; from the cages in Bombay where the prostitutes plied their trade (and probably still do), to the drug-fuelled atmosphere of hippie Goa. Then there is the relative calm of Bangalore, the IT city, where from the window in the gents' loo in the media stand at the cricket ground, you can still see an imperious statue of Queen Victoria. Not to forget those mouth-tingling, delicious, ever-changing curries – at their hottest in Madras – with the exciting, mingled tastes of the many wonderful spices. The poverty that was so immediately and shockingly visible in 1963 is today not so obvious, and has diminished or been hidden as India's wealth has grown. All these things, and so much more besides, have never failed to enchant, shock, fascinate and enthral me. It is hard to do more than touch the surface of this amazing country, but it is infinitely worthwhile to try.

Tummy troubles or 'Delhi belly', as it was rather cheerfully known by visitors, were another fact of life in India, but much more so fifty years ago than today. In those days Scotch whisky was the sublime disinfectant. Nowadays the water out of the taps in good tourist hotels is unimpeachable; if it was not, the tourist trade would fall apart. Some people used to go to India with iron rations in tins, so they would not have to eat the local food. In my experience they were usually the first to get into trouble, and to go diving for the cement bottle.

Poor old Brian Johnston got on the wrong end of this almost thirty years after I first went to India. Johnners made his first and only visit to the subcontinent when he was almost eighty, having been persuaded by Trevor Bailey to go and watch England play a couple of Tests there. It was surprising that he agreed, because Johnners was the most fastidious of eaters, and everything had to be the plainest English cooking. Anything remotely fancy was no good to him. His lunch during Test matches at Lord's was invariably the same: Nancy, a great character, who for many years presided over the players' and the committee's dining room, always made him the simplest mutton sandwiches, which he ate with relish. The likelihood of him getting on speaking terms with the curry and suchlike in India was not worth considering. Boiled eggs, boiled fish and the odd omelette became his staple diet during his visit. He was also told by a friend in England that his tummy would be helped by a large glass of Scotch after breakfast each day, a drink he loathed more than anything. It was great fun to watch him swallow this while holding his nose in an attempt to obliterate the taste. One morning during the Test in Madras he turned up looking like a ghost. When I asked him if it was really as bad as it looked, he said, 'If anything it's even worse. I invented a new curry last night. It's called Boycott curry. You get the runs just the same, but they come a great deal more slowly.'

There are times when India can be irritating, but getting angry is never the answer and is almost always likely to be self-defeating. I remember when India played New Zealand in the World Cup at Nagpur in October 1987. They had to score the 222 they needed to win inside thirty-six overs if they were to have a home draw against England in Bombay for the semi-finals. In the second over of the Indian innings Sunny Gavaskar came down the wicket and straight-drove Ewen Chatfield over the sightscreen and into the president's box, forcing its occupants to beat a panic-stricken retreat.

Gavaskar's 103 not out came in eighty-eight balls, and was almost as colourful. India won by nine wickets in 32.1 overs. Yet this was the man who perversely, or politically, batted through the full sixty overs for 34 not out in a match India played against England at Lord's in the first World Cup, in 1975. England had made 334 for 4 and in reply India reached 132 for 3. Gavaskar later said he was unable to adapt his mood to the requirements of a one-day game. He had no such problems twelve years later in Nagpur.

I was covering that match in Nagpur for the BBC with Trevor Bailey, and we flew down together from Delhi the day before. When we checked in at Delhi airport, I was asked to pay a lot of money for excess weight on the identical luggage I had been carrying around India without any extra charge for the previous two weeks. I am ashamed to say that I raised my voice in protest, and said more than a few things that would have been better left unsaid. Of course this got me nowhere, and with what little grace I could muster, I paid up. While this was going on, I could see Trevor sadly shaking his head and doing a bit of tut-tutting. After we had gone through to the departure lounge he told me firmly that I had not scored many points, and had behaved stupidly. I felt suitably chastened and rather embarrassed. We watched the cricket the next day, and the morning after that we gathered at the desk in the foyer of the hotel to pay our respective bills. Trevor had just acquired a brand-new gold credit card, and he was immensely proud of it – it had already cropped up a time or two in our conversations. Now, with the air of a conjuror producing a spectacular rabbit out of a hat, he thrust it at the cashier, who took one look at it, said, 'I am afraid, sir, this card is not acceptable,' and pushed it back.

After a brief attempt at negotiation, Trevor hit the roof, and volley after volley of pretty near-the-bone comments poured from his mouth. The cashier, shaking his head a good deal, listened politely, but stood his ground. Trevor revved up a gear or two before realising that he, like me two days earlier, was facing defeat, and there was nothing he could do about it. He had to beat a somewhat ignominious retreat and find another, more modest, slightly dog-eared credit card, which did the business. We didn't speak until we had settled into our taxi. He then turned to me and said, rather shamefacedly trying to muster a smile, 'I don't think I did very well.' 'On the contrary,' I replied. 'I thought you were in mid-season form.'

My most recent visit to India was in November 2012, to commentate on the first two Tests between India and England, in Ahmedabad and Mumbai. Ahmedabad is in Gujarat, a Muslim state, and prohibition is an ugly fact of life, although I think we all arrived with our survival kits. The city was dusty and disorganised, in a charmingly haphazard way. Taxis, mostly elderly post-war Morrises, belched smoke, and auto and manual rickshaws were as good a means of transport. In the streets cows, camels and elephants would turn up in the most unlikely places. We – Valeria was with me – had an intriguing Gujarati lunch at MG House, built of red-and-white-painted wood early in the twentieth century by a colossally rich Gujarati whose initials were MG. Our hotel assured us it was more or less around the corner, and we jumped into a manual rickshaw, but forty-five minutes later we were still not there. A passer-by told us it was just behind us, so our spirited driver did a U-turn and went back the wrong way up a dual carriageway. You soon learn in India that red lights, zebra crossings and so forth are there more for ornamental than practical reasons. Once we had located it, MG House proved to be a most impressive building. We sat on the balcony at the top of the tall red-and-white building looking out across the city. Lunch there was a remarkable eating experience. It came in a myriad of small dishes, containing powerfully spiced contents which varied between the excellent and the awful. As for the Test match, England were outplayed by India on a turning pitch, and lost by 9 wickets. But by the end, after the new captain Alastair Cook had made 176 in the second innings, we departed for Mumbai with just a glimmer of hope.

The Taj Mahal Hotel in Mumbai was bliss, as ever, and was matched by England's cricket in the second Test. India were given the spinners' pitch their captain had asked for, and when they won the toss and batted, the only question seemed to be whether they won in three days or four. England now had left-arm spinner Monty Panesar, who had been obstinately or obscenely left out in Ahmedabad, back in the side, and the bowlers kept India's total down to just over 300. Cook then made another hundred, Kevin Pietersen a much larger one, and in an astonishing partnership batted England to a good lead which effectively won the game. I must hold my hand up here, and say that I would never have had Pietersen back in the side after all he was reported to have said in tweets to the South African dressing room during the Headingley Test in the summer of 2012. He has however been welcomed back, and has settled down in the side. I am now happy with that, but if it should happen again ... Panesar and Swann then outbowled the much-vaunted Indian spinners, bowling faster and to a fuller length, and England won the Test by 10 wickets. For my money it was as impressive a victory as the one famously inspired by Ian Botham and Bob Willis against Australia at Headingley in 1981. By a happy coincidence I was on the air when England won both these games.

This victory gave us all an extra day and a half to enjoy Mumbai before we went our different ways. The English architecture in the centre of the city is sensational, and the shopping is not far behind. On one expedition on foot Valeria and I ran into Alastair Cook and his wife Alice doing their Christmas shopping, and it was lovely to watch the charming and friendly way with which they both coped with all the people who came up to photograph him or ask for his autograph. They told us that earlier that day they had come across a two-year-old boy who had been hungry so they had bought him something to eat. England's cricket is in the best of hands with Alastair Cook, who, as his batting in India in that series showed, is a hard man despite his gentle exterior. If KP should step out of line again, he may find Cook less sympathetic than his predecessor, Andrew Strauss. England went on to win the series by two matches to one and it was most gratifying for them when the following March Australia lost all four Test matches in India.

My second overseas tour was with Colin Cowdrey's England side to the West Indies in 1967–68. This was the first of many tours that I covered in the Caribbean, and it was the one that made the biggest impression on me, just as my first tour to India had had such an indelible impact. In the first Test at Port-of-Spain, which was drawn, although England should have won, Tom Graveney made the most perfect and beautiful hundred I have seen, while a young Clive Lloyd made his first century for the West Indies. This match was played in the amazing build-up to the city's annual pre-Lenten carnival. It was calypso in excelsis.

One of my jobs on that tour was to 'help' Jim Swanton, the fate of many a budding cricket writer, which meant, roughly, doing everything he didn't want to do. He was a tough, not to say bullying taskmaster. Our next port of call was Montego Bay, on Jamaica's north coast. I partied late in Port-of-Spain before attempting to catch an early flight to Kingston the next day. It had been arranged that I would be given a lift to the airport with Jim and his wife Ann, almost certainly in one of the Governor Sir Solomon Hochoy's cars. Jim was on more than nodding terms with Sir Solomon, to whom, despite their rather different origins and antecedents, he had a marked resemblance. On one occasion during this visit he had gone to Government House to have a drink with the Governor, and was left alone in a big reception room for a few minutes. An aide came in and addressed Jim as 'Your Excellency', a case of mistaken identity that would not altogether have displeased Jim.

I am afraid I overslept that morning, and was woken by the telephone ringing in my room in the Queen's Park Hotel. It was a furious Swanton, who told me he was not going to wait for me. I got a taxi to the airport, where I found I had had a great piece of luck because the aircraft was two hours late. I sought out the great man to apologise, but he was nowhere to be found – he and Ann were firmly ensconced in the VIP lounge. Where else? Later, when I stepped forward to say sorry to him, he turned his back, and for several days communicated with me only by message.

This caused a mild problem. Jim was not going to the game against the Jamaican Colts at Montego Bay, preferring to go with Ann to Ocho Rios and stay with Blanche Blackwell, a great friend of Ian Fleming's who was pretty much the uncrowned Queen of Jamaica. He had asked me to write a piece about the game for the *Sunday Telegraph*, but as he did not want the paper to know he was not covering the game, what I wrote would appear under his by-line. Jim always wrote with a certain pomp and circumstance, so I was pleased to be able to insert a 'notwithstanding', a favourite word of his, into the piece. As it happened, the MCC, as they were in those days when not playing Test matches, had to follow on against the Jamaican Colts, which was, to say the least, absent-minded of them, so I had a bit of a story to tell the *Sunday Telegraph*.

Jim and I resumed remote and distant verbal communication in time for the second Test in Kingston. For a time it looked as if England would win the match by an innings. The West Indies followed on, and when their fourth wicket fell at 174 and they were still 49 runs behind, the crowd on the popular side of the ground could take no more of it. Bottles began to fly, the players ran to the pavilion for cover, the police arrived and fired teargas at the rioters, failing to notice that they were aiming it into the wind. As a result the members in the pavilion on the other side of the ground had a much harder time with the teargas than the rioters. Sobers, who went on to make 113 not out, had had a great piece of luck. Tom Graveney had been catching everything at second slip but broke a fingernail and went off for repairs. Basil d'Oliveira took his place and dropped a straightforward catch from Sobers when he was on only 3. In the end England had to score 159 to win on a pitch which had broken up, and Sobers got rid of Boycott and Cowdrey in the first over. There was an unscheduled sixth day to make up seventy-five minutes lost to the rioters, and at the end England were 68 for 8. Phew!

The third Test was a boring draw in Barbados, where England's vice-captain Fred Titmus lost four toes in a speedboat accident at Sandy Lane, before we returned to Port-of-Spain. Another dullish Test match meandered on for four and a half days, at which point Sobers leapt up from his deckchair, clapped his hands and set England to score 215 in 165 minutes. Thanks to Boycott and Cowdrey, who was initially reluctant to go for victory, but was successfully persuaded to chnge his mind by Ken Barrington and John Edrich, they got there by seven wickets, with three minutes to go. There is a good Johnners story from this match too. A couple of days before the Test began he and I returned to the crumbling, colonial grandeur of our hotel to find one of our number and a highly toothsome lady sitting at the back of the colonnaded entrance hall. Being well brought up we went over; our colleague jumped up and said, 'Johnners, I don't think you've met Annette.' 'My goodness me,' came Johnners' reply, 'every time you've told me over the last few days you were going to have a net, I thought you meant you were going to go and play cricket.'

The final Test, played at Georgetown, was a six-day affair, as the series had not been decided. Sobers won an ecstatically acclaimed toss, and he and local boy, Rohan Kanhai, both made 150s. When England batted, the thirty-seven-year-old Tony Lock, Titmus's replacement, made 89, his highest first-class score, and England easily saved the follow-on. The West Indies now made 264 in their second innings, leaving England to score 308 to win or bat for five and half hours to draw the match and win the series. They progressed unsteadily from 33 for 0 to 41 for 5, and then 206 for 9. The final over was bowled by Lance Gibbs, the best off-spinner in the world, to England's last pair of Alan Knott and Jeff Jones, with Jones facing. Somehow he survived. The two batsmen met in mid-pitch before the over began, and had a long natter. Later, I asked Knott what they had been talking about. 'Talking about?' came the reply. 'We sang the first two verses of "Land of My Fathers".' Maybe it was divine intervention that allowed Jones to play out that final over.

Perhaps distance lends enchantment, but it does not distort facts and figures. That series remains the best I have ever seen, *pace* Australia in England in 1981 and 2005. Another reason I remember it so well is that in those days journalists and players mixed freely, and become good friends, which made the joy of winning the series against the odds taste even better.

There was also more humour about, both on the field and off, and somehow the game seemed more romantic than it does today. In all honesty, were those series against Australia any better? True, there is always something especially sweet about beating Australia, but even so, I will live and die by this series in the Caribbean.

My abiding memory of Georgetown on that tour, away from the cricket, is of a concert at which one of Trinidad's most famous calypso singers, the Mighty Sparrow, sang his lovely 1968 Carnival hit 'Good Morning Mr Walker'. He was followed on stage almost immediately by that irrepressible, rumbustious, but ultimately tragic figure, Colin Milburn. Colin never made the Test side in this series, but, resolute and cheerful to the end, he now gave his own vibrant and unforgettably Geordie rendition of 'The Green, Green Grass of Home'. It would have been hard to imagine a more sublime contrast.

Of all the Test-playing countries, there is something unique about Australia, because for an Englishman, the Australians are the oldest cricketing enemy of all. 'The Ashes' are two words which give Australia v. England Test matches a special feeling, and I have to say, tongue-in-cheek maybe, I still think that every other series England plays has only one purpose, which is to prepare us for the next time we take on the Aussies.

I will never forget the first Test I watched England play in Australia. We arrived for the 1974–75 series thinking we had an excellent chance of retaining the Ashes, and I believe many Australians would have agreed. What neither they nor we knew was that Dennis Lillee had fully recovered from injury, and that there was also another chap, who had bowled a wayward over or two for Australia a couple of years before, waiting in the wings. In Melbourne in 1972, Jeff Thomson had played a single Test against Pakistan, and in nineteen wild and expensive overs he had not taken a wicket. He had since moved from Sydney to Brisbane, and had been bowling successfully for Queensland, but when he and Lillee were picked to open the bowling in the first Test in Brisbane, no one expected a great deal. As it was, they blew England out of the water. Lillee bowled with pace and control, while Thommo ran in almost as if he was demented. They took 13 wickets between them, and bruised England so much in body and mind that by the time Australia had won this match by 166 runs, they had effectively regained the Ashes. I don't think Roberts and Holding, Marshall and Ambrose or anyone else has ever come on the scene together with such far-reaching impact.

Although England could not cope, this match did see a truly extraordinary innings. When Tony Greig came to the wicket in the first innings, England were 57 for 4, and Thommo had taken two of them. Greig was a wonderful all-round cricketer, and because of his later defection to Kerry Packer (of which more anon) when he was still a relatively new captain of England, he was never really given full credit for what he achieved as a player. As he strode out to bat now at the Gabba, the England dressing room must have been in a severe state of shock. But Greig had made up his mind to take Thomson and Lillee on. When the ball was short he pulled, slashed or hooked. When it was pitched up he drove like a man possessed – which he was. There was a lot of thrashing and missing too. This was one of the two or three most heroic innings I have seen. I can see him now, flailing Lillee through the covers and extravagantly signalling a four when the ball was still twenty yards short of the boundary, which did not exactly fill Lillee with joy. Whenever Lillee retaliated with a bouncer, Greig would duck out of the way and taunt him either by pretending to wobble at the knees in mock fear, or by walking far down the pitch and tapping vigorously with his bat at a spot not far from the bowling crease. It was electrifying stuff. In all Greig hit seventeen fours and batted for a few minutes short of five hours. These figures may seem a contradiction in terms, but there were long periods of excellent and watchful defence. This was the same Greig who, two years later at Calcutta, on a pitch made for the Indian spinners Bedi, Prasanna and Chandrasekhar, made a hundred in 434 minutes, an innings that won the match for England.

In that match at the Gabba, John Edrich and Dennis Amiss both broke bones in their hands. Desperate measures were called for, and Colin Cowdrey was that desperate measure. He had not played Test cricket for three years, but was called up from England to try to stem the tide in the second Test in Perth, a few days before his forty-second birthday. The day he arrived, he and Alec Bedser, the tour manager, had dinner with Johnny Woodcock, Michael Melford and me at the Weld Club. That would never happen today. After dinner we played snooker, and I had the impression that Colin didn't have a clue what he had let himself in for. When he went out to bat four days later, he went up to Jeff Thomson at the end of his first over with his right hand outstretched and said, 'I don't think we've met. I'm Colin Cowdrey.' Thommo's reply has not been recorded.

Two years later, in March 1977, the Centenary Test was played in Melbourne to commemorate a hundred years of Ashes rivalry. It proved to be a remarkable game. England won the toss, put Australia in and bowled them out for 138. On the second day Lillee bowled better than even he had ever done, taking 6 for 26, and England could only reach 95. In Australia's second innings Rod Marsh became the first wicket-keeper to score a hundred against England, who now had to make 463 to win. Derek Randall, playing his first Test against Australia, made an extraordinary 174, and from time to time on the last day gave England hope that they might just do it. In the end they lost by 45 runs, which, incredibly, was also Australia's margin of victory in the first ever Test match. On that final day the Queen and Prince Philip met the players during the tea interval. When Lillee asked the Queen for her autograph, she refused, but he was sent a signed photograph later. It all seemed like a cricketing fairy story – but while these events were being played out, the cohorts of Kerry Packer, who was soon to become the villain of the piece, were lurking in the corridors of the pavilion.

One of the most amusing things to have happened to me in all the time I have spent watching cricket in Australia occurred one morning at the Sydney Cricket Ground in 1978–79. England, under Mike Brearley, were effectively playing an Australian second eleven, as the best Australian players had joined Kerry Packer's World Series Cricket. At the beginning of the series I had been asked by the Australian Broadcasting Commission if I would have a ten-minute chat each day in front of the camera with their commentator Peter Meares. This was always an amusing brief interlude, as Peter was great fun, and ever ready to have a laugh. We had done this slot during the first three Tests, and in the first week of January we arrived in Sydney for the fourth. The SCG had recently been impaled by six vast black floodlight pylons, a Packer by-product, and I was sitting in the press box in the morning session when someone told me to have a look at something that had been attached to the lower part of the pylon on the famous Hill. I peered through my binoculars to see a sign in red paint on a white sheet that read 'The Bespectacled Henry Blowfly Stand' (in those days I wore horn-rimmed glasses with umbramatic lenses which darkened in the sun). I had to take another look to make sure my eyes weren't deceiving me. I was obviously thrilled, but also rather embarrassed, and there was much leg-pulling in the press box. The next day it was there again, with a second sheet underneath it which said, 'Come on over Henry, and have a pint'. This was not so much an invitation as a royal command, and during the afternoon I set off to the Hill. As I walked around in front of a small stand and then picked my way through the spectators sitting on the Hill itself, I was recognised, and there was much shouting and laughter, with people jumping to their feet and cheering. It was both embarrassing and pleasing. The crowd were making a considerable noise, and as this coincided with a rather dull passage of play, the players were all looking around to see what was going on.

I grinned inanely, and shook a few hands as I threaded my way along. When I finally got to the pylon I was greeted more warmly than I could believe by a group of students from Sydney University, who had put up the sheets. They were thrilled that I had come to see them, and a can of beer – a tinny – was thrust into my hand. I sat down with them, and it was terrific fun. I was deluged by questions, and at one point a lovely dark-haired girl with a heavenly smile threw her arms around me and gave me a smacking kiss. By now I had got my second wind, and thought the future was full of promise. My hopes were dashed when she drew her head back and said, 'The chap I'm really after is Geoff Boycott.' Talk about having a jug of cold water poured over one's head.

Anyway, I stayed for half an hour or so, and we arranged that they would all come round to my hotel on the edge of King's Cross one evening and we would have a party. After much hand-shaking and a certain amount of kissing, I set off back for the press box. By now everyone in the ground was aware of what was happening, and I think I received the loudest and longest cheer of the day – perhaps it was rivalled by the one that greeted Allan Border's fifty, but I hope not – as I wended my way back.

Those guys from Sydney University were admirably persistent. On the third day another sheet appeared. It read 'Our Henry can even outdrink Keith Miller', which did my reputation no harm, especially as Keith did the decent thing and didn't sue. On the fourth day there was yet another sheet. This one said 'Our Henry is to cricket what Tony Greig is to limbo dancing'. I wasn't sure about that one. That day my heart bled for my delicious, if fleeting, girlfriend on the Hill. Rodney Hogg ran in to bowl the first ball of England's second innings to Geoffrey Boycott, a stiff-muscled, half-pace loosener which had the great man palpably *LBW*. But then, all heroes occasionally have feet of clay, although that day Boycott's seemed to be stuck in something more solid, like concrete. England won the match, although long before that moment arrived we had all been put to sleep by an innings of 150 in nearly ten hours by Derek Randall. What a contrast to his effort in Melbourne.

There was another nice little vignette during a Test match at the SCG in the late seventies. I had written some pieces for the *Australian*, a Rupert Murdoch paper, which had been critical of Kerry Packer and his World Series Cricket. One day at about noon I went with the Australian commentator Alan McGilvray down to the bar on the ground floor of the Noble Stand for the day's first schooner of beer. As we were talking, an attractive girl came up to me holding a piece of paper. I had just taken it from her and started to write my signature when she protested that she didn't want my autograph, but was serving me with a writ for libel. Something I had written in the *Australian* had upset the supremely edgy Packer camp, and they had decided to fire a shot across my bows. In the end I apologised, and I don't think much money passed hands.

I dare say Packer did not want to upset the Rupert Murdoch lot too much.

I cannot leave Australia without mentioning the wonderful days I spent at the Yalumba winery, owned by Wyndham ('Windy') Hill-Smith, who played cricket for Western Australia between the wars. On the rest day of Adelaide Test matches both teams and all the journalists would be invited, and tennis, swimming, the most delicious lunch and splendid wines which never ran out were the order of the day. I remember one year when Windy invited Johnny Woodcock and me into his office/study, where we sat through a lovely, bright, air-conditioned afternoon drinking glasses of magnificent brandy. We talked for about three hours, expressed strong views about everything, and found ourselves in complete agreement. The abolition of rest days after the arrival of Packer and World Series Cricket sadly scuppered such wonderful adventures.

Although it may have increased the profits of the television companies, which no longer had to leave their equipment sitting idle for a day, the loss of rest days irrevocably changed the character of Test cricket. Every rest day all around the world had its own idiosyncratic and delightful traditions. In Trinidad we would potter around the islands on former West Indies captain Jeff Stollmeyer's boat, while the Sunday of Sydney Tests would be spent on the harbour in restaurateur Peter Doyle's magnificent boat on which he once taught me the most efficient way to peel a prawn, a lesson I have never forgotten. Another Australian adventure came in Adelaide, between two Tests in the 1990/91 Ashes series. The former Australian wicketkeeper Barry Jarman (and no nicer man has ever worn the gloves) had a houseboat on the Murray River. The match referee for that series was John Reid, who had captained New Zealand with great distinction. We spent three days on Barry's boat going up and down the Murray, and each night we would discuss Muttiah

Muralitharan's interesting bowling action. John said he did not throw; Barry, a match referee himself, said he did. Murali has a double-jointed wrist and a deformed right arm which he cannot straighten. Of course it looks strange. After many hours watching videos of him, Barry was uncertain if Murali was straightening his arm at the point of delivery. At the end of the trip I don't think any of us were any the wiser. I must also not leave out my annual visits to Houghton's attractive winery in the Perth suburb of Claremont to see Jack Mann, father of Tony, who was the first nightwatchman to score a hundred in a Test match. Jack made some lovely white wines there, which were not too hard on the pocket either.

On the other side of the Indian Ocean, I will never forget the first hour of the afternoon at Kingsmead in Durban, during the second Test of Australia's tour to South Africa in 1969–70. Graeme Pollock and Barry Richards matched each other stroke for stroke, putting on 103 in that time. It was a staggering exhibition of strokeplay – and how seldom it is that two great players bat at their best at the same time. The only other occasion on which I can remember such brilliant strokeplay in a long partnership was when Imran Khan and Wasim Akram put on 191 for the sixth wicket against Australia at the Adelaide Oval in January 1990. Pollock and Richards may have been the greater batsmen, but that day in Adelaide, Imran and Wasim were jolly nearly their equals.

That series against Australia in 1969–70 was the last South Africa played before being ostracised for their government's hideous apartheid policy. On that tour I experienced, all too briefly, the joys of the Mount Nelson Hotel in Cape Town, which was then resplendent in its white-colonnaded, aristocratic and palm-avenued magnificence. It still stands, but today it is naturally much more frenetic, lively and democratic both inside and around the pool. Those were the days in Durban, too, when the old Edward Hotel was still functioning at something like its best, while the Oyster Box, about twenty miles to the north at Umhlanga Rocks, catered for a lovely rest day of beach, golf and fish. It was, however, not until a later tour that I established an undying relationship with Hamilton Russell Chardonnay.

One year my old friend Dick Foxton arranged a fantastic visit to the Mala Mala game reserve in the Kruger Park. It was an amazing experience, setting off in the early morning and late afternoon in huge Land Rovers in search of lions, leopards, cheetahs, elephants, crocodiles, buffaloes and anything in between. On another occasion Dick persuaded the admirable South African Tourist Board to lay on fascinating visits to the Boer War and Zulu War battlefields. To climb to the top of Spion Kop with a guide who gives you a blow-by-blow account of the battle is unforgettable. Rorke's Drift was equally impressive, and I came away understanding why eleven Victoria Crosses were won in that extraordinary battle, in which 150 British troops successfully defied a force of 4,000 Zulus. The Blue Train from Pretoria to Cape Town, stopping at Kimberley and seeing 'the Big Hole', which produced such a wealth of diamonds, was also an incredible experience which cricket has allowed me, as was a visit to Robben Island to see Nelson Mandela's cell. This latter is something no one should miss.

My friendship with Commander Arshad Gilani, now a businessman from Karachi, who is the best chairman the Pakistani Board of Control for Cricket never had, has led to much enjoyment both of cricket in Pakistan and of the country itself. Paradoxically, and perhaps unfairly, my chief memory of cricket in Pakistan comes from the most boring game it has ever been my lot to watch. It was played in December 1977 at the Gaddafi Stadium in Lahore. Goodness knows why the ground should have been named after that brutal Libyan dictator, who I am sure never set foot on a cricket ground in his life. I can only suppose he must have coughed up lots of moolah for Pakistan.

This was the first of three Tests on that short England tour, and it would almost have been appropriate if it had been inspired by the dreaded Gaddafi. Boring it may have been, but it was considerably spiced up by rioting on successive days. The first was inspired by Mudassar Nazar attempting to reach the slowest hundred known to mankind. The situation was then seized upon by the supporters of Zulfiqar Ali Bhutto, the former prime minister and father of Benazir Bhutto. He had been imprisoned by his successor, General Zia Ul-Haq, a Terry-Thomas lookalike, and sentenced to death. While his supporters took advantage of the first riot, the second day's fun was all down to them.

Don Mosey was representing the BBC on this tour, and with some help from one or two others, he and I commentated on the series for *Test Match Special*. At the Gadaffi Stadium we were sitting on the roof of the pavilion. The deadly facts were that Mudassar batted for 591 minutes for 114 runs, taking 557 minutes to reach the slowest hundred ever made in the history of first-class cricket. As if this statistic was not bleak enough on its own, the situation became bleaker still in the latter half of the second day, although I have to say it broke the tedium of the game. Mudassar, with 98 to his name, played Bob Willis to third man for a comfortable single. The crowd, which had been geeing itself up for an explosion when Mudassar reached his elusive hundred, collectively thought that two runs were possible, and that this was it. A good many of them managed to scale the wire fencing on the popular side, and they poured across the outfield to congratulate their hero who was marooned at the non-striker's end with 99 against his name. In moments, he was submerged under a mass of people congratulating him on the hundred that was still one run away. This went on for some time, and then the police came running onto the ground in their khaki shorts and got to work with their lathi sticks. They whacked some of the invaders pretty hard, which didn't go down well. As a result a great many more came rushing out in protest. Pandemonium ensued, and before long police reinforcements arrived, bringing with them teargas canisters to try to quell the crowd. As I had discovered at Sabina Park in Kingston ten years earlier, teargas doesn't do you much good. Eventually the police gained control, and the spectators left the field of play. When the game restarted Mudassar at last reached his hundred with a quiet push into the covers. Mercifully, the crowd's response was more muted. I was on the air at the time, and was able to tell listeners that Mudassar had made a truly 'riotous' century.

On the following day, the riot erupted from the ladies' stand at square leg. Bhutto's supporters invaded the stand from the back, forcing the ladies, in their brightly coloured saris, to take flight like a cage of suddenly disturbed butterflies. The next moment the invaders were throwing the sofas on which the ladies had been sitting over the fence and onto the outfield. At this point a good many spectators decided that the time had come to join in. The established procedure now followed. The police appeared, vigorously waving their lathis and hitting a few people. They were followed shortly afterwards by more police, armed with teargas, and it was quite a while before play restarted. It was a surprise that we did not get a riot on the fourth day as well, when Geoff Boycott attempted to put Mudassar's record in the shade. He positively raced to his 50 in 290 minutes, which was twenty minutes longer than the Pakistani had taken to reach his, but succumbed to Iqbal Qasim's slow left-arm spin 13 runs later. The two first innings of the match were not completed until the afternoon of the final day, which might have been cause for yet another celebratory riot. Thank heavens there was no attempt to make up the time lost.

Of course, Pakistan and its cricket, which has produced so many wonderful players, has much more to offer than riots. I was royally entertained by Imran Khan's family, the Zamaans, in their private clan-like enclave, Zamaan Park. One early morning I drove with some of them out of Lahore for a wild-boar shoot. It was great fun without being impressively destructive – I think the boars will have been well satisfied with the outcome. My contribution to the day's bag was a poor, solitary sand grouse. In Lahore I was taken to tea with the founding father of Pakistan cricket, Abdul Hafeez Kardar, who before Partition had played for India. Even as an old man he was tall, formal and upstanding, with grey hair and forthright views on everything. I often stayed with Arshad Gilani and his family in Karachi, and we would sometimes eat at the old Sind Club, founded in 1871 by the British when prohibition was not the order of the day. It is so sad that terrorism has now made Pakistan an unsafe venue for international cricket. The country will always produce amazing players, and it is a great pity that their fellow countrymen may not have the chance to see them in action in the flesh for a long time.

It may not make me very popular in New Zealand when I say that their delicious wines have made a stronger impression on me than some of the cricket I have watched in those two lovely islands. Central Otago's Pinot Noir is up there with that splendid side of Jeremy Coney's in the mid-eighties, to say nothing of the Pinot Gris. Then there are all those wonderful wines from Marlborough, Martinborough, Waiheke Island, Hawke's Bay and elsewhere, just as on the cricket field there have been at different times the prodigious Hadlee family, Martin Donnelly, Glenn Turner, Martin Crowe and all the others. I also remember with particular joy New Zealand's Bluff oysters, and its unique form of whitebait.

Then there was the occasion at Lancaster Park in Christchurch in February 1978, when Ian Botham, on his first tour, was sent out early in England's second innings with the express order to run out his captain, Geoff Boycott, who was holding up the innings when quick runs were needed for a declaration. It took Botham two balls and I believe they had a lively verbal exchange during the run. Twenty-four years later at Christchurch, Nathan Astle, going in against England at number five, played an amazing innings of 222 in 231 minutes, with eleven sixes and twenty-eight fours. New Zealand needed 550 to win, and were beaten by 98 runs. By a happy coincidence Astle's cousin owns one of New Zealand's best restaurants, Antoine's in Auckland's Parnell Road, where I have greatly enjoyed myself on many happy evenings.

I have not been back to New Zealand since those dreadful earthquakes made such a mess of Christchurch between 2010 and 2012. I only hope the Valley of Peace, arguably the prettiest small ground in the world, has not been affected. Nestling in the hills outside Christchurch, it has been visited by many touring sides, including Douglas Jardine's after the Bodyline tour of Australia in 1932–33. Because of its diminutive size, fours count as two and sixes become fours. When I was last there, at the turn of the millennium, women were still not allowed at the ground – hence its name. That day, former New Zealand captain Jeremy Coney defied convention and brought a lady along. She was asked to leave. This rule had been handed down by the ground's founders, who controlled the Christchurch cinemas and plainly were nothing if not chauvinistic.

My only tour of Zimbabwe was in 1996–97. Apart from the beautiful country, which Mugabe's thugs were making less beautiful by the minute, and the Victoria Falls, which I only caught a glimpse of from the air, I have two particularly strong memories of that visit. One is of the second Test in Harare. Mugabe, who lived in the old Government House just around the corner, was coming along one day to watch the cricket for an hour or two. He was going to give a press conference at the ground, and the *TMS* producer Peter Baxter deputed me to interview him for the BBC. On occasions like this, at which there are many journalists present, the BBC reporter is allowed to ask the first three or four questions, giving listeners the impression it is an exclusive interview. Then the rest of the press join in and take over.

The interview was to be held in a room upstairs in the pavilion. At the appointed hour a cavalcade of cars arrived, and Mugabe was decanted from the largest and poshest. He was accompanied by innumerable goons wearing ill-fitting dark suits, each with a suspicious bulge up by the shoulder. Clutching my microphone, I went into the room with the other journalists, where we were soon joined by a great many of these villainous-looking thugs, who wandered about trying to look meaningful and occasionally talking in the sort of way spy films suggest the Gestapo engaged in their social chitchats. It was all extremely menacing. I had been warned beforehand that I was not expected to ask any questions that could have the remotest political implication. Eventually there was a sudden buzz of expectation; the moment was obviously

192

imminent. At that very second one of the guards shuffled up to me, asked me what I thought I was doing, and told me to follow him. Maybe he thought my microphone was an offensive weapon. The situation was saved by Mugabe himself, who entered the room a few seconds later and, steered by the chairman of the Zimbabwe Cricket Board, came straight over to me. The goon had no alternative but to make an ignominious retreat.

The first thing I noticed about Mugabe was that he had the worst halitosis it has ever been my lot to come across. I asked him about his love for cricket, which didn't go down especially well. Then I said I had heard that he had been a formidable tennis player in his younger days, and he was quick to agree. He said he loved to play singles matches against his immediate predecessor as President of Zimbabwe, who went by the lovely name of Canaan Banana, and added with great modesty that he usually won. I suggested that the Centre Court at Wimbledon would be the ideal venue for such a sterling contest. Mugabe grinned and nodded vigorously before unleashing the deepest of deep breaths, which I promise you was the most effective public-relations job ever to have been done on behalf of teargas. Apart from a few other pleasantries that was about it, and I thanked him before backing off and leaving his halitosis for the rest of the press corps. I think it was the closest I have ever come to an international stink.

I came out of my other big memory of Zimbabwe with no credit whatever. In the first Test at Bulawayo, England had been left to score 205 to win on the last day. I took up the commentary as scheduled, but became so shamefully carried away by the thrilling run chase that, looking neither to the right nor the left, I kept on commentating for an hour and a quarter. I will never know why Peter Baxter and Simon

Mann, my fellow commentators, ever spoke to me again and what would dear Johnners have said? To this day, if a commentator overruns his allotted twenty minutes, he is said to be 'doing a Bulawayo'. That match, by the way, was the first Test match to be drawn, with the scores level at the end. David Lloyd, the England coach, famously said afterwards, 'We murdered 'em.'

In early 1980 I went on an extraordinary tour of five South American countries arranged by Derrick Robins (DHR) a cricket benefactor who managed effortlessly to combine benevolence with malevolence. He was a one-time chairman of Coventry City Football Club, and a terrific sporting enthusiast – providing he was on the winning side. I was selected to go on this tour as a sort of social secretary, a job which, despite having lots of important qualifications for, I never really came to grips with. The side was composed of young and hopeful county cricketers, a few of whom would go on to play for England. The former England batsman Peter Parfitt, who had started his cricket career with me in Norfolk, was the manager, and Les Ames, famously of Kent and England and the dearest of men, came along as a benign guardian angel. The other official was Kelly Seymour, a South African doctor who had bowled off-breaks for his country a few times. It was his job to protect us from the dreadful diseases we were likely to pick up along the way.

To say the tour was fun would be a massive understatement. We started off in Caracas, the capital of Venezuela, then moved on too rapidly to Peru and the splendours of Lima, nearly ten acres of the most valuable real estate in the middle of which was occupied by the Lima Cricket and Football Club. It was in Lima that I caught the ultimate in tummy bugs, and had to be left behind when the others departed for Chile.

When I rejoined the party in Santiago, the Prince of Wales Country Club, in the shadow of the Andes, where we stayed and played cricket, was the perfect haven, especially for the walking wounded. My health was much improved by a bottle or three of vintage Chilean Merlot.

Argentina, and in particular the Hurlingham Club in Buenos Aires, was our next stopping point. The standard of cricket in BA, where there are a number of clubs, is good, and was steadily improving at that time under the guidance of the resident professional Brian Ward, who had opened the batting for Essex. Our indefatigable patron (DHR) fancied himself no end with a golf club and we had an in-house tournament. On the practice day Graham Stevenson, who bowled fastish for Yorkshire and a few times for England, showed he could hit a golf ball an uncommonly long way and in approxim-ately the right direction. The pairs for the next day's golf competition had already been decided, but a quick change now saw DHR partnering Stevenson. To the relief and amusement of everyone else, on the day of the tournament Stevenson hit the ball further and further, but this time it flew unerringly over cover point's head.

When we got to Brazil, things hotted up considerably, both on the field and off. Our first stop was São Paulo, where the local opposition were keen but hopeless. On the first evening one or two of our side were taken along to a nightclub, where they failed to spot the difference between a vestite and a transvestite until it was jolly nearly too late. Not always easy in the dark, I should imagine. In Rio, the ground at Niteroi, over the longest bridge in the world, was a delight, with its bank of flowering rhododendron-like shrubs. DHR was a hard taskmaster. When we bowled out Brazil for a modest 12, he was angry because it should have been only 8, but 4 byes were given away. He was even angrier when our captain turned up late for the start of play one day after experiencing the delights of the Copacabana the evening before. He had woken up the next morning to find that the associates of the young lady with whom he had become friendly had removed his clothes, and were demanding a heavy ransom for them. Negotiations had barely been completed by the time of the scheduled start, and when he arrived at Niteroi, via a quick change in his hotel, the lunch interval was pending. DHR's apoplexy was such that he only narrowly avoided swallowing his moustache.

As a final postscript, I remember playing in Corfu Town on an adventure organised by Ben Brocklehurst, who had captained Somerset one year soon after the war. I managed to put on a hundred with an elderly but still considerably chirpy Bill Edrich. The ground was in the centre of the town, and a good quarter of the outfield doubled up as the municipal-bus park. The great thing was to bat second, because when the buses returned for their night's rest, the boundary on that side of the ground became a good deal closer. One of the Corfiot sides – the players were mostly locals – was captained by a short, stocky, amiable, dark-haired bandit called Contos, who carried his bat rather as if it was a gun, came in at about number seven or eight, and liked to spend a bit of time at the crease. He was clean-bowled shortly after he had arrived, whereupon without any fuss he put the bails back on the stumps and got ready to face the next ball. No one dared say a thing, not even Bill, although much biting of his tongue went on at first slip.

NINE

A Modest Dinner at Alresford

People often wonder if we have as much fun in the *Test Match Special* commentary box as most of our listeners think we do. The answer is that we probably have even more. In-jokes abound, and suppressed giggles are a constant fact of life – as, of course, are those which are inadequately throttled at birth. It is the most delightful form of organised chaos.

Brian Johnston was the man who changed *TMS* irrevocably. He first joined the team in 1966, then switched back and forth between the television and the radio commentary boxes until he was sacked by BBC Television in 1970 'for being too funny', which argues a sad lack of humour in those who controlled the sporting affairs of the screen. He was instantly snapped up as a permanent member of *TMS* by Robert Hudson, the head of radio sport, who had the vision to see what Johnners would do for the programme.

Johnners would have liked more than anything to have been a stand-up comic. Laughter, and the ability to make others laugh, was a huge part of him. He could not resist seeing the funny side of almost everything, and his appearance, with his enormous nose and big ears, was part of that. The lobes of his ears were so big that one of his favourite party tricks was to tuck them into their respective ears. He would occasionally do this in the commentary box, and the giggles would start. Johnners loved the corny old music hall jokes.

As I have already shown, I was quick to collide with Johnners' sense of humour when I did my first Test commentary for *TMS*. During the same game I also had an anxious moment because of his penchant for saying things he didn't quite realise he was saying . . . or did he? Tony Greig was bowling to Sunny Gavaskar in India's second innings. Johnners was at the microphone, and near the end of his twenty-minute spell, his commentary went like this: 'Greig's coming in to bowl to Gavaskar in that slightly awkward, stilted way of his. And he bowls, and Gavaskar plays forward and the ball goes gently to Hendrick at mid-on. Hendrick picks it up, looks at it before throwing a little underarm catch to Greig. And as Greig walks back to his mark he polishes the ball on his right thigh. He turns now and starts in again, arms and legs flying, and bowls to Gavaskar, who plays forward and the ball again runs down to Hendrick, who polishes it briefly before giving it back to Greig. And this time to ring the changes as he walks back to his mark, Greig polishes his left ball.'

Led by Bill Frindall, who was a giggler and snorter of no mean order, the box was consumed with laughter. Realising what he had said, Johnners giggled as helplessly as anyone. He managed to control himself for a moment, but all he could say was, 'And after the Prince it will be Henry Blofeld.' Talk about being thrown in at the deep end. The box was still heaving with laughter, both suppressed and not so suppressed, as I sat down in Johnners' pew, and leaned as far forward as I could to avoid catching anyone's eye. As I was still pretty nervous, I was not so much in danger of laughing as of being cast into utter confusion by the chaos around me. It was a great deal more by luck than by good judgement or anything else that I got away with it.

The 'Prince' in the box was Fatesingh Gaekwad, the former Maharajah of Baroda. He had managed a recent Indian side in England, knew his cricket well, and *TMS* had decided to use him as our Indian summariser. Peter Baxter, who was in his second year as producer, told me a delightful story about the signing up of the Maharajah. He had met with Baxter and Robert Hudson, who was a considerable broadcaster and commentator in his own right. The Maharajah happily agreed to join us as an expert summariser and was then asked how he would like to be addressed on air. He thought for a moment before saying, 'I think His Highness Lt. Colonel Fatesingh Gaekwad, the former Maharajah of Baroda, would be appropriate.' 'Every time?' asked Hudson, raising his eyebrows. The Maharajah again became thoughtful, then said, 'No, for the first three or four times, and then "Prince" will do.' So Prince it was. Many of our listeners must have thought we had a Labrador in the box.

TMS was not sombre in the pre-Johnners years, but eruptions of laughter certainly became more frequent after his arrival. From the start he brought a great many listeners with him, having been involved in numerous radio and television programmes since the war, and in 1972 he would take over *Down Your Way* from Franklin Engelmann. These new listeners, who included a large number of ladies, initially tuned in to hear the much-loved Johnners, and after encountering the genius of John Arlott they never went away.

I first entered the box two years after Johnners had become a permanent part of *TMS*, and I was amazed by the relaxed atmosphere I found there. In all the years I have been a part of *TMS*, it has never changed. We have all got along pretty well together, and I am sure that that friendship has communicated itself to our listeners. Peter Baxter, who produced us for thirty-four years, took over in 1973, the year after I started, and he did much to create this enjoyable state of affairs. As we have seen, his rather pompous predecessor Michael Tuke-Hastings was a more divisive character, and was not universally popular. He also didn't much like cricket, which was no help. I soon saw him meet his match in Jim Swanton, another imposing figure with a somewhat similar disposition. In the second of my first two one-day internationals, at Edgbaston, Jim came into the commentary box about fifteen minutes before the end of the match in preparation for his close-of-play summary. No one has ever done these summaries better than Jim. He was concise, he told the story well, with the odd flourish thrown in, and he never failed to leave the listener with an accurate account of what had happened as well as the flavour of the day.

He always made a bit of an entrance, and would make his not inconsiderable way to the end of the commentary box, sit down and look at his notes. It was the producer's job, once Jim was seated, to place on his right-hand side a glass which contained a large measure of Scotch whisky, water and ice. Tuke-Hastings duly delivered, and while reading Jim reached instinctively for the glass and took a sip. No sooner had he done so than he hurriedly put the glass down and, looking over his shoulder, whispered forcibly, 'Michael, Michael – no ice, Michael!' Tuke-Hastings moved over quickly and whispered, 'Jim, it's been a hot day, and they've run out of ice in the bar, I'm afraid.' Jim didn't consider this to be a satisfactory reason, and was quick to reply, 'Er, Michael, did you tell them who it was for?' Game, set and match to Swanton.

Jim Swanton – he keeps cropping up in these pages; but then, he was like that – may have been a trifle overbearing, but he did a lot for the game of cricket, in his writing, his broadcasting and his encouragement of young players. During the Second World War he was a member of the Bedfordshire

Yeomanry, and was captured when Singapore fell. His appalling experiences as a prisoner of the Japanese must have helped him develop his strong faith as a Christian. Not the least of Jim's achievements was to found his nomadic cricket club, the Arabs, in the mid-thirties. He himself was wholly responsible for deciding who should be elected as members. They were almost all pretty good amateur cricketers, and one or two, like Richie Benaud, a great deal more than that. There was no doubt that Jim was a snob, and in some ways the Arabs was a part of this. He preferred members to have been to smart public schools like Eton, Winchester or Harrow, and to have gone on to Oxford or Cambridge. Jim himself had not actually made it to any of these, but in spirit he had been to all of them. Arab cricket was some of the most enjoyable I ever played, and this was enormously to Jim's credit. When I first played for them in the early sixties, Jim turned out as often as he could. Like most owners or patrons of private cricket clubs, he did not enjoy losing, and after a poor result, the post mortem would be a prolonged affair. But his very presence, as player or spectator, at an Arab match always improved the day. His unbridled determination that we should win – not quite at any price, but almost – gave us all great joy, as did his leg-rollers, which he bowled in stately fashion, although his delivery had not been helped by the effects of his treatment as a prisoner-of-war. He was at his best when he took the Arabs to his beloved Barbados for a month's tour in 1967, about which I have already written.

Peter Baxter helped to put together a team of commentators and summarisers which blended extremely well. It combined a range of different personalities, styles and voices. Although the team has changed over the years as age has taken its toll, this happy blend continues today under Adam Mountford, who succeeded Peter after the series against the

West Indies in 2007. I am often asked who my favourite commentator is, who is the summariser I like working with the most, and what I think of so-and-so as a commentator. These are questions I never answer, because it is invidious to attempt to compare commentators or summarisers. There is the temptation to think that because someone does things in a different way to you, it is not as good. That is nonsense. The most important thing for any commentator or summariser is to be himself, and not try to be anyone else. If everyone on *TMS* sounded the same, or commentated in exactly the same style, it would not be as entertaining for the listener as it is. After each commentator's twenty-minute spell, the listener needs the break a new commentator – another voice talking in a different way – gives him.

As well as the blend of commentators and summarisers, I am sure that another, almost paradoxical reason for *TMS*'s longevity is its non-cricketing content. During a day's play, a lot of things are discussed which have little to do with the cricket. There is no doubt that a great many listeners – both male and female – appreciate these extraneous bits and pieces at least as much as discussions of the complicated intricacies of leg-breaks and googlies. The listeners are just as much a mix as the commentators, and the one thing that is certain is that nobody can please everyone all the time. Every commentator makes a few listeners reach for the switch-off button, although it seems heresy to suggest that anyone would ever have wished to silence John Arlott or Brian Johnston for a single second.

As a commentator I always become hopelessly caught up in the game. There is an element of excitement in almost every situation that develops in front of you. A long spell of maiden overs, a stubborn rearguard action, a pointless afternoon session when the batsmen can't find their strokes and the bowlers can't get it right either – are all a part of the game. So too are clumsy and inefficient moments, when catches are dropped, or long hops and full tosses go unpunished. All of these incidents are important to certain of the players, whatever the reason, and it is my job to try to spot that reason. There is always a personal battle going on somewhere within the larger battle. I try to locate it, and build my commentary around it. This doesn't always work, but if it does, I like to think it makes the listener feel a little bit more involved, and therefore more attentive. If a commentator has genuine excitement in his voice, only the most stony-hearted of listeners won't react.

It was this that made Johnners so easy to listen to – and John Arlott too, although they went about it in entirely different ways. Johnners was like a bottle of champagne which has just been opened, and the bubbly is spraying out of the top. He would always spot anything unusual that was going on, be it the umpire scratching his behind, backward short leg blowing his nose, the captain trying to catch the attention of a fielder in the deep, any strange behaviour in the crowd, someone walking past the window of the box and looking in at us – particularly at Edgbaston, where before recent renovations changed things, the committee balcony was just below and in front of us. He was a great spotter of the famous. On occasions it would be, 'Oh, look. There's a chap down there I was at school with. Can't remember his name.' Then he would turn to his summariser and say, 'I hope I don't look as old as that, Fred.' It was all wonderfully jolly, and not a bit intrusive. For all their differences, Johnners and Arlott did have one important thing in common: they were never unkind to a player. If a fielder dropped a catch or a batsman departed to a really ghastly stroke, they did not dwell on it and rub the wretched chap's nose in it. 'We've all done it,'

Johnners would say, while Arlott's take would more likely be 'Spare a thought for whoever-it-was. He didn't do it on purpose.' In my first years I often handed over to Arlott, and I would stay in the box to listen to him. After five minutes I would leave, wondering why I even bothered to try.

In many ways John Arlott was the complete opposite to Johnners. Everything about him was more measured, except perhaps the amount of wine in his glass. Johnners, an Old Etonian but never self-conscious about it, was abstemious, which was not a word that found a home in Arlott's vocabulary. Arlott's genius lay in his ability to find the right adjectives and other descriptive words to grace the situation unfolding in front of him. The rest of us would leave the box fearing that we might have found a better, more descriptive way to portray a particular incident. It would then come to us in bed that night when there was no one around to tell.

Arlott would have found the right words instantly, and have delivered them in those ringing Hampshire tones which grew richer and richer over the years as his vocal cords were increasingly marinaded in ever more spectacular bottles of claret. His pace of delivery never changed much; he merely sharpened his words a fraction when a wicket or some other drama occurred.

In 1975 at the first World Cup final at Lord's his description of Clive Lloyd going to 99 with a six into the Mound Stand lives on. 'He hit that like a man knocking the top off a thistle with a walking stick.' And also, 'Dickie Bird is signalling everything including "stop" to traffic coming on from behind.' He had such a compelling voice and turn of phrase that there was never any need to deliver extra excitement or, when relevant, more bathos. To say that Arlott commentated with an exciting and irresistible *de profundis* is not a contradiction in terms.

He left behind so many memories which, because he stopped commentating in 1980, fewer and fewer people now remember. One of my favourites, which underlines his ability to come up instantly with the right words, happened during the Lord's Test against Australia in 1975. On the fourth afternoon Arlott was commentating after a lunch with his literary agent which would almost certainly have involved four bottles. When he returned to the box he found that Ian Trethowan, the Director General of the BBC, was among those present. So as Arlott settled over the microphone a few minutes later, he was mellow and more than happy to show off. Soon after he had played himself in, he had the greatest gift of his entire commentary career. An ample young merchant seaman improbably called Michael Angelow, who had been watching from ground level underneath the grandstand, jumped the fence and, wearing only trainers and socks, ran towards the middle. Arlott did not see him at once, and was alerted by Trevor Bailey, summarising alongside him, who couldn't remember the word for what he was witnessing, and said in a loud voice, 'Ah, a freaker!'

Arlott was happy to run with that, and took up the chase. 'Yes, we've got a freaker. It's not very shapely, and it's masculine, and it's seen the last of its cricket for the day.' He described the 'freaker' vaulting the stumps at the Nursery End, watched over by umpire Tom Spencer. I'm pretty sure that from the back of the box Johnners said, not so quietly, 'All's well. Umpire Spencer hasn't signalled "one short".' Arlott continued his description: 'And now he's had his load. He is being embraced by a blond policeman and now he's being led away in front of about 8,000 people in the Mound Stand, some of whom have never seen anything quite like this before.'

While Johnners' humour was always up-front, Arlott's was more measured, and was conceived with a greater subtlety.

He was not one for the slapstick approach, and his stories, while always pithy, took a time in the telling. When something really amused him he produced a marvellous chuckle, accompanied by a beaming smile. Arlott's briefcase was usually full of letters and catalogues from wine merchants, which he would look at from time to time when he was not on the air, occasionally murmuring, 'I like that,' marking the list and nodding his head in satisfaction.

He also had the habit, which was both splendid and disturbing, of visiting a local wine merchant on his way to whichever ground we were broadcasting from. He liked a companion on these expeditions, and he was very persuasive too. During a Test at Old Trafford early in my career, he twisted my arm, I fear more easily than he should have done, and I followed him to Altrincham one morning – this was before all those motorways had been built around Manchester – on the way to the ground. He had obviously alerted the shop to his impending arrival, because we were met by an impressive reception committee, who had already been limbering up with their corkscrews. A glass of Puligny Montrachet was soon in my hands. Somehow I managed to limit myself to a couple of fairly hefty sips; John, on the other hand, was of the view that it was bad manners to leave a bottle with anything in it. He took away with him a case of this and that, which willing hands put into the boot of his car – although I am not sure that any money changed hands – and we continued on our way to Old Trafford. I felt a trifle uneasy at having had a drink so early with a day's commentary ahead of me, but one of the advantages of youth is that a couple of mouthfuls has no discernible effect. For my companion, however, three-quarters of a bottle soon after breakfast, if not par for the course, was clearly not an unusual event, and was part of a throat-clearing exercise. In fact, it was not unlike rubbing the sleepy dust out of his eyes. When he took to the airwaves that day, there was no sign that it had had any effect on him. In fact he seemed in top form. Maybe that was the effect it had: it was medicinal after all.

There was another occasion, during a Test trial in Hove, when Arlott made a similar diversion on the way to the ground. This time he managed to persuade Tony Lewis, who was playing in the match, to accompany him. Tony would have been hard-pressed not to have had a taste, and when he later had a bad day with the bat Arlott was remorseful, and felt he had led Tony unforgivably astray. I also remember an early-morning tipple while watching the New Zealanders begin their tour at the Saffrons in Eastbourne. Yet, as far as the listener was concerned, Arlott managed never to allow his passion to interfere with his broadcasting output. Later on, he would commentate for just one spell after lunch before retiring to the press box to service the needs of the *Guardian*. Those were busy days for him, and goodness knows how he coped so well. I dare say those around him in the commentary box were able to detect the signs of the usual heavy lunch more easily than the listeners. But that magic voice transcended such minor details. It was as redolent of cricket as that lovely smell of linseed in the days when bats still had to be oiled.

Arlott lived in Alresford in north Hampshire, and appropriately his house was a retired pub, the Old Sun, with an impressively large cellar. Once when I stayed with him I discovered that it was not, however, quite large enough. It was in the seventies, when I was working for the *Daily Telegraph*, and they sent me down to the United Services ground in Portsmouth to watch the last two days of a Hampshire game. I rang the great man to ask him if he would be there. His immediate reply was 'Would you fancy a bed?' I said I would, and he told me that I would have to share a room with Clive Taylor, by now the cricket correspondent of the *Sun*, whom we have already met. Arlott told me that he would not be working at Portsmouth himself, but he expected to go to the ground in the middle of the afternoon, and we could drive back in convoy at the end of the day.

The day progressed, but well into the last session Arlott still hadn't turned up. There was less than an hour to go when his black Mercedes edged into the ground. He parked and plodded round to the press box, where Clive and I had begun to thumb through the AA book in search of a hotel, just in case. 'Sorry I'm late,' he said, pushing his way breathlessly into the box. He was a large man, and his unbuttoned jacket made him look even bulkier. 'Valerie and I are having a few people to dinner tonight, and I wanted the wine to breathe.' I asked him how many were coming. He thought for a moment, and settled on eight, which he quickly changed to nine, because his son Timothy was coming in for a 'jar' after dinner. Clive then asked how many bottles he had left breathing on his dining-room table. 'Before I left I pulled twenty-two corks,' was the spirited reply. Seeing the look of horror on our faces, he was quick to go on, 'But I can assure you there's a more than formidable second eleven on the sideboard.'

It was as thirsty an evening as I can remember, and terrific fun, as I am sure all his dinner parties were. One of the guests was a friend of all of us. Bill Shepherd was not tall, but he was comfortably built, with a stomach that retirement from the world of insurance had done nothing to diminish. He now helped Desmond Eager in the Secretary's office at the County Ground at Southampton, and was the most delightful of men, with smiling eyes behind his heavy glasses. He was a particular chum of Arlott's, and was something of a straight man for him. At dinner, Bill, who always drank his share with enthusiasm, would prompt Arlott from down the table: 'John, have you told them about so-and-so?' or 'You must tell the one about someone-else.' Arlott did not need much encouragement in this way, but even so, Bill's promptings seemed to heighten his stage just a fraction. We all listened, spellbound, and the bottles kept coming. It wasn't easy to get a word in oneself, but it was all so amusing that it didn't matter, although those who were regular visitors to his dining-room table probably had to suffer a certain repetition. By the time the evening finished we were all exceedingly mellow, and I'm not sure that the more than formidable second eleven on the sideboard wasn't three or four wickets down. Clive and I somehow made it to our room, where we immediately passed out. I suppose some of the others must have driven themselves home, but that doesn't bear thinking about.

It seemed only about two minutes later that the bedroom door was opened by Arlott, wearing the most hirsute of dressing gowns. He drew back the curtains, then asked in a voice which showed no signs of being affected either by the amount of wine that had passed over his larynx the night before or by the lengthy soliloquy he had so eloquently delivered, 'Would you fancy a glass of champagne?' As he spoke, he pulled a bottle of Bollinger from one of his dressing-gown pockets. In unison and with conviction, Clive and I declined the offer, to the obvious disappointment of our host, who was therefore able to use only one of the three glasses he had brought with him.

After a splendid but rather late breakfast, Clive and I paid the obligatory visit to our host's cellar. This was when we discovered it was not big enough for his purposes: we had to start picking our way in between the bottles even before we had reached the bottom of the stairs. After declining another glass of something white, we discussed the previous day's county cricket scores before departing for Portsmouth. Our host, who was by some distance the liveliest of us all, then went straight to his study to write his weekly wine column for the *Guardian*. He had plenty of material.

A visit to Johnners' house, while not a teetotal affair, was rather more orthodox. For many years he and his wife Pauline lived close to Lord's, first in Hamilton Terrace, from where he could have reached the Pavilion with a well-hit three-iron, then further away, towards the end of Abbey Road, from which he would have needed more than one club to arrive at the same destination. He always had a party on one evening of the Lord's Test match, and these evenings, when drinks in the garden moved on to a buffet supper, were the greatest of fun. Many of the great and good from the world of cricket would help make up the numbers, including a few from overseas who were on their annual pilgrimage to Lord's, and it would be catch-up time around the coronation chicken. Johnners, resplendent in his brown-and-white leather shoes, was a marvellous host. He was always just as he was on the air, and laughter followed him wherever he went. He had a good word for everyone, and could never bring himself to be seriously critical about anyone – at least not in public. I remember one party in his lovely long garden in Hamilton Terrace not long after I had joined *TMS*. Johnners had been in the Grenadier Guards during the war, and had won the Military Cross. That evening one of his brother officers came to the party, and towards the end he asked Johnners what sort of chap he thought Hitler really was. Johnners was quick to reply, 'Adders? I think old Adders was what I would call only a fairly nice chap.'

I can only recall one occasion when I ever saw Johnners seriously upset. He was always fiercely protective of *TMS* – as I'm sure he was of any programme with which he was involved. We were staying at the Swan at Bucklow Hill, as we always did for a Test at Old Trafford. This was at a time in the eighties when the future of *TMS* seemed to be continually up for discussion within the BBC. On this occasion the Head of Outside Broadcasts, Slim Wilkinson, had come up from London at Johnners' request to talk to us all about the principal problem, which was finding us a permanent home on the airwaves. Radio 3 medium wave had been accommodating us, but that station's Controller was not convinced that he wanted us any longer. Wilkinson tried to convince us that the programme was safe, but failed to come up with what we regarded as a worthwhile assurance. Johnners went for him in fine and flowing style, and more or less told him to go back to the drawing board with the other heads of departments and to come up with a realistic solution. I am not sure that Wilkinson fully appreciated the huge popularity of *TMS*, in this country and wherever the game is played. There had been comments in the press about the future of the programme, and an Early Day Motion had even been tabled in the House of Commons. I never again saw Johnners come out of his corner like this, and Wilkinson was way out of his depth. We eventually moved to Radio 4 long wave, although this was never going to be a permanent home. *TMS* was a remarkably successful programme, with a hugely appreciative and growing audience. It seemed extraordinary that its popularity did not make those who control these things realise that it had to be protected and secured, come what may. I have no doubt that Johnners' outburst that evening set a lot of people thinking.

There are some people who like to think that John Arlott and Brian Johnston were not exactly the greatest of friends. I think the truth of this was, quite simply, that they were not each other's sort of person. They may seldom have dined together or visited each other's houses, and they may not have been naturally attracted to each other. Their contrasting views on alcohol may not have helped. But this is nothing more than a reflection of human nature, which explains the relationship between the two greatest commentators in the history of *Test Match Special*. They were truly two old pros, and I am sure there was never any hostility between them, just as I am sure that each of them hugely respected what the other brought to the programme. I wonder if Hengist and Horsa or David and Jonathan were forever asking each other to come round and take pot luck, or to stay the weekend. Together, Arlott and Johnston made *TMS* what it is today.

While Arlott and Johnston were the first among equals, they would have been quick to acknowledge that they owed a lot to their supporting cast. For most of the time I have been with *TMS*, the two principals of these were Trevor Bailey ('the Boil') and Fred Trueman. They could hardly have been more different as characters, yet it was because of this difference that they complemented one another so well. Having played for England together, they were good friends, and Trevor's dry, crisp comments contrasted happily with Fred's rich, lingering Yorkshire tones.

Trevor did his first Test for *TMS* in 1967, and Fred came on board seven years later, in 1974. It was a year or two before they settled into their famous partnership, which rivalled that of Norman Yardley and Freddie Brown in the fifties and sixties. At first I found Trevor the more difficult to work with, until I understood where he was coming from. In their different ways neither of them had any grey areas. Trevor was more sparing in his praise than Fred, and was every inch as devoted an Essex man as Fred was a patriotic Yorkshireman. They both spoke just as they had played. Trevor dotted all the 'i's and crossed every 't', while Fred's brush had a broader sweep.

I am not sure Trevor had much sympathy for young commentators feeling their way, and more than once I was thrown by his sharp but economical replies. When you asked him between overs for a comment on a new batsman or bowler he had not seen before, it was disconcerting to have two words – 'Can't bat' or 'Can't bowl' – fired back at you, although after a pause he would go on. Occasionally there would be a grin as he leaned forward, turned towards you and said, 'Like him in my side,' and then after a pause would tell you why.

Trevor was succinctly clinical. He spoke like the man who had batted through that last afternoon with Willie Watson to save the second Test against Australia at Lord's in 1953, then a month later in the fourth Test at Headingley had batted for 261 minutes for 38 runs before bowling wide down the leg side to frustrate Australia's batsmen as they chased 177 for victory. We must not forget, either, that in 1953–54, in the final Test at Kingston's Sabina Park, the West Indies won the toss on a belter of a pitch. Trevor opened the bowling with Fred, and took 7 for 34 in sixteen overs, enabling England to win the match and draw the series. Trevor loved to remember that game, and if ever I brought it up he would turn to me, smile broadly and produce a happy, satisfied 'Ummmmmmmmm', which took a moment or two. By contrast, there was always more than a touch of the tearaway in Fred, who had helped to reduce India to 0 for 4 in their second innings at Headingley in 1952, his first Test. Also a bit of the rebel who was docked his good-conduct money after the 1953/54 tour to the West Indies – and missed out on tours to Australia and South Africa, and some Tests at home as well – for an unwise verbal sortie or two in his early years with England.

Trevor's arrival in the box before the start of play would usually be accompanied by a long-drawn-out 'Good moooooooorning,' while Fred would make more of an entrance. There would be a couple of friends with him, he would be carrying a bat he wanted to have autographed, and there was a bit of good-natured bluster. His faithful pipe was never far away, and the wretched thing should certainly have had a health warning permanently hanging round it. I've never come across another pipe that managed to produce as much smoke as Fred's, or to give off such an evil smell. When he had it in his mouth it was as if he was preceded by something that would have been a star turn on Guy Fawkes' Night. There used to be a time when there was a fair bit of smoke in the box. Trevor, Don Mosey and I all wielded cigarette lighters, and a number of the visiting commentators and summarisers from overseas were smokers, led by the indomitable and excellent Alan McGilvray from Australia who seldom had one out of his mouth when he was not commentating. In those days, as we have seen, before Political Correctness tried to sweep our sins away, alcohol, in modest measure of course (pace John Arlott), was also a happy accompaniment. A resounding 'pop' around midday would disconcert Peter Baxter, but Trevor Bailey wheverever he was would save the day by saying in a loud voice "Ah, the medicine."

As a summariser, Fred was at his best when rain or bad light had stopped play, and matches, tours, players and personalities from the past were up for discussion. He had a wonderful memory, and when he was talking about Test matches early in his career, he really brought them to life. To listen to him talking about that first Test of his against India at Headingley was a joy – unless you were a passionate Indian supporter and had been one of their top-order batsmen that day. After only fourteen balls of the innings India were 0 for 4 and Fred had taken three of them in eight balls. One of their touring party that year was a certain H.R. Adhikari, who batted in the middle order. He didn't play at Headingley, but took his place in the last three Tests (there were only four that year). Not only did he not prosper, but he showed considerable apprehension when facing Fred. Twenty-seven years later, H.R. Adhikari, who by then had become Colonel Adhikari, returned to England as manager of the Indian side. When there was a break in the play during the Test at Old Trafford, Johnners brought the Colonel into the commentary box.

Fred was smoking his pipe, and Johnners said to him, 'Fred, you remember Colonel Adhikari, don't you?' 'Ay,' said Fred, smiling, and as he shook him by the hand he went on, 'Glad to see yer got soom o' yer colour back, Colonel.' The box shook with laughter, and no one thought it funnier than the Colonel himself, although I am not sure how much he then enjoyed being reminded about his dismissal at Old Trafford. He probably needed his glass of champagne after that.

Fred always called me 'H', and I was flattered that he singled me out for special treatment and was a good friend to me. When anyone questioned whether I had ever played cricket myself, he would spring to my defence, saying, 'H got a first-class 'undred at Lord's.' I was glad he never asked who bowled for the MCC that day, otherwise his support might not have been so readily forthcoming. Another lovely feature of Fred's broadcasting was that he always came up with his own distinctive phraseology. If there was a hold-up in play for some obscure reason, or the umpires had a long chat, or a twelfth man came on with a message for the batsmen, and you asked Fred what it was all about, he would say with great emphasis and mild annoyance, 'I don't know what's going off out there, sunshine.' There was one lovely occasion during a break in play when Fred and I were discussing the various skills of fast bowling. We found ourselves in complete agreement, and I brought the topic to a close by saying there could be no doubting our opinions, as we had taken 307 Test wickets between us. For a moment Fred didn't quite get it, and glared at me as if I was an umpire who had just said 'Not out'. He was about to come in with a verbal bouncer when he saw what I was getting at: he was the first bowler to take three hundred Test wickets, and finished with 307.

When Fred first came into the box it was never a good idea to bring up the name of Geoffrey Boycott. Fred would wax eloquent on the subject for at least three overs, and it was always a job to get him onto something else. In those days he had it in for his fellow Yorkshireman, but happily they were to become good friends and when Geoffrey had his long and frightening battle with throat cancer in 2002–03, Fred was a great source of encouragement, and was in constant contact with him. A few years later, when Fred himself went through his long final illness, Geoffrey was in turn a real comfort to him, and there was no greater admirer of Fred as a bowler than Geoffrey.

One of my best memories of Fred came after his death. He was a devout Christian, and went to church at Bolton Abbey, where he now lies buried. In 2007, a year after his death, I visited a second-hand bookshop in the nearby village, and the owner asked me if I had seen Fred's grave. I had not, so I walked round to the churchyard. It would not have been a surprise if Fred had organised a pretty fiery headstone, with all sorts of embellishments, but when I found it I was moved by its wonderful simplicity. It said: 'F.S. Trueman, A Cricketer, Yorkshire and England'. There was no side about that. It said it all, with endearing modesty, and told anyone who saw it a great deal about Fred.

Trevor, too, was a terrific admirer of Fred, who not surprisingly more than appreciated Trevor's own canny way of playing cricket. When he was at Cambridge, Trevor went on a football

Left: Soon after it all began: I am with my producer, Peter Baxter, now my inestimable stage partner, broadcasting at a county match in Canterbury – fresh-faced youth!

Right: It was not always that easy or comfortable. Here I am telephoning a minute's report from the Sydney Cricket Ground to BBC Radio Somebody.

Left: CMJ and I discussing affairs of state and maybe a technical problem in some commentary eyrie during a Test match.

Right: Bulawayo 1996 when, to my huge embarrassment – unaccountably of course! – I kept going for an hour and a quarter on my own. Trevor Bailey on the left and Simon Mann (His Grumpiness!) on the right.

Above: On the road to Bombay in October 1976. A puncture had halted the Rolls, in Greece. Ady changes the wheel while Judy, Michael and the Rover have a watching brief.

Above: Ady behind the wheel and Wooders teaching the local youngsters a thing or two somewhere in Afghanistan.

Above: With the Maharajah of Baroda outside his Palace. From the left: a retainer, me, the Maharajah, Michael, Judy and Ady, grinning fit to bust.

Above: TMS *in excelsis*. At Lord's, at the back of our wonderful old box we should never have been made to leave. From left: Alan McGilvray, Don Mosey, Tony Lewis, Johnners, Trevor Bailey, CMJ and me.

Above: Sadly, my last sighting of Keith Miller. Colin Ingleby-Mackenzie and I organised a lunch in London on his last visit, in 2004. Johnny Woodcock, talking to Miller, also came along.

Left: I am talking in the new box at Lord's with Iain Galloway, a Dunedin solicitor who was a wonderful commentator and became President of the New Zealand Cricket Council.

Above: With a formidable pair of fast bowlers in the commentary box at the WACA ground in Perth. Fred Trueman on my right and Peter Loader on my left.

Right: Cricket commentary on an ice floe in Iceland. It was probably just as well I was kept on a lead. Surprisingly, the ice took a bit of spin!

Left: With Sir Viv, always a joy to work with, in the box at Lord's. We were dressed more for ratting than for watching a Test Match.

Right: Ready, Steady, Cook. I am with my charming opponent, Phillip Silverstone, a wine expert, with dear old Ainers (Ainsley H) keeping us on the straight and narrow.

Left: A bit more name dropping now. Aggers and I are with Nigel Havers to whom I talked in *A View from the Boundary* during one lunch interval.

Right: And while I am at it, here's another. HM presented us with an amazing fruit cake when she came to Lord's in 1961. From left: HM, Peter Baxter, me, CMJ, Aggers and the Bearded Wonder (Bill Frindall).

Above: Well really! A sign put up on a balcony during a Test at Headingley. It might mean, when the time comes, I shall have a lively chat when I touch base with St Peter.

Below: A bizarre and lively invitation to the launch at The Sheraton-Wentworth Hotel in Sydney, of my book, *Wine, Women and Wickets*.

James Fraser Publishing
invites

....

to the launch
by Kate Fitzpatrick
of WINE, WOMEN & WICKETS
by Henry Blofeld
and to sample the inaugural
SHERATON BLOWFLY COCKTAIL.
To be held in
the Perth Room of the
Sheraton-Wentworth Hotel
on Tuesday, February 14
from 5.30-7.30.

R.S.V.P. Roxanne (02) 212 1677

Memories of TEST MATCH SPECIAL

Above: When I commentate on the Chelsea Arts Club's short tour to St Moritz in July 2012, the local pigeon population gave me a handsome welcome by kind permission of John Springs' drawing skills.

Left: Need I say more! Two old farts on the road: Peter Baxter and me. Brilliantly cartooned by John Ireland.

Left: My daughter, Suki, with her husband, Olly, enjoying a well-earned rest outside The Old House at Home, in Newnham, Hampshire, their restaurant-cum-pub which has caught the eye of the Michelin guide, where she cooks like an angel.

Right: My seventieth birthday party at the Albert Hall made famous by Stephen Fry's huge generosity. I stand behind the bar in the second act while Aggers talks to my brother (in the middle) and Edward Lane Fox.

Above: In 2012 I clocked into the Paddock at Royal Ascot where I had been asked to present the trophy to the winning owners of that race.

Above: Valeria is the best thing ever to have happened to me. Big in the world of fashion, she opened Moschino in Mayfair and looks the part. Has converted me to all things Italian and she loves cricket. I rest my case!

tour to Switzerland. The programme for one of the matches mis-spelt his name as 'Boiley'. He was then referred to as Boiley by the ground commentator and his close friend Doug Insole, also of Essex and England, who was playing in the football match, called him 'the Boil' from that day on. Johnners always called Trevor 'the Boil'; the rest of us had to wait until we had qualified.

It was after Fred had been left out of the tour to South Africa in 1955–56 that he went down with the Yorkshire side to play a game against Essex. Fred was bowling pretty quickly, anxious to remind the selectors that England were not sending their most hostile attack away that winter. The Boil was being his usual obdurate self at the crease, when Fred bowled him a nasty bouncer which hit him on the head. He went down in a heap, and there was some blood about. Being Trevor he realised that if he stayed down long enough, there wouldn't be time for another over before lunch. As he lay on the ground he was conscious of a figure with a tousled head of black hair bending over him and saying, 'Eh, Trevor lad, there are many I would rather have hit than thee.'

In the box, Trevor never let anyone get away with a mistaken view, and his corrective tones brooked no nonsense. My first game at Lord's for *TMS* was the second Test against Australia in 1975. In the end it was a boring finish, and we had to watch Australia batting out the match for most of the last day. I was commentating in mid-afternoon when Peter Lever was bowling off his enormous run to Greg Chappell, who launched himself into a glorious cover-drive for four. I described the stroke, and went on to say that I was sure the ultimate coaching book, which those of us lucky enough to make the grade would probably find in heaven, would contain more photographs of Greg Chappell playing that stroke than anyone else. Trevor came in one ball later, at the end of the over. 'Of course,' he said, 'the stroke that Greg Chappell is best known for is the on-drive.'

What fun it was to have worked with both Trevor and Fred. There were so many of these amusing moments in the box, for they both always had a twinkle in their eye, and of course their vast knowledge of the game greatly enhanced the quality as well as the entertainment value of our output. The saddest thing about their splendid partnership was the ending of it. In 1999 another round of bidding was coming up for the television and radio rights to broadcast cricket in England for the next few years. The England and Wales Cricket Board (ECB), who control these things, had let it be known that they thought some of the *TMS* team were a little long in the tooth, and that too much time was being spent saying that things weren't what they used to be. The powers-that-were at the BBC decided to dispense with Trevor and Fred's services and bring in some younger summarisers who would be more in tune with younger listeners, and more recognisable to them too. One of the saddest things about this was the way it was done. Instead of making a great fanfare about their departure and giving them a terrific send-off after their final Test match on the air, nothing was said. It was left to Peter Baxter to tell them both before the start of the next season that their services would no longer be required. Both of them were understandably most upset by this, and they had every reason to be. Trevor had been part of *TMS* for thirty-three seasons, and Fred had done twenty-six.

For many years, one of the things that made the mix of the programme so perfect was the interaction between Arlott and Johnston and Trueman and Bailey. The knowledge, the banter, the humour and the atmosphere these four created made the job a lot easier for the rest of us. Easier, but also in a way more difficult: they may have made sure the audience were on our side, but how could we compete with them? How could we do any more than come up to their ankles? But that is all water under the bridge. *TMS* still does a great deal more than just exist, and it is to the immense credit of all those I am about to talk about in the next chapter who have made this happen. The kings are dead; long live the kings.

TEN

The Traffic Cop in Faisalabad

Every Test match takes on a life of its own, and for a commentator, ordinary life has to be put on hold for five days or however long it takes. For me, now that Anno Domini is taking its toll, the adventure of a Test in England starts the evening before, when the second bottle remains unopened and it's early to bed. I have never enjoyed the 6.30 alarm call, and then there is breakfast. I am at my worst in the early morning. I am grumpy, disinclined to talk, and almost blatantly hostile if someone comes and sits at the same table. It's bad enough if it is a friend, but if it is a stranger – they have a way of saying, 'I've so enjoyed listening to you over the years . . .' which means they must have been dropped on their head as a baby. We are told that flattery gets you everywhere, but not with me in the early morning it doesn't. I scowl, try to look forbidding, and say something along the lines of 'I like to read the paper at breakfast,' but it seldom has the discouraging effect I am hoping for. If whoever-it-is is both adhesive and loquacious, I bolt my food and flee, hoping there is time for a cup of coffee in my hotel room before I set off.

The drive to the ground is more enjoyable when the countryside is involved, as it is for Trent Bridge, which is a lovely twenty-five-minute drive from that peerless billet at Langar

Hall, where the browsing and sluicing and stage-management are perfection. It can also be a pleasant drive to both Edgbaston and Old Trafford. The car parking at the various grounds has become less confrontational over the years, as ticket inspectors have grown accustomed to my face. That was not always the way of things at Headingley, where they seemed to enjoy keeping you out rather more than letting you in. 'Yes, I know who you are, but you can't come in here without the right ticket,' sort of thing.

I have always been reasonably punctual, and I like to get to the box a couple of hours or so before the start of play. In the old days I sometimes found myself arriving even before Bill Frindall, who would clock in early with a trolley or two of equipment. He would set up his considerable stall at one end of our long commentary desk, amid guffaws and snorts. Pity the man who tried to rein him in. Latterly I have sneaked in ahead of Bill's successor, the eternally good-humoured Malcolm Ashton. He covers something like the same acreage as Bill, but with a good deal less noise. Of course, producers clock in early. Peter Baxter – always a blur of motion, with a mop of white hair: by the time he retired he had almost joined the blue-rinse brigade – would burst through the door before rushing off to have a word with Andy Leslie, Brian Mack, Dave Sherwood or Nick Bell, all great men, one of whom will have been in charge of the engineers' box next door. His successor, Adam Mountford, makes a more stately entrance, but then he has the figure for it. He too is full of good cheer, but in a more measured way.

The jaunty, angular Aggers comes next, sitting down and starting things off with a, 'Well, how are you, Blowers?' before branching off into a problem with his hotel room or a story about someone who was 'trolleyed' in the hotel the night before. A cheerful 'Hello' will announce the arrival of Vic

Marks, who will already have staked out his position in the press box, for he flits tirelessly from one to the other as the day progresses. I cast a provisional eye over Vic's apparel, which is invariably well worn, full of unintended creases and comfortingly familiar, both the creases and the garment. If the Australians are over here, Jim Maxwell checks in enthusiastically and heartily. He has never believed in whispering, and is quick to state the Australian point of view. If it is a West Indian year, Tony Cozier makes a quieter, but still smiling and friendly, entrance after peering hesitantly around the door. He is always full of cheerful optimism, latterly more about life in general than the immediate future of West Indies cricket. Another early arrival if the West Indies are touring will be Sir Viv Richards, with that uproariously infectious laugh. There are always some risqué suggestions between us about how last night was spent, how tonight is shaping up, and more laughter. 'Grumps', otherwise known as Simon Mann, will make an easy, relaxed appearance, saying 'Good morning' to us individually before sharing whatever adventure he had that morning on the way to the ground. Then, to general acclaim, Tuffers bounces in, usually in a pair of jeans, with a 'Morning all,' and an exploit to recount from one of his many radio or television programmes. David 'Bumble' Lloyd will almost certainly put in a quick head-round-the-door on his way to the TV box, with a story to tell or a successful hoax to reveal.

There will be a measured entrance from Geoffrey Boycott in one of his wide-brimmed sunhats, which come in a variety of colours. He wants to know from Adam what the roster is, and when he is on air. About now Adam will walk quickly, with commendable determination, back and forth between the various television boxes to make sure the commentary times for one or two of his summarisers fit in with their television obligations. He then bustles off to make sure the Five Live box is up and running. Shilpa Patel always used to be there too as assistant producer; now it is Henry Moeran. In their ways both have done a lot for the programme.

We're usually on the air at 10.45, by which time, if it's the first day of the match, Aggers has covered the toss and talked to the captains. He now stands at the side of the pitch and kicks the programme off with Victor and maybe Tuffers beside him, or a smartly suited Michael Vaughan, who always seems to be doing three things at once, in addition to firing off a constant stream of tweets. I am usually asked to start the programme on one day of each Test – and what fun that is. You can get the day under way with a good laugh, and the likes of Vic and Tuffers and Alec Stewart, who sometimes lends a hand in the middle, are all happy to join in. While this was happening, a breathless and mildly harassed CMJ would come bustling into the box, looking around and saying, 'I'm not late, am I?' This was always said more in hope than confidence. With CMJ, sudden traffic jams, Acts of God or mechanical failure, and sometimes all three, took their toll, and he was almost always their only victim – sod's law. Then, as the players are taking the field, Aggers, who has walked back to the boundary's edge with his accompanying entourage, hands over to Grumps in the commentary box, who has just marked out his long run in front of the microphone, and we're buoyantly away.

As a commentator myself, I am never on air with any of the other commentators. I only make this obvious point because people often ask me who I most like to commentate with. But I have been lucky enough to work with many versatile and excellent performers over the years. Although I only shared the box with him once, in one of my first two one-day internationals in 1972, I will always remember Alan

Gibson as a good friend and an important but underrated commentator, and if I don't pop something about him in now, I am not sure when his chance will come. He was a commentator in the mould of John Arlott, with a deliciously obstructive streak. He never cared for authority, and was always ready to kick it into touch. When I began my career at the microphone, it was an unwritten law that the commentator who covered the last overs of the day should never read out the full scorecard, because that was how Jim Swanton liked to begin his close-of-play summary. If Alan was doing the last stint of the day, he invariably read out the scorecard, preferably after Jim had arrived in the box. On one occasion he greeted Jim's arrival with the words, 'The close of play is nigh, because the Angel of Death has arrived.' Alan was nothing if not mischievous.

Once, in the north, where *TMS* was produced by Don Mosey, he told Alan that pints of bitter were no longer allowed in the box. 'Aren't you being a trifle pompous, old man?' was Alan's reply. Later that day he came into the box with a brimming pint mug. At the end of his session, Mosey said brusquely, 'Alan, I thought I told you that pints of beer were no longer allowed in the box.' 'I don't see any beer in here,' Alan replied innocently. His tipple was a pint of neat Scotch. He had a wonderful turn of phrase, a pointed and erudite sense of humour, and a thirst which rivalled Arlott's, although he adopted even more of a devil-may-care approach to the business of quenching it and, indeed, to containing it. Norman Yardley, who had captained England and then worked on *TMS* as a summariser, became a wine merchant in Bradford. One year when an Indian touring side was playing at Park Avenue against Yorkshire, he asked Alan and Pearson Surita, the Indian commentator who hailed from Calcutta and had an impressive thirst of his own and a voice to rival Swanton's, to visit his shop before the start of a day's play. The consequences were disastrous. Incidents like that accounted for Alan having a shorter life-span in the box than he would otherwise have had. He only did twenty-seven Test matches in fourteen years – not nearly enough.

Alan was a most amusing man, and would go on to write delightful and idiosyncratical pieces about county cricket for *The Times*. In those intriguing articles he described his own adventures during the day as much as what went on in the middle. Tallish, thin and florid, with a cheerful face and a most disturbing habit of sometimes losing it completely if lunch had been entirely liquid, as it usually was, he was one of the wittiest, most enjoyable and more irresistible of the characters I have met in the world of cricket. He had been President of the Oxford Union, and had the intellect that suggests. It was always a joy to find him working at the same match, as it guaranteed a long pork-pie-and-beer or whisky lunch just around the corner from the ground in some dark, rundown Victorian pub presided over by an elderly lady called Violet or some such who had been serving him for years. What fun it was, too, to read the account of his adventures that day in the next morning's copy of *The Times*. The pick of them have now been published in book form, and are not to be missed.

Don Mosey, whom we have just met as the cricket producer in the north, joined *TMS* as a commentator in 1974. Johnners said that when he first saw him he reminded him of an alderman, so 'the Alderman' he became, to Johnners and therefore to everyone else. Don described himself as 'a bowler's commentator', whatever that may have meant. His manner was irascible and sometimes grouchy and not always tightly controlled. He was a Yorkshireman who lived in Lancashire, which may not be quite as drastic as having a sex-change operation, but almost. He always closely espoused Northern values, and was more than a trifle suspicious of those who came from the South. He and I had no problem over this, because he was prepared to concede that Norfolk was not conspicuously one of the Home Counties.

The Alderman and Johnners got along famously – he made Johnners an exception to his rule about effete southerners – and they endlessly played what was known in the commentary box as 'the word game'. They would both begin with a blank sheet of paper on which they drew the same number of squares. Then, in turn, each nominated a letter which they both had to use; the winner was the one who came up with the largest number of three-, four- or five-letter words. It was an ongoing contest which continued for many seasons, but the Alderman was never able to match Johnners' technique, and overall was a heavyish loser.

It was sensible to tread delicately with the Alderman, who in the end let himself down by writing a book saying that few of his colleagues were really up to anything much. As far as he was concerned the rest of us were all part of a Machiavellian public school plot. Even Johnners, who was the most good-natured man in the universe, felt that this was a bit steep, and the word game petered out. The Alderman was not plagued by self-doubt, and if anyone disagreed with him he became even more certain he was right. For all that, he was a good commentator, and his North Country humour had a lively glow to it. He was the only member of *TMS* (to date) to have married the same woman twice: he and Jo were married and divorced, and then took the plunge a second time, which argues all-round bravery of the highest order.

Tony Lewis, who achieved fame as a batsman for Cambridge, Glamorgan and briefly England, was with us for a few years before going on to greater things with television. He was another commentator who told it as it was, with a gentle smile and without going down the pitch more than he had to. Every morning when Peter Baxter drew up the rota for the commentators he used their initials – 'JA', 'BJ', 'CMJ', 'DM', 'HB' and so on. Tony went down as 'ARL', so in no time Johnners was referring to him as 'Arl', and of course it stuck for as long as he was with us. Arl was a good friend of John Arlott, that visit to the wine merchant's in Hove having long since been forgotten and forgiven, but the *TMS* box was never going to be more than a temporary resting place for him. For some time he will have had his sights on the BBC television box as Peter West's successor. While he was with us he added greatly to the quality of our output. He had of course a vast knowledge of the game, and was always interesting, with the fresh insights he was able to produce from his Welsh perspective. He was good fun behind the scenes in the back of the box, and was another who constantly trod the path between the commentary box and the press box, usually on behalf of the *Daily* and *Sunday Telegraph*.

Christopher Martin-Jenkins, tall, thin, angular and likely to list in a breeze, invariably late for any appointment and adopting a mystified air of injured innocence if anyone should point a finger, was one Test senior to me. CMJ was dedicated to cricket, with an almost schoolboy passion for the game that never left him. He was always wide-eyed and enthusiastic, yet terribly correct at the same time. He exemplified the amateur ethic in a charming way, and was audibly shocked whenever he felt the highest ethical standards had not been maintained. It was appropriate that he was selected in 2009 to give the Colin Cowdrey Memorial Lecture on 'The Spirit of Cricket', a subject that was so dear to him, to MCC members at Lord's. In 2010–11 he received the ultimate cricketing honour when he was made President of MCC, and with terrific dedication he did a first rate job in a difficult year.

CMJ was a man who, in every aspect of life, would walk if he snicked the ball to the wicketkeeper. He did not take chances: if ever there was a player who would never have been run out at Lord's for 99, it was CMJ. Yet, playing for Marlborough against Rugby in 1963, that was precisely what happened. Even so, anyone who scores 99 at Lord's has to be a pretty impressive batsman. CMJ was certainly that, and he went on to play for Surrey Second Eleven. If a career in commentating and journalism had not taken over, who knows what he might not have gone on to achieve. A straight talker who commentated without too many flourishes, he had a lovely voice which was very easy to listen to. He was extremely accurate in his descriptions: if he told listeners that a batsman had worked an inswinger off his pads to midwicket, you knew that was exactly what had happened. CMJ also had the rare attribute of making every listener feel he was talking personally to him.

Away from the commentary box he was a brilliant mimic, and in high demand as an after-dinner speaker. He brought a great amount of good humour to the box, even if he was a stickler for old-fashioned cricketing standards, and let no one off if they let him down in the middle – or indeed in the commentary box. He was never averse to taking on his expert summariser and expressing an alternative point of view. I remember him once having the temerity to argue with Fred Trueman, who was, to say the least, most surprised. If all commentators met the standards set by CMJ, *TMS* would go on forever. His was truly the voice of cricket after Brian Johnston did his last commentary in 1993. He had a wonderful vocabulary, a great way of constructing a sentence, and a marvellous instinct for choosing the right word for the right situation. He had a lovely chuckle, too, and was always ready to pounce on a moment of humour. CMJ was scrupulously polite and charming – the strongest oath I ever heard him employ was a muttered 'Fishcakes'. The only criticism that could be levelled at him concerned his inability either to read his watch, or if he did read it, to pay any attention to what it said. His arrival time was always a matter of conjecture, and if you were following him as the next commentator, it was anybody's guess when you would get on the air. It was a grievous blow, for the programme and its followers, his many friends and, most of all, his family when he was struck down by the dreaded cancer in January 2013, at the age of only sixty-seven. CMJ was a dear man, and the world of cricket will miss him very much – nowhere more than in the *TMS* commentary box. He may not have been Arlott or Johnston, but in his own way he was just as special and just as important.

Perhaps the most inspired decision Peter Baxter (who was himself a most reliable commentator when pressed into service) ever made was to make Jonathan Agnew the BBC's Cricket Correspondent in 1991, when CMJ retired after his second stint in the job. There is no one I have felt happier or more relaxed with in the box than Aggers – it took Johnners less than a second to come up with the nickname. While he was still playing county cricket Aggers had done some work with BBC Radio Leicester, and had quickly built up a good reputation. When the correspondent's job came up, there were others who were closer to the centre of things who may have felt that their turn had come. But Aggers' easy, friendly style, his knowledge of cricket, his palpable sincerity and his ability to bring out the best in people made him the right choice. The fact that he had played a few Tests for England had nothing to do with it. Aggers was not being employed because he was a former international cricketer, but because he was an able broadcaster and was the best man for the job.

Aggers fitted into the *TMS* box as seamlessly and effortlessly as if he had been there for years. Although he has never needed luck, he did have one great piece of good fortune almost before he had got his feet under the table. In his first year, 1991, he was used as an expert summariser rather than a commentator, to allow him to settle comfortably into the job. England were playing the West Indies, and the final Test at The Oval saw Ian Botham make one of his comebacks. In England's first innings he had made 31, and was beginning to bat well, when Curtley Ambrose bowled him a nasty bouncer. He shaped to play a hook, but the ball bounced more than he expected, and he tried to pull out of the stroke. In doing so he overbalanced, and realising he was in danger of treading on his stumps, he attempted to jump over them. The back of his trousers just caught the off-bail, which fell tanta-lisingly to the ground, and he was out hit wicket.

When play ended for the day, Johnners and Aggers did the close-of-play summary. They discussed Botham's dismissal, and were just about to move on when Aggers remembered a phrase he had heard earlier that day in the press box: the correspondent of the *Sun* had said to him that Botham had just failed to get his leg over, and Aggers had stored it away. Now, just as Johnners was about to move on to the next part of the summary, Aggers quietly slipped in, 'Yes, he couldn't quite get his leg over.' According to Peter Baxter, Johnners immediately gave a hiccough, which Backers, as I always call him, feared was ominous. Johnners later claimed that for the next thirty seconds he was the most professional he had ever been in his life. But it was only for thirty seconds – and then came the first 'Oh, do stop it, Aggers.' Tears began to roll down his cheeks, and he lost control. The situation degenerated into a succession of squeaks, giggles and snorts, and little else. If you listen to a recording of it now, more than twenty years later, it still reduces the listener to giggles almost as much as it did to Aggers and Johnners while it was happening. At one point you can just hear a bemused producer saying, 'For God's sake, someone say something.' That evening both Baxter, as producer, and Johnners left the ground thinking they may well have ended their broadcasting careers. The next morning, to their grateful astonishment, they woke to find that recordings of the incident were being played on almost every network. By the time they had reached The Oval, there was little doubt that Johnners and Aggers had become heroes. It was later voted by Radio 5 listeners as the greatest piece of commentary ever. The one thing it certainly was not was a piece of commentary. It was, though, a moment that perhaps only cricket, and maybe only *Test Match Special*, could have produced.

I was not in the box to hear this, because for three years I shamelessly defected to Sky Television. I was asked by Sky in 1990 if I would commentate on the Sunday League matches they covered. I agreed to do so, as it did not affect my relationship with the BBC who did not have the rights. The following year Sky gained a share of the rights to broadcast all international cricket in England, and asked me to be a part of their team. It was put together by David Hill, who had masterminded Channel Nine's coverage of World Series Cricket in Australia and was now working for Rupert Murdoch organising Sky's coverage of sport in the UK. Hill's principal lieutenant as far as cricket was concerned was Tony Greig, whom Kerry Packer had presumably leased to Murdoch for the purpose. I was offered a lot of money to join Sky; and it was an offer my bank manager felt unable to refuse. Sadly, as I later discovered much to my cost, it was only for one season.

Because the normal broadcasting boxes were BBC property,

we had to commentate from some strange places, including a ladies' loo in the Warner Stand at Lord's. This was not unique: in his early days Johnners had broadcast the controlled blowing up of an unexploded wartime bomb in St James's Park near to Buckingham Palace while peering through the window of a ladies' loo. He had been sent there by a policeman who considered it the safest spot and, being Johnners, he emerged saying he was 'just a little bit flushed'. At The Oval we were perched in a temporary hut at the back of the terracing just inside the Harleyford Road, and temporary and rather unusual accommodation was also provided at other grounds.

My days with Sky always began well before the start of play, sitting at a small table on the outfield and having a cup of tea with Geoffrey Boycott while trying to work out what would happen that day. I don't think the Great Man needed any assistance from the tea leaves. Greig and Bob Willis were two of my fellow commentators, and Charles Colville was the link man. It was good fun, and the fact that we were pioneering something completely new gave it a certain tinge of excitement. Alas, though, I was never any good at television commentary. For a start, I talked too much, a common failing of radio commentators if they move on to television. And I found it almost impossible to confine my commentary to events on the monitor, which showed what was being seen by viewers at home. It is bad television to talk about things people cannot see. I was unable to avoid talking about something funny I had spotted happening in some remote corner of the ground, and as a result the cameras had a frantic time trying to follow me, when I should have been following them.

At the end of my last stint on any day's television commentary, whether it was in England, the West Indies, on the subcontinent or in New Zealand, where I worked for TVNZ in the eighties and nineties, the producers must invariably have reached for the smelling salts, or maybe something stronger. My career as a television commentator was not exactly stillborn, but it certainly didn't flourish. During the winter of 1991–92, Sky and David Hill made the decision that they were only going to use former Test cricketers as commentators for international cricket, so in 1992 I was back to a few Sunday League matches, and the following year I didn't even get any of them. Whenever I rang David to find out what, if anything, was going on as far as I was concerned, he was never in the office. So in 1993 I was, in aviation terms, grounded. As Sky had made rather a meal of it when I joined them from the BBC, I had effectively outlawed myself from my previous employers. 1993 was a bad year.

1994 made a sad start, for in January, Johnners, who had had a stroke in the back of a London taxi the previous month, put his cue in the rack. South Africa were making their first tour of England since being readmitted to the International Cricket Council following the end of apartheid. After the first Test, the BBC felt that they were prepared to hold their noses and recall me to duty. I was thrilled and nervous, and felt like a new boy all over again. In fact, it was worse than that, because I now had to do well enough to atone for my heinous crime of leaving *TMS* for Sky. As luck would have it, I think everything went reasonably well. I will not forget my first match back in the *TMS* box because of one specific over. This was the first time Jonty Rhodes had come on a tour to England, and his fielding was little short of miraculous. The best fielder ever, in my view, was another South African, Colin Bland, who in the sixties was able to throw down the stumps about three times out of five; but Rhodes was not far behind, and he was great entertainment. When South Africa were fielding he was always in the thick of it, at cover or backward point, and I decided to commentate on one over entirely from his perspective. He was a continuous blur of motion even if the ball went to another fielder, and it made for an amusing, and I think well received, diversion. Anyway, I managed to avoid blotting my copybook, and I was back with *TMS*. I can say, hand on heart, that I will never again be lured away – although at my age the chances of that happening are far to the other side of remote.

As he was the Cricket Correspondent at the time, Aggers will have had a say in my return, and I can only doff my cap to him. Aggers, inspired by his stunning and elegant wife Emma, has always been a mildly snappy dresser, although even he might agree that his choice of suit when we met the Queen in the Committee Room at Lord's in 2001 was questionable. But that is the only blemish I can recall. He has a disarming and deceptive smile, for he is usually actively engaged in preparing to pull someone's leg. I have cause to know this better than most, as I am often the butt of his efforts. He hands me emails sent in by listeners such as 'Hugh Jarce', 'Ivor Biggun', 'I.P. Freely' or 'R. Sole', and expects me to read them out over the air. When it looks as if I am about to reveal the name at the bottom, which is the only way I can get back at him, he dashes forward and tears the piece of paper from my hand. He has always been a joy to work with, and humour and enjoyment have never been far below the surface. He is also a splendid companion when we are commentating overseas.

Cricket commentary, like almost everything else in life, is involved in a constant evolutionary process. In its early days before the war, with Howard Marshall, it had more than an element of 'Movietone News with Lionel Gamlin reporting'. Everything sounded as though it was being read by Big Ben, or perhaps by Laurence Olivier playing Jim Swanton. Johnners brought about a considerable change. His humour made commentary much less formal and more relaxed. It became more conversational, too, for Johnners brought in his summariser more often than other commentators. Aggers has taken things a stage further. In the old days the summariser would come in at the end of the over or when a wicket fell, and not otherwise, unless the commentator asked him a direct question. While Aggers is a superb commentator, he likes to carry on an almost continuous chat with his summariser, which does not intrude on the game, because he breaks off to describe each ball as it is bowled. If nothing significant happens he will immediately resume the conversation. But if something exciting occurs he will give it full value, and he and Vic Marks – they are the perfect combination for this – may wait for a couple of balls before going back to their previous topic.

CMJ and I were brought up under the old regime, when summarisers were used less. CMJ liked to regale listeners with a pet cricket theory, or some interesting aspect of a field placing he had spotted, in between giving details of impending charity matches or that morning's traffic jam. For my part, I tend to rush off with red double-decker buses, pigeons, seagulls, helicopters, butterflies and other such extraneous visual delights around the ground. I think it is good that the programme has these contrasts in style, which help to give it variety. Commentators must tell the story in the way that suits them best.

Another character for many of the later years I have spent in the box, and who made an important contribution to the success of *TMS*, was Shilpa Patel. For many years she was Peter Baxter's assistant producer, and then Adam Mountford's, until the BBC decided to move itself pretty well lock, stock and barrel to new studios at Salford, not far from Manchester United's ground. A number of people understandably decided that they were not prepared to move from London to Manchester, and Shilpa was one of them. Extremely attractive and always beautifully turned out, she would buzz around like an energetic bee from the commentary box to the engineers' box and back again, a journey she must have made many, many thousands of times in her years with us. She knew all the players, and one great strength was her ability to persuade whoever Aggers wanted to interview to come and have a chat with him. Each morning when the programme began, one of the joys was to see Shilpa out in the middle of the park, flitting about persuading coaches, managers, chief executives, groundsmen and many others to come and have a brief talk during the opening sequence.

When I started with *TMS*, hardly anyone was allowed onto the field before the start of play. Nowadays it's like Oxford Street at sales time, and you never know who you're going to run into. Shilpa also had a genius for finding where any member of the great and the famous who had come along to watch a day's cricket was sitting. In no time at all whoever it was would be in the commentary box and Aggers would be unleashed upon them. Aggers is a brilliant interviewer, and although he must have diligently researched many of his subjects, he chats with them so easily and conversationally that it seems to be entirely off the cuff. He often does it without a single note too. On one occasion Shilpa managed to get Daniel Radcliffe, a great cricket lover, up to the box at the time when he was at the height of his Harry Potter fame. Goodness knows how she located him and then managed to winkle him out of whatever box he was watching from. Aggers did a splendid interview, although he had had no time to research anything. Shilpa's efforts did much for the programme, and it is marvellous that her successor, Henry Moeran, although nothing like so pleasing on the eye, should have assumed her mantle as well as he has. When needed, he has shown that he can do a good job as a reporter too.

This brings me to Grumps, otherwise known as Simon Mann, who in his understated way is one of the most delightful people with whom I have been in the box. I am not sure how he came by his nickname – it was probably because of something that happened back in the studio when he first joined the BBC. He is a true Mr Reliable in the box, the sort of commentator that producers go to bed praying they will be working with the next day – and forever, if it comes to that. He has an impeccable broadcasting technique, and is always fun to work with. Nothing gets past His Grumpiness, who has a lovely, slow, almost on-the-back-burner sense of humour. Whenever I hand over to him, I know he is going to put me to shame by never failing to identify third man as well as thingamajig who has just been moved from third slip to somewhere you never expected to find him. Every commentary team needs a Grumpy, and preferably two of them. He can turn his hand to anything, be it starting the programme or interviewing an unexpected guest when Aggers is AWOL (usually hobnobbing in the President's box with the rich and famous, where he and Emma have been asked to lunch). Grumps will interview somebody on the telephone in Australia, do a forty-five-second piece for the *PM* programme, twenty seconds for the six o'clock news, and whatever other broadcasting chores come along. He does it all so easily, and with a smile too. He has a lovely wife, Alex, and two delicious daughters, Isabel and Marina, who sometimes embellish overseas tours. Grumps is truly a man for all seasons.

The scorer is an important figure in the *TMS* box. The commentators rely on him for the figures and more than a few of the facts. Usually we can see the scoreboard from where we are sitting, and the only problem when you look at it after runs have been scored is whether the operator has added those runs or not. As a general rule, scoreboard operators are quick, and by the time you've recounted all that has happened and look up to see the score, the extra runs have been recorded. But if there's any doubt, our scorer will instantly put us right. I don't think any of us give the score or recap enough on what has happened earlier in the day, or give the bowling figures often enough. But these things are almost impossible to get right: new listeners are tuning in all the time, but a commentator would annoy the existing audience if he gave the score after every ball. For most of my time with *TMS*, Bill Frindall, also known as the Bearded Wonder, a name and a character inevitably created by Johnners, was in the scorer's seat, having taken over during the series against the West Indies in 1966. Bill developed a system of scoring which had been handed down to him by Arthur Wrigley, one of his predecessors. He wrote in a lovely italic script, and his scorecards were works of art that any museum would have appreciated. I think Bill found the scorer's role a trifle restricting, and after a time he began to see himself as an extra commentator. At first he had a microphone which was always live, but give him an inch and he took a yard. His frequent interruptions, though mostly pertinent in their way, tended to interrupt the flow of the commentary.

I think it is fair to say that Bill's timing could sometimes let him down. I was commentating at the finish of the Boxing Day Test match in Melbourne in 1982. Australia were nine wickets down when Jeff Thomson joined Allan Border at the crease, and they still needed 74 runs to win. Bob Willis, who was captaining England, set his field deep when Border was facing to allow him a single, so that Thomson would be on strike. This did not work, and the pair added 70 runs, taking them to within 4 of victory. In desperation, Willis brought back Ian Botham, and immediately a lifter found the edge of Thomson's bat. The ball flew at waist height to Chris Tavare's right at second slip. He could not hold on to it, and the ball ballooned upwards to his right. Geoff Miller, at first slip, ran round behind Tavare and held the rebound. England had won by 3 runs. You can imagine the excitement, and the devastation among the Australian players and spectators. Knowing that this was one of the great moments in my commentating career, I went over the top, and gave it everything. I was just getting into my stride when the Bearded Wonder's purposeful voice came in over the top of me, announcing that this was Botham's hundredth wicket against Australia, completing his double of a thousand runs and a hundred wickets against the old enemy. Of course this was a relevant fact, but it should not have been allowed to interrupt the drama of the moment. I was cut off in midstream, and it is not easy to recapture these highly charged moments.

In the end Bill was allocated a microphone which he had to pick up and switch on before he went live on air. Even so, his frequent noises off, whether giggles, snorts or corrections, came through loud and clear to the listeners. His perfectionism as a scorer meant that no mistake from the commentator would ever go uncorrected, and he could sometimes make the life of a new commentator harder than it might have been. It was bad enough if you failed to read out one of the many notes he would pass over to you, but God forbid that a commentator should dare to disagree with him, or even worse, spill some tea or water over his immaculate scoring sheets. For all that, Bill set a new standard for the job, and was deservedly the first scorer to be awarded an MBE. He said that when the Queen invested him, she asked, 'Where is my cake?' As listeners know, Johnners' sweet tooth meant that the *TMS* box became an extraordinary repository for cakes of all descriptions, although chocolate was always his favourite.

The Bearded Wonder, who sadly died in 2009 of Legionnaires'

Disease, was a hard act to follow, but Malcolm Ashton, a large and cuddly solicitor from Lancashire with the readiest of wits, has made a brilliant successor. He gives the commentator everything he wants without thrusting it down his throat, and is commendably *sotto voce*. He has a lovely, easy manner, and his handwriting is good, if not madly beautiful. The scorer with the worst writing I have ever come across is Andrew Samson, who lives in Johannesburg and often scores for us overseas. Even so, he is brilliant. You can ask him the most obscure question, and he will come back instantly with the answer. He comes to the ground each day having anticipated pretty well all of those beastly questions that commentators have a habit of asking scorers. He is understated to a point, and in the important matter of demand and instant supply he is perhaps the first among equals. The one stumbling block is his handwriting, which requires considerable deciphering skills to make anything of. On the 2012 England tour of India I christened him Erasmus, and I think it fitted – I am sure Erasmus had bad handwriting.

The commentators may be the main pillars of the box, but the blend could never be achieved without the input of the summarisers. Since Fred and Trevor disappeared, Vic Marks has grown into a splendid successor. He has an easy, relaxed voice, and he seldom fails to put his finger on the spot. His comments are shrewd, but leavened with a light touch and a jolly sense of humour. When Vic is on with Aggers I always think that *TMS* is as good as it gets. The two of them interact brilliantly, and however grim the picture they may be painting, a smile is always just around the corner. Vic never pontificates, he only seems to suggest. If the news is not good, his voice slows and takes on an almost ecclesiastical tone, as if he is thinking of becoming one of those splendid Old Testament characters. I have an idea that Agag, the King of the Amalekites who 'came unto him delicately' might be his man, although Agag went on to reach a somewhat sticky end at the hands of Samuel. I have spent many happy hours on air with Vic, and I have already mentioned his idiosyncratic dress sense, which tends to be more casual than smart.

One of my favourite memories of him is from the Gabba in Brisbane in November 1998. Australia had had the better of the match, and by the middle of the last day it looked as if they would win, with England trying to hang on in their second innings. After lunch it became clear, looking into the distance from where we were sitting high up in the main stand at the Cricketers' Club end of the ground, that a big tropical storm was building up. Electric storms in Brisbane at this time of the year are not to be trifled with, and this one approached inexorably as the afternoon wore on. The lightning drew closer and closer, the light grew rapidly worse, and English wickets continued to fall. It got to the point where play was continuing in virtual twilight, yet still the umpires, Darrell Hair of Australia and K.T. Francis from Sri Lanka – in those days only one neutral umpire was used – refused to come off. They consulted after just about every over, and kept deciding that at least one more was possible. It began to look as if the two of them must have had built-in night vision. The most remarkable thing of all was that although the black clouds overhead made the phrase 'stygian gloom' look like a good way of describing a half-decent sunset, it obstinately refused to rain. On air, I was as bewildered as anyone as to why the weather gods were mocking England in this way.

One of the local landmarks, usually visible to the right of the commentary box, is the old Boggo Road Gaol, the sternest of Victorian structures, and in its way a part of the scene at the Gabba, even if it doesn't quite match Table Mountain's importance to Newlands. The prison, which has been enjoying retirement for quite a while, was fast disappearing from view when suddenly a streak of prodigiously forked lightning was followed by a rolling clap of thunder that would have made Mounts Etna and Vesuvius, off their longest runs, look like mere beginners. The sluice gates of heaven opened, and in under a minute it was impossible from where we were sitting to see even the pitch, let alone the Clem Jones Stand at the other end of the ground. The Boggo Road Gaol was now a figment of the imagination. It looked as if the world was going to end some time within the next minute and three-quarters. England's two not-out batsmen, Dominic Cork and Robert Croft, almost needed lifejackets by the time they got back to the pavilion.

I'm afraid I let my hair down a little in my commentary, for I had never seen anything like it. On one of the rare occasions that I paused for breath, I remember Vic saying in his mildest manner, 'Yes, it is raining fairly hard. We don't get anything quite like this in Somerset or Devon. But then, this is Brisbane, isn't it? Anyway, I think it's saved the match for England, don't you?' After that, his cheerful chuckle took over as we enjoyed our relief at England's salvation. In the face of both natural and unnatural disasters, on the field and off, Vic always manages to keep both feet firmly on the ground, shrugging off hat-tricks and violent tropical storms alike as 'just one of those things'. But I think even his Devonian phlegm was shaken by this example of nature having a strenuous coughing fit. Soon the ground was completely flooded, and down to our right the water was halfway up the white boundary fencing – the pickets, as they are known Down Under.

One piece of understatement was followed by another soon afterwards, when Vic's place as summariser was taken by dear old Thommo, the most ferocious fast bowler ever, and now the most charming, cheerful and skilful landscape gardener, as well as a considerable scourge of the fish off the Queensland coast. 'Yes, mate,' he said, 'I've seen plenty of these. You don't want to be out fishing just now.'

'They won't play cricket here for a week after this,' I suggested.

'I'll tell you what, Blowers, if you turn up at ten o'clock in the morning, you'll find they'd be playing by half past.'

I have never enjoyed a storm so much, and our description of it managed to win a place on that week's edition of *Pick of the Week* on Radio 4. For those who live in and around the Tropics it may have been nothing remarkable, but for anyone used to a more sheltered life, there were not enough superlatives with which to describe that downpour. As this was the last day of the match, I did not return to the Gabba the next morning to see if Thommo's prediction was on the mark. Instead I drove to the airport under a cloudless sky on the stillest of mornings. I dare say that if necessary they would have been perfectly able to bowl that first ball of the day.

Vic and Thommo are both gems to work with, and there are many others too who have been good companions, stalwart drinking mates and the best of friends. At the head of the list are Graham 'Foxy' Fowler and Mike Selvey, but the rest of the field are stepping on their heels: Gus Fraser, Ray Illingworth, Jack Bannister, Robin Jackman, Graham Thorpe, Colin 'Ollie' Milburn, Bob Taylor, Mike Hendrick and Peter Roebuck, to name but a few of our home-grown experts. Then there are our friends from overseas, led by Ian Chappell, Keith Stackpole, Farokh Engineer, Mushtaq Mohammad, Sunil Gavaskar, Ravi Shastri, Richard 'Prof' Edwards, Everton Weekes, Clyde Walcott, 'Tiger' Pataudi, Jeremy Coney, Glenn Turner, Barry Richards, Sean Pollock, Kerry O'Keeffe, Ranjit Fernando, Henry Olonga, and the rest. 'Prof' Edwards, who bowled fast for the West Indies, was a local commentator I worked with in Barbados. On one occasion when I was having trouble identifying the birds which flew frequently across Kensington Oval, 'Prof' told me they were known locally as mahogany birds. I stuck with this for the rest of the match, assuming that the giggles in the box when I mentioned yet another mahogany bird flying over were no more than a sign of appreciation that I had got it right. I only discovered after the match that in Barbados they call cockroaches 'mahogany birds'.

I have left to the last the summariser who makes the greatest impact on *TMS*, Geoffrey Boycott, who, in his way, has become a gem. There is no cricket broadcaster who invites more comment, produces more contradictory opinions, is more outspoken, some would say cussed, in his views than Geoffrey. That is him and he is simply being himself. He is controversial and loves it. He batted like a snail, he talks on air like a vampire. There is never a doubt whether discussing the futility of selectors, a captain, a bowler or a batsman or the future of Test cricket about which, in its present form, he can be particularly outspoken and pessimistic. There is not a single shade of grey with Geoffrey, let alone fifty, and that's the way he is. He believes passionately that he is right and he usually is. The question this begs is if he had been as clear-thinking in his playing days as he is now, why was he not the best captain of them all? Hindsight gives you an advantage.

Geoffrey has always had this same feeling of invincibility whether batting or commentating. There was one highly amusing occasion when it did not work for him. He and I did a fair amount of television commentary together in the Indian subcontinent in the eighties and early nineties. We were covering a Test match in the Pakistani city of Faisalabad where the traffic chaos was, on a daily basis, worse than I have seen it anywhere else in the world. We drove one morning in the same taxi to the ground – it would usually have been quicker to walk – and became embroiled in a traffic jam of gargantuan proportions. Geoffrey watched for a while as horns blared and tempers began to flare. Then he could stand it no longer, got out of the front seat and made a valiant attempt waving his arms like a traffic cop to create some order in the prevailing chaos. One result was that the horns reverberated with even greater velocity. King Canute did something similar although more silently, with the incoming tide in the Wash, and he would have sympathised with Geoffrey now. The horns became ever noisier and it was as if Geoffrey's presence had given the drivers a common purpose. They seemed hellbent on running him over. It was not long before he leapt back with an oath or two into the safety of the taxi. If they had opened the batting together, I wondered how King Canute and Boycott would have got on running between the wickets.

It is impossible to ignore Geoffrey's forthright views. You are either with him or against him. When he began with *TMS* he was not the easiest summariser to work with because he barged in regardless after pretty well every ball. He was not a Victor Marks who did it by persuasion and suggestion. Geoffrey gripped you round the throat, saying in effect, like it or leave it. He can sometimes be wrong and he is now happy to have a smile and a chuckle if his attention is drawn to it. If ever we remind him of a time when his partner, through no fault of his own, was run out, Geoffrey will say with a grin, 'He didn't run fast enough'. It is fair to say that when he first joined *TMS* he didn't fully understand the gentle nature of the programme and he carried on where he had probably just left off in the television box. He would burst into *TMS* just before his stint exclaiming loudly and not always jokingly, 'Come on, let's get rid of the rubbish.' He would take over from whoever was summarising and attack the microphone with strong and forceful opinions. He never committed the

245

ultimate sin of being boring. He tended to consider that the two sides of an argument were his own and the wrong one. He did not suffer disagreement gladly. And he still doesn't, but now he does it less insistently.

When he first came to us, Geoffrey was not unlike that tropical storm at the Gabba. He made his point forcefully, there was much lightning and thunder in what he said and he spared no one from his criticisms. All this was fair enough. But was it *Test Match Special*? He has now come round much more to our ways and not only fits in more happily, but in some ways he has changed things for the better. He has given *TMS* more of a cutting edge, which is no bad thing. I sometimes find myself wondering how John Arlott and Brian Johnston would have got on with him when he first came to the summariser's seat. After an initial raised eyebrow or two, they would both have enjoyed his company and would soon have had him laughing because both of them were such consummate broadcasters. They would have won him round. Geoffrey too, has suffered from, fought through and won a brave and amazing battle with cancer of the throat. Don't underestimate anyone who has done that. Neither Arlott nor Johnston would have made that mistake.

As the years have gone by I believe the essential ethos of *TMS* has come across to Geoffrey, who has become an integral part of the team. He is at his best doing his close-of-play podcasts with Aggers when he has a habit of hitting almost every nail on the head. Because he now lets his sense of humour come through and is prepared to laugh at himself, I believe that what he says comes across with a stronger effect. He undoubtedly talks a great deal of cricketing sense – but then he always has. It is simply the way he first put it across that was the problem. He has now come to accept *TMS* for what it is and has become a most welcome member of the family. I hugely enjoy working with Geoffrey. When he first came to us, I was apprehensive when he joined me on the air. Now I look forward to it. This change is greatly to the credit of both Geoffrey and the essential nature of *Test Match Special*.

In the last few years we have been joined on a regular basis by Phil Tufnell who is a complete natural. He has a brilliant sense of timing, wonderful humour, is a good reader of the game and puts it all across to easily and so cheerfully. You can see why he won *I'm a Celebrity . . . Get Me Out of Here!* and twinkled away with surprisingly electric footwork on *Strictly Come Dancing*.

Michael Vaughan is nothing if not a Yorkshireman even if he was born in Lancashire. He comes into the box, takes over between Tweets and keeps us all on our toes with his splendidly forthright opinions. You would never accuse him of sitting on the fence and as a successful England captain he brings a great authority to the box.

In 2013, Ed Smith who batted at different times for Kent, Middlesex and England, joined the commentary team. His erudite views are always interesting, he has a ready turn of phrase and a nice manner with it even if he belongs to the CMJ school of timing. He has made a good start and it's never easy coming into the middle of the piece of the mosaic that is called *Test Match Special*.

ELEVEN

A Heavenly Rejection

Of the many Test matches I have watched, does any single
one stand out from them all? If I was to answer this question
from a strictly cricketing point of view, it would have to be
either Headingley 1981 or Mumbai 2012. At Headingley,
England looked like losing to Australia by an innings and
plenty before Ian Botham hit 149 not out. Australia were left
to score 129 to win. Bob Willis then took 8 for 43, and England
won by 18 runs. In Mumbai in December 2012, the most
recent Test I have watched at the time of writing this chapter,
the odds were stacked against England. The previous week
they had lost the first Test in Ahmedabad by nine wickets,
and now at the Wankhede Stadium in Mumbai, India won
the toss on a spinners' pitch that had been prepared in accord-
ance with the specific wishes of the Indian captain Mahindra
Singh Dhoni. England proceeded to win by ten wickets in
three and a half days, outplaying India in every department
of the game, including spin bowling. In my view it was just
as extraordinary a victory as Headingley, even though the
margin of victory was huge.

For all that, the Test match I remember more fondly than
any other was played at Edgbaston against New Zealand,
starting on 1 July 1999. England won by seven wickets, but
that had nothing to do with it. I had flown back from New

Zealand in April, and had gone straight home to Norfolk. The lawn badly needed its first mow of the year, and on the Sunday I set about it. I had a huge, unwieldy, elderly motor mower which required strength and willpower to control, especially when turning it around. The job took an hour or two, and I was getting towards the end when I felt a strange constrictive sensation across my chest. I thought I must have strained something lugging the mower round in one of those 180-degree turns, and did not worry. That evening I drove up to London, and the next afternoon I decided to visit the World's End Nurseries to see my old friend James Lotery.

It was a short walk down the King's Road, and on the way that strange constriction again spread across my chest. I stopped and then started again, but if anything, it was worse. It so happened that there was a bench nearby, and I gratefully sank into it. I still didn't think anything much was wrong with me, for it was more a sensation than a pain. I waited a few minutes, and then set off again. I must have gone about a hundred yards when I was again stopped by the horrid feeling. There was no bench around this time, so I had to lean on a lamp post for a few minutes before I thought I was again fit enough to travel. At last I reached the World's End Nurseries, and pushed my way past masses of shrubbery and greenery and through the sliding door into James's office, where I immediately threw myself into a chair. James fussed around, and soon came up with his invariable remedy for everything – from a broken heart, to a bad result for England at Twickenham, to a lost Test match, to an ingrowing toenail – which was to be located in a brandy bottle. I found myself refusing this offering, which in itself should have made me seriously worried. James assured me that it couldn't be anything serious, and that brandy would provide a certain cure. But for some reason I still refused.

My wife, Bitten, who had arranged to meet me there on the way back from her office, now arrived. She didn't think it was much to worry about either, and drove me home. That evening we were going to dinner with Suki at the Chelsea Ram, which in the days of Rupert Clievely and Nick Elliott was an excellent gastro-pub. Suki arrived, heard my story and tried to make me ring my doctor, Trevor Hudson. I said I would try to go out to dinner, but if it happened again I would go home and call him. We were three quarters of the way there – it was only a short walk – when it returned with a vengeance. I shuffled back home and rang Trevor, who said at once that he knew exactly what it was, and that I was the perfect candidate for it. He told me I had angina, and ordered me to go straight to bed, and not to move unless it was to go to the bathroom, until I had heard from him the next morning. He rang soon after nine o'clock to tell me that I had been booked into the Harley Street Clinic in Weymouth Street, and to get there as soon as I could. I would be under a cardiologist called John Muir, who he assured me was up there with the best of them when it came to this sort of thing. I still didn't have the slightest idea that I might have been on the point of drawing my last breath.

Bitten came back from her office took me to Weymouth Street, where I waited in reception for a long time before I was shown to a room. The Harley Street Clinic is a bit of a rabbit warren, having originally been three or four mews houses. Over the next three weeks I was to have several rooms, and they were all tiny and uncomfortably hot. I had been told to bring some pyjamas with me, but I couldn't find any as I always sleep naked. As a result they provided me with an austere pair which had been given a touch of upright formality by some starch, popular stuff in hospitals. This pair had obviously encased the limbs of a great many people during a long, and I hope blameless, career.

Soon after I got into bed, John Muir, a solid-looking chap, well into his fifties, smiling and immensely competent with swept-back dark hair, appeared. He was in skittish form, and told me roughly what was likely to happen, although I dare say he spared me some of the juicier details to stop me fussing. I don't think I was ever in the least worried, then or at any other time, which was greatly to his credit, for hospitals can be unnerving places. He told me that the following day he would be doing an angiogram on me, which meant sticking a tiny camera into a vein in my groin and pushing it up to my heart, where it would behave as if it belonged to Metro-Goldwyn-Mayer and take photographs from pretty well every angle – of my good side as well as my bad. He told me that the surgeon who was going to do the heart bypass which he thought was likely to be necessary would soon be visiting me. He was called Christopher Lincoln, and was a sort of Field Marshal Montgomery in terms of open-heart surgery.

While I had been throwing some essentials into a zip bag before being carted off to the clinic, I remembered that I had been given a dozen bottles of Château Gruaud-Larose 1982 a few days earlier. Bitten never touched a drop of red wine unless we had run out of white, and as I felt that would be a rotten waste of Gruaud Larose '82, I shoved the remaining eight bottles into my bag. When I got to the clinic the nurse was surprised it was so heavy, and set off ahead of me like a mountain goat on a bad day. After I had got under the covers another charming nurse unpacked my bag, and plonked all eight bottles with some emphasis on the small table at the foot of my bed.

Half an hour later there was a perfunctory knock on the door, which then opened and admitted a procession of two. At the front was a tall, slightly stooped man with whitening hair. He smiled and introduced himself as Christopher

Lincoln. The more formal part of the procession came next. A sister (at least) in a splendid and imposing uniform which seemed to contain a good deal more starch than my pyjamas, stood just behind the great man in the way that consorts usually do. He asked me a few questions in a firm but charming manner, then talked about the likely course of events over the next couple of days. I was, by the way, being heavily monitored, and the state of my heart had clearly become one of the major attractions of the hospital, with its progress being shown on screens all over the place. I suppose this was rather comforting, but I still didn't think I was in mortal danger. In fact I was rather enjoying it all.

Christopher Lincoln was talking away when he noticed the bottles of wine. He stopped in mid-sentence, and turned to his companion. 'Sister,' he began, 'you see that red wine?' I thought, 'Oh, blast. You win some, you lose some,' but he went on, 'Mr Blofeld can have as much of that as he likes, at any time he wants.' He then turned back to me and said, 'The benefits of red wine with heart illness are only just beginning to be understood.' He made me feel like a conjuror who had just pulled the Ace of Spaces out of thin air – especially when he asked if I had remembered to bring a corkscrew with me.

To think that a man who had trained under John Arlott could have made such an elementary mistake.

Next morning, the arrangements for John Muir's angiogram were revealed to me. I was told that I would be able to watch the whole performance on the screens above my head. No thank you, that wasn't for me. I have always been squeamish, and I had no wish to see the camera cavorting round my body, or indeed what it found. By this time I was beginning to feel more than a little frightened. I was getting nearer to the coalface, and although everyone kept trying to reassure me, I could not believe that things were not going to be extremely uncomfortable, not to say excruciating. John Muir came to see me again, and told me that it was really no more than a gentle net before the start of play. He then left me, presumably to set the field.

I must have been given some tranquillisers, because I was quite relaxed by the time I was wheeled upstairs. John Muir was waiting for me, and told me again that it would be child's play. I lay down on a sort of medical couch, and he gave me a local anaesthetic to the inside of my groin, then began to thread something not unlike a fishing line up one of my veins. A good deal of clanking was going on overhead – either it was the bank of monitors, or perhaps something to do with the camera. I had a very quick look, and there, believe it or not, were my guts coming into view, in glorious Technicolor. It was the strangest of feelings, not least because I could not feel anything. It did not seem right, and I kept my eyes tight shut for the rest of the show. One good thing was that those standing around seemed happy enough, and I had the impression that things were going according to plan.

The camera must now have been getting pretty close to my heart, because the chatter around me became more intense. It was all complete gibberish to me, but it was a bit like Geoffrey Boycott discussing the pitch just before the toss, finding one or two points of interest and being concerned that it might take spin before the end of the first day. Every now and then John Muir gently assured me that everything was going well. Eventually they decided they had seen enough, and reeled in the camera, again just like a fishing line. I lay there wondering what they had caught. When John Muir told me in his most comforting bedside manner that there were one or two things they wanted to check again, I feared for a second that they were going to shove that blasted camera all the way up again, but of course they had recorded it all, so there was no need. He told me he would come and tell me the score once they had had another look. I was wheeled back to my room, uncomfortably aware that the main game was about to be played.

Later that afternoon John Muir appeared holding some large negatives, and told me there were a couple of things Christopher Lincoln needed to have a look at. He also said there wasn't by any means an open-and-shut case for bypass surgery. Later still, there was a significant conference in another room, to which I was lugged in a wheelchair. With all the wires sticking out of me I looked and felt like an antiquated telephone system. Bitten was there, and so were Trevor Hudson and John Muir. My sister Anthea, who was herself a doctor, was also present, with her husband Anthony, a vicar who a day or two later would have more than just a walk-on part to play – which he did with his usual flair. The subject now up for debate was whether Christopher Lincoln should operate or not. If he didn't, there was the chance of a repeat performance, and maybe of a heart attack which had every chance of being conclusive.

I was a good deal more gung-ho than anyone else, and was adamant that I should have what looked like being a double bypass. I knew I lived a hectic, on-the-edge sort of life, and it would be no use asking me to live surrounded by cotton wool. Most of the others advocated a more cautious, wait-and-see approach, and the discussion went on for a while. But in the end I carried the day, and it was agreed that I would be operated on the following morning – I suppose the chap whose life is on the line should be allowed the major say. I don't think there was a show of hands, but if there had been, I probably would have been in a minority of one, and would by now almost certainly be dead.

It may seem strange, but even at this stage it never occurred to me that I might be about to die. Trevor Hudson, who had probably already saved my life, said to me just before he departed, 'Don't worry. It'll be over in no time at all, and you'll be home before you know it,' or words to that effect. After that, I sank back into a mood of peaceful acceptance. The evening passed with the help of P.G. Wodehouse and Mike and Psmith, which took my mind off things. I even had a glass or two of claret for dinner that night.

Life made a brisk and early start the next morning, as nurses fluttered about getting me ready for the operation. I had to swallow some pills, and the anaesthetist paid me a smiling visit. He told me not to worry, and that he would be back later to give me an injection. Then I spent a little longer with Mike and Psmith before it was time to get down to serious business. Whenever I have a general anaesthetic (which has been too often for comfort), I always lie there as the needle is being taken out and think, 'Well, I'm not asleep yet.' No sooner have I thought this than I am asleep – as I was this time.

The sequence of events that followed is a touch tricky for me to describe. A lot of things happened before I took any further interest in life, and by no means all of them went as they should. The next thing I remember is opening my eyes and finding myself lying on a sort of trolley bed in a rather bare room with lots of things hanging down from the walls. There were several other beds like mine in the room, and they were probably full of comatose patients. There seemed to be a lot of other people about too. The first thing I can clearly remember being said to me was by John Muir, who told me that my family had been through an awful time. I don't think I had any idea what he was getting at. I could vaguely see Bitten, Anthea and Anthony in the middle distance, and I later learned that by then Anthony had had his moment. He had brought with him a phial of holy oil with which to administer the Last Rites should the need arise. When it was generally felt that it had, he stepped forward, like God in a dark suit, to do his stuff. He must have got into a bit of a tangle with the phial, because he ended up pouring gallons of the stuff all over me. He must have known what he was doing, though, for it was surely the quantity of oil that forced his boss to sit up, have a look and decide to do the decent thing.

I was conscious of a fair number of pipes which seemed to be going into various parts of my body, and there were nurses and sisters all over the place. For a time after my return to the world, events drifted into one another. I don't think anything dramatic happened for a day or two, but I soon began to realise that I had caused quite a stir, and that I was extremely lucky still to be in the land of the living. I was, however, much more concerned about what was going to happen next than about the fact that I had jolly nearly shaken my maker by the hand. I spent a couple of pretty drowsy days in intensive care before going to my room.

In the days and weeks that followed I heard a number of different accounts of all the excitement that had gone on while I had been unconscious. If I jump around a bit now and things aren't in chronological order, all I can say is that I wasn't in chronological order either.

On my initial journey from my room to the operating theatre, my heart had apparently gone into heart-attack mode, whatever that may mean. One thing it did mean was that Christopher Lincoln had to roll up his sleeves and get a move on in double-quick time. I believe I had a double bypass, because in the end two of the three blockages were coped with by the same bypass. Shades of getting around Watford and Rickmansworth, or perhaps the twin cities of Hyderabad and Secunderabad, on the same dual carriageway. My chest, which had been sawn apart so they could get at my heart, was clipped together again, and when all the other more minor details had been attended to, I was ferried to intensive care.

If I had then behaved properly, I would have been transferred from the heart-lung machine, which had been my life-support system while they chopped me up, back to my own heart, which should have been rearing to give of its best. But as I understand it, it was now that the real problems began, as I showed no signs of wanting to come round. Next comes a hotchpotch of things I heard or was told, and which I may have got muddled or inadvertently made up.

They tried to put me back onto my own heart a time or two, but it showed not the remotest interest. I suppose that may have meant they had either to kick-start me, or to kick-start the heart-lung machine. After that, they decided to open me up again, there and then, in intensive care, to see what they could do. That must be the reason why, when I came to, there was a certain amount of blood about the place, although that was the least of my worries. My blood pressure had plummeted, and someone told me that when I eventually surfaced, it was lower than it is in the residents of most cemeteries. Bitten, who had been told to go home when things seemed to be happening normally, was rung up in the middle of the night and summoned to the hospital, which can't have been a pleasant journey for her. She enlisted the help of Victoria Tinne, a real friend who didn't hesitate to come round the moment she was asked.

When Bitten arrived in intensive care, they had pretty well given up on me. She persuaded them to have one last try, and lo and behold, it did the trick. I've no idea exactly what happened, and I'm sure that among all the things I have heard, many were medically impossible. For those who are present at the time, such moments are charged with suspense, drama and foreboding. But who cares exactly what happened, as long as things have a happy ending. Mercifully, it all worked out, even if it was considerably later than the eleventh hour. One thing that is certain is that it is impossible for me to thank John Muir, Christopher Lincoln and their assistants enough for all they did for me during those murky hours. Between them they did plenty more than just save the follow-on. Their efforts were a combination of Botham and Willis's best at Headingley in 1981. And in the end Geoffrey had just about got the pitch right too.

Some people have asked if I had any out-of-body experiences while I was deeply unconscious. Many of those who have been near to death say they have had a sensation of going into a tunnel, presumably en route for the next world, or of seeing bright lights. I did not experience anything like that, but I do distinctly remember feeling that I was somewhere wonderfully warm, friendly and comforting, although I have no more precise memory than that. Many of my Richard Dawkins-like friends have shrugged their shoulders at this and told me that that is what morphine does for you. Don't ask me to explain it, but after all I went through I would now be amazed if this world is not a staging post. Is the wish the father of the thought, or is religion the last resort of the elderly? We all just have to wait and see what turns up, but I am optimistic.

This was not quite the end of the dramas. It was discovered three or four days after I had left intensive care that my chest had not joined up properly, so they had to have another go at that. I was assured by Christopher Lincoln that this was nothing to worry about. I don't think I was unduly fussed, and I'm glad to say it went off without a hitch. The only trouble was that it meant I was going to have to stay in the clinic for even longer, when all I wanted to do was go home. I'm afraid I had one or two strong exchanges of opinion on this point with Christopher Lincoln, who found my petulance difficult to understand. Of course it was post-operative nonsense and unreasonable of me to argue like that with someone who had just saved my life, but I had had enough of hospital, and I wanted to get on with life. While I was in the clinic, Peter Baxter and Shilpa Patel came to see me, and their visits made me long to get back into the commentary box. I told Backers that he could jolly well write me in as a commentator for the first Test against New Zealand at Edgbaston on 1 July. It gave me a goal to aim at, and I was determined to make it, come what may.

I eventually emerged from hospital sometime in the second week of May. I had to stay in London for a couple of weeks, just in case. Then came four weeks of gentle and happy recovery in Norfolk, although they got off to a questionable start. I had been there for less than two days when the telephone rang. I answered it, and it was a journalist friend who asked me if he could speak to Bitten. When I asked him why, he said he was writing my obituary and he wanted to ask her a thing or two about me. I said that, happily for both of us, I had missed that particular boat, and that if he asked Bitten, after all she had gone through, to help him with my obituary, I would not be responsible for her actions. That didn't put him off the trail, and he said that in which case he would like to talk to my brother John, because they would want to keep my obit on file. This didn't seem much of a vote of confidence, and it certainly contributed to my feeling not quite as chuffed as I might have done. I told him it was up to him what he did. John was a High Court judge, and I was not sure how the conversation would go. He called me later and told me he had been rung up by a journalist who was writing my obituary and wanted to ask a few questions. 'I don't think I'd ever heard of him, but he seemed to think he knew me, because he called me John.' Overall, it was not perhaps the greatest exercise in tact.

In those days, for matches at Edgbaston the *TMS* team stayed at a lovely hotel called Brockencote Hall, at Chaddesley Corbett in north Worcestershire. I'm keeping my fingers crossed that one day we shall return. It's quite a journey from Norfolk, but I cannot think of any drive I have enjoyed so much in my life as that one on 30 June 1999, from Hoveton to the Brockencote. By then I knew how lucky I was to be alive. This was underlined when, after taking my bags upstairs, I went down to the terrace for a glass of wine. I was in mid-sip when my colleague 'Foxy' Fowler, a great friend who had opened the batting for Lancashire and England, came down the steps, saw me, gasped, rushed over and gave me an enormous bear hug. It was a truly touching welcome, and it could not have mattered less that my glass was knocked over. I was alive, I was back – and on schedule. John Muir later told me it was probably a bit too soon, but as I had set my mind so firmly on it, they thought it would be good for me to go ahead.

My health has always had a habit not of plaguing me with minor ailments, but of messing things up in a big way. Maybe it has been paying me back for having pedalled it into that bus all those years ago. At Christmas in 2005 my gall bladder got up to all manner of tricks. I had had a high fever and various pains in my tummy, so my doctor, then the redoubtable Tony Greenburgh, sentenced my gall bladder to death, and arranged for a charming surgeon, Arjun Shankar, to attend to the details. I was going to be on my own over Christmas that year because Bitten and I had recently split up, so it seemed a good idea to have it done at that time. It was going to be keyhole surgery, and a room was found for me in a well-known West End hospital. I didn't think it was going to be the worst way of spending Christmas. If the browsing and sluicing was going to be up to scratch in any hospital, it looked as if this would be the one.

I was under starter's orders a couple of days before Christmas, and as usual I was told I would be out of hospital in two or three days at the most. The assembled company of nurses and anaesthetists got down to it, and I was carted off to the operating theatre. When I next opened my eyes I did a double take. It was intensive care all over again. Arjun arrived, and told me that he had set out to do keyhole surgery, but had found that my gall bladder, which was in a particularly nasty state, had somehow got itself inextricably entangled with a main artery which went from my heart to my liver. He rapidly abandoned all thoughts of keyhole surgery and instead made a whacking great incision of the sort that Sir Lancelot Spratt, aka James Robertson Justice, favoured in that lovely old film *Doctor in the House*. At some stage, in what had become a tricky operation, the artery burst. I think I have been told that if that happens and the chap standing over you doesn't know what to do, you bleed to death in about ten minutes. Arjun Shankar had learned his trade on the medical equivalent of uncovered pitches, and knew exactly what stroke to play. So all was well – up to a point. Arjun told me he liked difficult cases, but not quite as difficult as this one. It meant intensive care for a short time, and then I was back to my not very grand room – I think the best ones were either occupied by or were being kept in readiness for rich overseas patients.

Christmas Day came and went, and a few days later, although my wound was not healing, I was allowed out of hospital. I had to go back and see Arjun every other day in his consulting rooms in Harley Street to have my dressing changed. No matter what he tried, it leaked, and I needed three or four clean shirts a day. It didn't smell too good either. On one of my visits to Arjun he did some tests, and came back to me with the worst news possible: I had caught MRSA, the dreaded hospital superbug.

I felt lifeless, listless and ghastly, and the constant leaking of the wound made it an even more unpleasant experience. Arjun gave me antibiotics in ever-increasing strengths, but nothing seemed to work. I was more worried now than I had been at any time during my interesting bypass experiences, or indeed during the present episode. It went on with relentless horror, and no one could do anything. I had been operated on before Christmas, and with Easter approaching I was still swallowing antibiotics by the sackful. One morning I woke up feeling so ill I thought I was going to die. I rang Arjun at home, and he told me to stop taking the pills. The following week he did a test in his consulting rooms, and was able to give me the wonderful news a day or two later that I no longer tested positive for MRSA. Not long afterwards, though, on the Easter weekend, I noticed a nasty swelling just below my ribs on the right side of my tummy. Now it was instant panic on a big scale. I was convinced I had cancer of the liver, and rang the dear man again. Although it was Easter he promised to come straight round, as he did not live far from me. A bad half an hour followed, during which I thought of everything short of ringing up the undertaker. At last Arjun arrived, I had my shirt off in a flash, and he told me I had an operational hernia. MRSA weakens the body's defences, and my stomach had burst through the surrounding wall and was now presenting itself in a not so neat bulge. I am pretty sure we then had a large drink. At least, I hope we did.

The hospital never admitted that it was responsible for the MRSA, although one surprising fact emerged. All the staff nurses there are continually tested for MRSA, as are the agency nurses, who probably come to work in their uniforms. Whether or not they are tested with the same frequency as the permanent staff remained something of a grey area. One thing is for sure: MRSA is a beastly infection to pick up.

Since then, my medical adventures have continued to cause regular red alerts. A lumbar decompression for a painful back was, unusually for me, both successful and uneventful. A couple of months later my right hip went walkabout, and was singularly painful. I needed an artificial hip, and found myself in the King Edward VII Hospital for Officers ('Sister Agnes', as it is known, after the nurse who in 1899 turned her house into a hospital for officers injured in the Boer War. She was a friend of King Edward VII, who also lent a helping hand. Of all the hospitals I have been to, Sister Agnes, inspired by a splendid and beautiful matron, comes in first past the post by several lengths). The operation seemed to go well, but while I was lying in bed a few days later I reached for a book, and as I did so I felt the ball of the joint slipping, almost in slow motion, out of the socket. My new hip was dislocated. I have never known such excruciating pain. I was unable to reach the bell to summon help, and had, rather shamefacedly, to resort to howling my head off. Several of the nurses immediately broke the Sister Agnes all-comers' record for the hundred-yard dash, and the hip was put back again under anaesthetic later that evening.

A few days later I was discharged, but with Christmas approaching I was writing in my conservatory when the bloody thing dislocated again. I fell under the table, and got my leg entwined under the crossbar between the table legs. As luck would have it, I was able to reach my mobile, and rang Valeria (of whom more later), who had a set of keys. I then dialled 999, and had a painful wait before Valeria and an ambulance breasted the tape together. It was back to Sister Agnes, via a somewhat painful session in the Chelsea & Westminster A & E, which for some strange reason was determined to hang on to me for the night.

The surgeon on call that evening at Sister Agnes was the famous Sarah Muirhead-Allwood. She was one of the surgeons who helped give the Queen Mother her two new hips. When the first one was done she was William Muirhead-Allwood. When she donned her mask and gown for the second, she was called Sarah Muirhead-Allwood. No need for an explanation, but a bit unusual all the same. In any event, she put my hip back together, but told me the next day that it needed revisiting, which seems to be hospital-speak for being redone. So off I went again, to an operating theatre I was beginning to feel I was on first-name terms with. At the time of writing, the joint has since managed to stay in one piece, although I fear my days of doing the Charleston are over.

Looking back on my rich and varied collection of medical experiences, I can only say that they all had a funny side to them, except for the MRSA. Even that brush with the bus back in 1957 had its moments.

In the last year or two my eyesight has been getting worse. Unfortunately I have a macular condition, although it has not yet turned into macular degeneration. My splendid doctor, Michael Sandberg, sent me to see Lyndon da Cruz at Moorfields Eye Hospital in the City of London, whose main place of work it was. His first reaction was that we should wait and see, but after I had had a few problems during the first two Test matches in India in November 2012, I went to see him again, and he decided the time was right to do my cataracts. So, a fortnight apart, in January 2013, I twice caught the bus to Moorfields. I did so with some trepidation, because the idea of my eyes being opened up made me decidedly squeamish. I need not have worried. After lots of eyedrops, some pethidine to quieten me down, and a massively dilated right eye, I hardly felt a thing. A slight buzzing feeling suggested that a saw was removing my original lens, and then for about half a minute towards the end something went on which I wished would stop. When it did, both sides of my eyeball were injected with an antibiotic, which for a second was excedingly painful. Then, after I had had something to eat in my room, Valeria shepherded me home. There was a repeat performance with my left eye two weeks later. While I may not be as sharp-eyed as I was when I bicycled into that bus in 1957, but I hope am not far behind. Adam Mountford has bravely allowed me back into the commentary box and I have been more on the ball (at the time of writing) during the first two Tests against Australia in 2013. It is simply amazing what these medics are able to do, not only these days, but as far as I have been concerned, for nearly sixty years, and how can one adequately thank them?

TWELVE

The Man in the Stocking Mask

One of the delightful advantages of growing old is that the passage of time softens memories and offers them up in a different, more relaxed and humorous perspective. The biggest schism in cricket in all the years I have been involved in the game came in the late 1970s when Kerry Packer, the billionaire Australian media magnate, turned his not-to-be-ignored attention to it. His aim was to buy the exclusive rights to televise cricket in Australia for his rapidly expanding Channel Nine network, and he was prepared to pay a great deal more money for the privilege than the Australian Cricket Board were receiving from the Australian Broadcasting Commission, who held the existing rights. This seemed straightforward enough.

There was nothing to suggest that this simple scenario was going to lead to a prolonged and bitter saga which had in it many of the ingredients of a James Bond novel, almost in reverse. It is easier to envisage Packer as one of James Bond's lethal opponents than as 007 himself, who represented the establishment, something that Packer would not have done in a million years. Simultaneously he played the parts of Goldfinger, Oddjob, Ernst Stavro Blofeld and Bond's other adversaries. I will settle for my namesake, Ernst Stavro Blofeld – without the white pussy, perhaps – who also weighed getting on for twenty stone and who, like Packer, was teetotal. Whichever Bond villain he was playing, though, Packer would not have needed to visit the make-up department before the cameras rolled. He was huge, with a manner which accurately proclaimed him to be a bully who unashamedly ruled his own world by intimidation. There was a rubbery hostility about Packer's face: he was admirably described in the *Daily Mail* by Ian Wooldridge, whose genius as a writer never allowed him to miss a trick, as 'the man in the stocking mask'. As with most bullies, for Packer the two sides of any argument were his own side and the wrong side. He did not like to be crossed.

In the other corner of the ring, sheltering behind the small but formidable figure of Sir Donald Bradman – who also had a liking for getting his own way – were the profoundly indignant members of the Australian Cricket Board (ACB). They saw their heritage being threatened by a vulgar upstart to whom they would not have given house room: three-piece suits versus an open-necked shirt waving indecent amounts of money. This was something up with which they were not prepared to put. 'How dare he?' was their rallying cry. The result was that common sense flew out of the window, and it was a long and exceedingly expensive time before it returned – if it ever has.

The ACB behaved like a bunch of First World War generals who were unable to see that a whole new game was unfolding in front of their eyes. They formed squares, and told Packer to go to hell and mind his own business, which showed they had not done their homework. People who told Kerry Packer to mind his own business often ended up walking the streets. It beggars belief that not one member of the ACB, or at least not enough of them, realised that Packer, if handled sympathetically, could have been an answer to their prayers. Cricket at that time was perennially strapped for cash, its popularity was falling all over the world, nothing was being done to bring it into the modern era, and its best players were still being paid sixpence halfpenny. But perish the thought of sitting down to negotiate with Ernst Stavro Blofeld's alter ego, let alone offering him a place on the board, and making use of him to their mutual advantage. With cricket's administrators so stuck in their ways, this was a major accident waiting to happen.

The battle lines were swiftly drawn up, and it didn't take Packer long to decide how best to get his own way. As he saw it, it was simple: if the ACB would not sell him the exclusive rights to televise cricket, he would get hold of the best players in the world and set up his own international competition in Australia. He was immensely rich, so money was no object. His first step would be to gather around him certain key people who could help him acquire the services of the players he needed to give his scheme credibility. Obviously, it all had to be kept strictly under wraps. Not the least difficult part of the whole undertaking would be to ensure that secrecy was maintained, not only by those who signed on the dotted line, but especially by those who turned Packer down. I am surprised he did not ask John le Carré, or at least George Smiley, to lend a hand.

Thanks to the ACB's obstinacy, Packer's cause had become a crusade. Almost at once the venture took on a semi-religious, whispering-behind-hands fervour as the conspirators, with Packer as their fountainhead, made their plans and swore to keep them secret from the rest of the world. Cricket's best players were soon off to what they perceived to be the Promised Land, led by Ernst Stavro on a gleaming white charger.

Packer would not have taken long to make up his mind about those he needed to have on board as fellow conspirators and recruiting agents. Ian Chappell, who had retired early as captain of Australia, and who was always ready to take on anyone and anything, was a natural choice. His influence, and that of his brother and successor as Australian captain, Greg, must have been a big help in persuading Australian players to join up. The West Indies side would not have been a great problem, for they were paid peanuts in spite of the fact that they were the strongest side in the world. Nonetheless, Packer would presumably have wanted to have had Clive Lloyd and Viv Richards on board at an early stage in order to encourage the other players.

Having secured the services of the Australian and the West Indies sides, Packer's next objective was to sign up a Rest of the World eleven so he would be able to field three sides for the Supertests and one-day games he planned to stage. There was an obvious candidate to act as his recruiting officer.

Tony Greig had come to England from South Africa in the late-sixties to try to find a way into Test cricket at the time that his own country was becoming ostracised from international sporting community because of its hateful policy of apartheid. His father was Scottish which meant that he had to wait four years with Sussex rather than seven before he had qualified to play for England. He came into the side in 1972, taking over the captaincy in 1975. As well as being an extraordinary all-rounder, Greig was a larger-than-life figure, and no stranger to controversy. Packer knew that if he could win over the reigning captain of England it would give great impetus to his plans. Their initial discussions about Greig joining Packer may have taken place during the Centenary Test in Melbourne in March 1977 – the disruptive Ernst Stavro would have approved. I doubt if it would have taken Greig long to come round to Packer's way of thinking, and like every recruit Packer signed up, he must have welcomed the prospect of being paid a good deal more money than he was currently receiving. But he was astute enough to realise how crucial he was to the success of Packer's plans, and told him that he would only desert England provided he had a guarantee of gainful employment for the rest of his working life – he died in 2012 aged 66. For many people it will always be unthinkable that the captain of England could agree to desert his country in the middle of one of the greatest ever celebrations of international cricket – or come to that, at any other time. But that was Tony Greig, who was nothing if not an opportunist, and was never troubled by sentiment. Greig rapidly became Packer's most important lieutenant, and – at any rate in these early days – the two of them formed a mutual admiration society. It was Greig who helped Packer assemble his Rest of the World side, which of course he captained himself.

The bond of secrecy which Packer had imposed upon his players held firm until May 1977. The story was broken in England in the *Daily Mail* by Ian Wooldridge, who swore never to reveal his source, and with admirable loyalty took it to the grave with him. I sometimes wonder if, for Machiavellian reasons, it was not Packer himself. It is more likely, though, that a loose tongue revealed all during the course of Sussex's game against the Australians at Hove in May 1977. The revelation caused immediate shock among the game's establishment and its supporters around the globe. The cricketing world was divided as never before – and even now it has not fully come together again. To many, Packer became the dirtiest of names, and Greig was not far behind. Of course, Wooldridge's revelations caused much fluttering of wings in Packer's camp too, although the boss must have been prepared for this (even if it was not he who let on in the first place). His henchmen, who would have thought that exposure was not planned until every last detail was in place, were caught unawares.

Packer, leading from the front as always, immediately came over to England, and went straight to Hove, where Greig invited several journalists, myself among them, to come up to the captain's room at the top of the pavilion. There Packer, looking more than ever like Ernst Stavro, told us quietly and decisively what he was intending to do and why he was intending to do it. All the while, Greig gazed on adoringly. Packer returned the compliment when he turned to Greig and said he had never been honoured by being asked to visit the captain's room before. This was when I discovered that Packer had a tiresome and patronising habit of calling everyone 'son' – all part of the intimidation process.

At that time I had been a journalist for fifteen years, and instinctively found myself on the establishment side of things. I was as horrified as anyone in the room by what I had just heard. Looking back now, with the advantage of hindsight, I blame myself not for failing to grasp Packer by the hand and offer him my congratulations, but for not taking a step back and being prepared to see what might happen, to give him a chance. I am afraid it was the manner of 'the man in the stocking mask' that made me, and I am sure many others, recoil from his barbed blandishments. That day at Hove, he and Greig were trying to win over a few journalistic friends, but it did not work. Packer's aggressive, pugilistic attitude and appearance did him no favours, and Greig's smug smile and air of slavish devotion did not help. In fact, one of the more unattractive aspects of what Packer was doing was the syco-phantic fawning of all those who supported and worked for him. They helped make the job of opposing these revolu-tionary plans even easier. Then of course there was the clandestine, underhand nature of the whole business, although I dare say that to have had any chance of success it had to be done in this way.

Many successful revolutions have had unpleasant beginnings, and I am not sure that anyone came away from that meeting in the captain's room feeling he had witnessed the start of a new order in cricket. Rather, it looked a pretty grubby affair, and one that we did not want to think could possibly succeed. But like the Australian Cricket Board, we had seriously underestimated Packer – a trap many fell into over the years – and the lengths to which he was prepared to go to win the day. There was no doubting his determination to get his own way, or the amount of money he was prepared to throw at the project. He had certainly shown that he could snarl most unpleasantly if he had to. Looking back on that occasion from this distance, there was something about it faintly reminiscent of the lions and the ancient Christians in the Coliseum.

For all his apparent crudity, Kerry Packer was one of life's more complex and extraordinary human beings. He had undergone a tough upbringing, with a martinet of a father: compromise was not a word that was understood in the Packer household. And while Packer, like Ernst Stavro himself, ruled by intimidation, he displayed a fierce, unflinching loyalty to those who stood by him. This showed itself, for example, in the way he stood by his initial group of commentators on Channel Nine, long after some of them had passed their sell-by date. They may have grasped eagerly at the money Packer was offering them, but it was a two-way relationship, because their names helped to give the enterprise respectability.

When Tony Greig gave the Colin Cowdrey 'Spirit of Cricket' Memorial Lecture at Lord's in 2012, he spent a long time at the start of his speech attempting to justify his decision to join Packer at a time when he was captain of England. He said that the money he was offered had nothing to do with it, and that he did it to safeguard the future of his family

– which, as anyone can see, is an entirely different matter. To honour his promise to give Greig employment for the rest of his working life, Packer founded an insurance company in Sydney, and put him in charge. It was not long before it ran into the ground. Greig liked to ape Packer. I remember once travelling with him from Sydney to Melbourne in an Ansett jet. We were in the front row, and there was an expandable belt which pulled out from the bulkhead in front of us. Greig put the belt through the handle of his briefcase, then reattached it to the wall. 'It took me three years to persuade them to put these in,' he told me. What he should have said was that it was Kerry Packer who took three years to persuade the airline to put them in, as one of the cabin crew later told me.

Packer could be extraordinarily generous, but usually in a self-serving way. There are many tales of his incredible largesse. Late in his life he became obsessed by the game of polo, and in spite of his mountainous size, he made a brave and whole-hearted attempt to play himself. One can only imagine the poor polo pony's feelings when it realised the identity of its burden for the afternoon. It was a clear case for industrial action. Packer set up a vibrant polo establishment in Sussex. One day play went on until late into the evening, and when it was all over he instructed one of his minions to ring a nearby restaurant and book a sizeable table for dinner. The restaurant said brusquely that it was too late, and the kitchen was closed. Another establishment in the neighbourhood was then tried and they said they would be delighted to remain open. At the end of the evening, when Packer paid the considerable bill, he left the staff a tip, on the condition that they told the restaurant that had turned his party away how much it was. It was £10,000. Was this a handsome gesture? A simple matter of showing off? The knee-jerk reaction of a man who could not tolerate being crossed, and wanted to get his revenge as swiftly as possible? Or was it just the expression of an enormous ego? Probably a bit of all four.

Packer was also a dedicated and compulsive gambler, and the stories of his flying around the world from one casino to another, winning or losing staggering, utterly indecent sums of money, are legion. It is one definition of a true gambler that he is prepared to stake more money then he can afford to lose, but with the money he had behind him, it would hardly have mattered to Packer whether he won or lost. But he liked to be seen to be gambling enormous stakes, and he loved the glamour and buzz of it all. He never shirked publicity, and always made sure he was noticed wherever he went. One story has it that he was once playing baccarat in the *salle privée* of a casino in Las Vegas. There was a Johnny-come-lately sitting next to him whose business had just made something like $40 million, which enabled him to take his place beside Packer. The man could not stop boasting about his good fortune, and Packer grew increasingly irritated with this. When his neighbour mentioned his $40 million for the fourth time, Packer said quietly, without looking up, 'I'll toss you for it.'

There was another occasion in Las Vegas when Packer had had a particularly successful evening at the tables, and gave a female croupier a tip of many thousands of dollars. When he returned the following evening, he asked her what she was going to do with the money. She replied that she had only actually received a small percentage of it, because all the casino's tips went into a common pot. Packer immediately summoned the casino manager, and told him to sack the girl on the spot. Because Packer was such an important client, the manager did as he asked. Packer immediately gave her the same amount as the night before: as she was no longer an employee of the casino, she was now entitled to keep it all.

He then demanded that the casino manager re-employ her. Stories like these tell you a lot about the man. Whether they make him more loveable or not is another matter.

Packer had a great love for beautiful women, and never felt that the small print – or the large print, for that matter – in the wedding service put him under any constraints. A beautiful girl was always on his arm, wherever he went. Although he was a heavy smoker, he was not a drinker. Apparently he had been involved in a messy car crash early in his life, in which alcohol had played a part. From then on he had never touched a drop, which says a lot for his willpower; and also for the power of parental persuasion, for it was said that his father was less than happy about what had happened.

Packer needed a big name to manage the cricket side of things in what became World Series Cricket. Rumour has it that the first person he approached was former Australian captain Bobby Simpson, who turned him down. By all accounts, he then had a lucky break. Richie Benaud had always been a great establishment figure, which was probably what persuaded Packer to go for Simpson first. At that time Benaud was apparently involved in a food business, which had not been going too well. So when Packer offered him the job, he jumped at it. Maybe it was a bank-managerial decision. Anyway, for whatever reason, Benaud joined Packer, to whom he always displayed an admirable loyalty.

In 1977 Packer went to Lord's to meet the game's powers-that-were. He strode with his usual determination through the entrance at the back of the Pavilion and on into the Committee Room. In his wake came Benaud, who must have been experiencing a considerable conflict of emotions. He knew that most of his long-term friends in England regarded his new boss as Public Enemy Number One, yet here he was, walking with him as his principal lieutenant into the Pavilion at Lord's, of all places. This called for considerable courage, and whether or not people disagreed with his new role, Benaud had to be admired for the way he carried it off. That meeting ended with everyone present only more firmly entrenched in their original positions, and with the members of the establishment regarding Packer with an even greater loathing, if that were possible.

The next battle was in the High Court. The various national Boards of Control had decided to ban all their players who had signed for Packer, and in retaliation he took them to court for restraint of trade. The case lasted for three weeks, and cost a great deal of money. Packer was represented with considerable brilliance by Robert Alexander, who went on years later, as Lord Alexander, to become the President of the MCC – one of the more striking ironies of this whole affair. Packer won the case, which cost cricket's establishment a fortune. Ernst Stavro would have been proud of him. Like him or loathe him, here was further proof, if any were needed, that it was unwise to make an enemy of Kerry Packer.

To some, Packer will always remain a villain – not that he would have given a damn. Yet I think there can be no doubt that good came from what he did, and the game was certainly jolted forward into the second half of the twentieth century. First and foremost, players began to be paid a more realistic amount of money, although this took some time to filter down to the game's also-rans below the very highest level. Television coverage was transformed: the hero here was David Hill, who is now one of Rupert Murdoch's principal television moguls in America. Coloured clothing, white balls, black sightscreens, day/night matches, more cameras, slicker camera-work and the introduction of exciting new gadgetry were among Hill's legacies to the game. Before he went to America, Hill ran Sky Sports for Murdoch in its early days in the UK. It was he who had snatched me away from the BBC to commentate for Sky, which was some way from being the best decision he, or I, ever made, as I was never any good at television commentary, as I have already shown.

World Series Cricket kicked off in November 1977. The next six months told us a lot about a super-sized ego which had been pricked, and even more about a stuffy, holier-than-thou establishment which felt as though the Holy Grail had been snatched from its hands. I found myself in the thick of it from the moment I boarded an aeroplane at Heathrow with Johnny Woodcock to go and watch the opening encounters between Packer's superstars. It all seemed distinctly surreal. The Australian cricket authorities were not going to let this circus perform on Test grounds if they could help it – which they could, but only for a while. The first Supertest was played on a drop-in pitch in the middle of Waverley Park, the Australian Rules football ground in the Melbourne suburb of Mulgrave. Not many spectators turned up to watch what was a pretty bloodless affair. Packer himself was there to sneer at those who had opposed him. The game, between Australia and the West Indies, pitted the best players in the world against each other, but as they all now came from the same stable it had an incestuous flavour, and did not give off the aura of being a proper, red-blooded Test match. The players themselves all said that it was the toughest cricket they had ever played, but that was probably just part of the script.

Wooders and I then hightailed it to Karachi, where we met up with Mike Brearley's England side, who were about to play three of the more boring Test matches I can remember, against Pakistan. We may have been a few thousand miles away from the battles going on in Australia, both on and off the field, between World Series and the establishment, but it was not long before we were embroiled in the same conflict in Pakistan.

A number of Pakistan's best players were in Australia, having signed up with Packer, and the country's Board of Control, like their counterparts all over the cricketing world, had banned them from playing for Pakistan. There was uproar in Pakistan because of the high-handed way in which the perceived rebels had been treated by their own board. Packer, who could never have been described as a pacifist, mischievously released some of his Pakistani players so that they could play for their national side. I believe one or two of them actually flew back to Pakistan, probably accompanied by Austin Robertson, a former West Australian Aussie Rules player who was a favoured lieutenant of Packer's. The Pakistan Board stood firm, however, and it was not long before the players returned to Camp Packer.

After the third Test in Karachi, Wooders and I flew back to Australia for another dose of Packer cricket. A Supertest between the Rest of the World and the West Indies was being played at the Gloucester Park trotting stadium, just across the road from the WACA, the main ground in Perth. Barry Richards and Gordon Greenidge batted magnificently, scoring a pile of runs on another drop-in pitch, and generally speaking, in spite of the venue, it all seemed more purposeful and genuine than the earlier game in Melbourne. After two days in Perth we flew to Adelaide to watch the last two days of the fifth Test between the official Australian side and India. This was exciting enough too. India were left to score 493 to win in their second innings to win, and after several times hinting that they might just get there, were bowled out for 445, which at that time was the second-highest fourth-innings total in Test history. There was a reasonable crowd at the Adelaide Oval, but not as big as is normal for the annual Australia Day Test match. There was no doubt that Packer's World Series

Cricket was limiting the interest in the official Test team, which was in fact nothing more than an Australian second eleven. It was captained by the forty-one-year-old Bobby Simpson who had been lured out of a long retirement and did pretty well, scoring centuries in the second Test in Perth and then in this game in Adelaide.

At the end of the Australian season, Ernst Stavro had every reason to be pleased with the way things were turning out. It was then over to New Zealand, where England were playing a three-Test series. Packer had not so far made much of an impression in that country, but now he focused, to the great concern of New Zealand's cricketing establishment, on the great all-rounder Richard Hadlee, who toyed briefly with the idea of World Series Cricket, but decided against it.

As soon as this series was over I flew to the Caribbean, where the non-Packer Australians under Simpson were doing battle against the West Indies. The West Indies had begun the series by picking their Packer players for the first two Tests, both of which they won by huge margins. The West Indies Board were under considerable pressure from around the world to jettison those who had signed up for Packer, and finally agreed to do so a few days before the start of the third Test in Georgetown. This led to a series of acrimonious meetings between the Board and the players, led by Clive Lloyd. Rumours were rife that Packer himself was flying in, but I think it was again Austin Robertson who made the journey, although you may be sure that Packer stayed close to his telephone in Sydney.

The leading officials of cricket in all the main Caribbean islands flew in to Georgetown. Most of the drama was played out at the Pegasus Hotel on the city's Sea Wall. Everyone was frantically second-guessing everyone else, and the country's supply of Scotch whisky must have barely held firm. Large cars kept driving up and disgorging hurried figures who disappeared into a lift which worked only intermittently. One of the chief participants was Sir Lionel Luckhoo, the head of a famous Guyanese legal family who was also Prime Minister Forbes Burnham's private lawyer. Luckhoo was the shrewdest of men, and had a sparkling sense of humour which, thank goodness, was in no way dampened by the seriousness of what was going on. His splendid house in the upmarket Belle Air Park was a venue for endless clandestine and unofficial meetings. Luckhoo had twice been knighted, and told how on one of the occasions the Queen, having dubbed him, said, 'Sir Lionel, you are looking a little nervous.' He replied, 'I was just thinking, Ma'am, what might have happened if you had taken the sword on the shortest route from my right shoulder to my left.' 'It would not have been the first instance of a headless knight,' was her answer.

In the end, presumably after being advised by their new Australian bosses, Lloyd and his fellow World Series players decided to make themselves unavailable for selection for the remainder of the series. The last three Tests were played between the Australian and West Indian second elevens and after all the off-field dramas, the cricket was inevitably an anticlimax.

By the time I returned to London early in May, my round-the-world journey had taken in eleven official Test matches and two Supertests. By then, Ernst Stavro was having the better of the argument, although none of his opponents were prepared to concede that fact, which, looking back now, seems ridiculous.

By the time England visited Australia the following winter, in 1978–79, World Series was using most of the main grounds. England, playing Australia's second eleven, easily won the Ashes, such as they were. There was no doubt that Packer and

World Series were doing enormous damage to Australian cricket. Something had to give. After this twin-forked season it did, and although it was made to appear that an even truce had been declared, there was no doubt that Packer had won the peace. England went out to Australia again in 1979–80, and this time lost every match of a three-Test series to the full Australian side. Packer had not won outright, because it was agreed by the two boards that the Ashes would not be at stake in this truncated series. But this was only postponing the inevitable, for Packer had clearly won through, even if it had cost him a lot more money than he had at first envisaged. Of all Kerry Packer's victories, I daresay this one gave him the greatest satisfaction.

THIRTEEN

Norfolk at the Albert Hall

Going onto the stage had never occurred to me, until in the early summer of 2001 I had a telephone call from Dudley Russell, a theatrical agent who lives in Gloucestershire and is probably best-known for being the husband of Pam Ayres and for putting on her theatre shows. He asked me if I would be interested in doing a one-man show. Johnners, who was the master of these things, had died eight years before, and the gap had not been filled. I was nearly sixty-two.

Although my first reaction was 'Help!', I was flattered to be asked, and we agreed to meet and talk about it. The more I thought about it over the next few days, the more I came to think that perhaps I should have a go. It was a challenge which it would be cowardly to ignore. Dudley came along to Lord's, where I was working, and we met in the bar in the Media Centre. He was much more confident about the whole thing than I was, and was sure it would work. He suggested that I rough something out that contained the type of humour that floats about in the *TMS* box, but not to stick religiously to cricket. I agreed, and we arranged to meet again after I had done this.

My first thoughts led me to Tom and Grizel, Hoveton, and my upbringing, which the closer you examine it from today's perspective, the more absurd it looks. My education at

Sunningdale, Eton and Cambridge could lend a hand, and then there was that unfortunate excursion into the City before I ventured upon writing and broadcasting. I trawled through my life and came up with the people like Noël Coward and Clive Dunn whom I had been lucky enough to meet. Then, of course, there was John Arlott and Brian Johnston, who had been such great sources of fun, and all the other figures from *Test Match Special*. Things didn't come anything like as easily as those few sentences might suggest, but I cobbled my ideas together, and Dudley seemed to think there was something there. Having always been a show-off, I have to admit that I found the idea exciting, and when a call from Dudley's office told me that I was booked to appear at the Everyman Theatre in Cheltenham on Sunday, 16 September 2001, I was both thrilled and terrified. My dreams alternated between taking a succession of curtain calls, and drying up completely. I didn't attempt to script myself – I never have – but I wrote down a list of headings which would lead me into the stories I was going to tell.

As that first evening approached, my material seemed to grow thinner and thinner. Bitten came with me, and we stayed at the Queen's Hotel in Cheltenham, which was a pleasant stroll from the Everyman. I had been to the theatre earlier that afternoon to have a look round, and I was terribly nervous. I changed into my smoking jacket and black tie at the hotel, and walked down a good two hours before the start at 7.30.

I now met Martin Mitchell for the first time. He worked for Dudley, and was my tour manager for that night, which meant he had to make sure the sound and the lighting and a host of other things were in working order and, above all, that he had to hold my hand and keep me calm. He was to become my regular tour manager, and a good friend and confidant. Martin was a small man with a ready smile who had once been a member of pop groups. I now did a microphone test, standing at the lectern in the centre of the stage while Martin, cheerful as ever, flitted around the theatre to make sure I could be heard by all those present. Then came the lighting test. I just stood there, nerves ajangle, feeling stupid, while Martin made sure I looked all right from every possible angle in the theatre. Then I retreated to my dressing room, had a cup of tea, and studied my notes. Martin had asked me how long each of the two acts would be, but I hadn't a clue. With a wild guess I suggested that they would both run for about fifty minutes.

I kept looking at my watch, but the hands obstinately refused to move. It was still only six o'clock. There was an hour and a half to go. My mind was all over the place. I had been told that about six hundred tickets had been sold, which seemed an awful lot of people to stand in front of and make a fool of myself. Being an old hand I am sure Martin will have realised at once that I was more than a little anxious, and he visited my dressing room once or twice with words of encouragement and more cups of tea. There were some sandwiches too. It was still a long wait. When the time had dragged itself round to 6.45, I found my way back to the stage, tiptoed onto it and arranged my notes on the lectern. I then returned to my dressing room, feeling like a chap who discovers he has left the house with no clothes on.

But by now there was nothing I could do to get out of it. At five to seven, a disembodied voice told me from the loudspeaker in the corner of my dressing room that there was half an hour to go and this was soon followed by an announcement that 'the house was open'. I glanced at the plate of prawn and tuna and sweetcorn sandwiches, which had a look of good old M&S about them. I calculated that if

I had one, it would while away a minute or two. Then I began to hear chatter coming out of the loudspeaker, which indicated that the first few intrepid souls were taking their seats in the auditorium. After about ten minutes the noise had swelled considerably, reassuring me that a few more ticketholders had decided not to stay at home. That voice now told me there were fifteen minutes to go – actually there were twenty, but they always leave you with five minutes in hand. Martin put his head around the door to see how I was bearing up, made sure my microphone was clipped to my shirt front, and told me to come up to the stage when I got the final beginners' call at twenty-five past seven. By now the noises from the loudspeaker told me that the auditorium was buzzing. The last five minutes seemed to go more slowly than ever, but at long last the final beginners' call came, and in a state of extreme trepidation I started to thread my way up to Martin, who was waiting in the wings.

He greeted me with his usual smile, and said something about it being a good audience. He talked intermittently to the front-of-house staff through a microphone, then took his headset off, turned to me and said, 'We've got clearance. Are you ready to go?' I nodded, and tried to smile. Suddenly the music stopped, the house lights went down, and the audience stopped talking. Martin was standing by a microphone out of sight in the wings and with great spirit he said, 'Ladies and gentlemen, please give a big welcome to Henry Blofeld.' I walked onto the stage feeling just as I had done when I walked down the Pavilion steps at Lord's for the first time all those years before. I moved as resolutely as I could towards the lectern, on which, thank God, I could see my notes. I was faintly aware of what seemed a far-off round of applause. I took up my position, and after a moment the applause died.

'My dear old things . . .' I began. Those four words were

greeted by a really good round of laughter. I couldn't believe it. My feet were on the stage, and I was away. I have to confess that I was not particularly good. I spoke too fast, my timing was all over the place, and once or twice I almost got stories the wrong way round. But I made the important discovery that if you treat the audience as friends, they will enjoy the odd mistake. Don't try to cover them up. I won't say my dressing room seemed a place of beauty by the time I got back to it at the end of the first act, but it was more warm and welcoming. The audience had clapped me off the stage too.

Dudley paid me a visit during the interval and said, 'Well done,' and so did one or two others. Maybe it had not been too bad after all. It seemed only a few moments before the loudspeaker flushed me out of my dressing room for the second act. By now, I was much more relaxed. When it was over, I not only had a most generous round of applause, but Dudley, who was in the wings, made me go back on stage for the first curtain call of my life. It was a great moment. The general feeling seemed to be that I had just about got away with it.

Martin Mitchell was to become an important figure in my theatrical career, such as it has been. He was my tour manager for several years, until Neil O'Brien who had become my agent felt that the bottom line did not justify the position, so sadly we parted company, although he will always remain a good friend. In the early days he was an unfailing source of encouragement, and whenever I got lost on the way to a theatre – which was almost every time – I would ring him, and he would talk me up to the stage door. He is a brilliant technician, and knows more about sound engineering than most of those whose job it was in the theatres. Sandwiches and Earl Grey tea were just two of the things Martin never failed to organise for me in my dressing room. I wonder if there can ever have been a better tour manager – of course, until I taught Valeria how to do it some years later.

A few weeks after my debut at Cheltenham I did another show, at the lovely Yvonne Arnaud Theatre in Guildford, where we had a half-decent audience. The Yvonne Arnaud, like the Everyman, is a well-run theatre, and once again the mixture I had come up with seemed to work. To start with I did very few shows, although it was not long before I came down to earth and discovered that audiences were often much smaller than those at my first two performances. I remember turning up at a theatre in Kettering which the local paper had said had been pulled down, which was not the best of advertisements. Under the circumstances, I suppose it was something of a triumph that as many as 37 people had come through the door, although the theatre could hold more than four hundred. It is at times like these that you really earn your keep. People in a big audience, all packed in together, are not self-conscious or inhibited, and will happily laugh their heads off – as long as they find you funny. By contrast, a tiny audience sitting in isolated groups of three and four in a sizeable auditorium will not do much more than snigger. One result of this is that for a small audience you need more material than when you are playing to a full house, because laughter uses up time.

It is always disappointing to find a small audience, and when I do, I wonder how the show has been promoted locally. The more well-known a theatre is, the more likely it is to have its own following in the neighbourhood, and a good mailing list. The better the organisation, the better the results. Each week when I am doing shows my agent sends me the advance booking figures for my forthcoming appearances. One thing I have learned that nearly all box offices have in common is the ability to exaggerate. The advance numbers may be minuscule, but the theatre will almost inevitably tell you that they are confident of at least twice that many people coming along – which hardly ever happens. When you turn up on the evening they will still exaggerate the size of the audience. For a long time this made me angry. It is disappointing, after playing one night to a full house, to drive a long way the next day and find you are playing to fewer than a hundred people. But that is the nature of the business, and the sooner you learn to live with it, the easier life becomes. I now find that much the best thing to do when I arrive at a theatre is never to ask how many people they are expecting, but just to get on with it and do the show. Another habit theatres have when they look like having a poor turnout is to tell you they are expecting a large number of walk-ups, people who have not reserved tickets in advance and just turn up. I have never known a significant number of walk-ups, and it is not wise to let yourself think that they will save the evening. Although full houses may be less frequent than I would wish, they do mercifully crop up from time to time, and the box office then makes a healthy contribution to my wellbeing. A big audience also makes my job so much easier. If people are prepared to pay to come and see me, I can be confident they are on my side before the curtain goes up. I think, too, that the more experienced I have become, the more my confidence has grown. My timing has improved, I have become better able to read an audience – all audiences have their own special ways – and to adapt if necessary.

It is a performer's job to send his audience home happy, and I like to think that I have always managed that – although it may of course be that what I have thought was a nice round of applause at the end was nothing more than an expression of relief that it was all over. I hope not. One of the most enjoyable aspects of travelling all over the country from theatre to theatre is the wonderful places I have found to stay. There are a number of guidebooks which steer you to private houses that take paying guests, and they are usually delightful, charging much less than hotels, while their breakfasts are in a different class altogether. Valeria and I have made good friends with some of these most hospitable people. I always try to drop my bags off before we go to the theatre, so that when we come back in the dark after the show, I have a good idea of the way to go. There is nothing worse than making a good getaway from the theatre, only to find that twenty-five minutes later you are still in the same town having passed the same church for the third time. Valeria, who has become a brilliant tour manager, has a good bump of locality and has turned into an excellent satnav too, even though we once spent nearly three hours trying to find the road out of Bordeaux, and on another occasion saw more of Brecon than we need have done.

Some of the hotels I have stayed in over the years have been truly memorable. Perhaps the greatest delight of all is the aforementioned Langar Hall, in the Vale of Belvoir, which for me, has at least six and a half stars for everything, with comfortable rooms and superb food. It is presided over by Imogen Skirving, whom I describe, in a foreword to her book about Langar, as a benevolent despot. She moves around the hotel with an air of aristocratic insouciance, but she misses nothing, and takes a personal interest in anyone who stays or eats there. Her character permeates everything, and some of her staff are as delightfully idiosyncratic as she is herself. Without her unobtrusive bossiness and attention to detail, Langar would not be Langar. She is a genius who claims she has no idea how it all works so smoothly, but I can assure you, she knows only too well. She is one of Valeria and my closest friends.

I drive everywhere, because I sell a certain amount of merchandise, including copies of my more recent books, during the interval and after the show, and I carry it all around in the boot of my car. I also have three different wines with my own distinctive label on the bottles. The Wine Company in Colchester helps me find these wines: after much delicious tasting, I now have a white Burgundy, a Côtes du Rhone and a splendid champagne made by Guilleminot near Troyes in southern Champagne. The punters are happy to have them, they are all more than half-serious wines and each bottle sold is a good PR exercise. Valeria, who has been a considerable figure in the fashion world, sells the merchandise for me and does it with great panache and success. Moschino's loss is my gain.

I now do far more 'Memories of *Test Match Special*' shows with Peter Baxter although I still love doing a few one-man shows. I find it surprising that I am sometimes asked if these shows are the same every evening. My rather portentous answer to this implied criticism is that if you go and see the same play twice, do you expect the plot to have changed? My shows are all one-night stands, so I never play in front of the same audience twice. Since I began performing on stage in 2001 I have changed and updated the show four times, and I shall soon do so again. A show probably has a two-year shelf life. Some stories – my bankers – will always stay, because you become known for them, people expect to hear them and they can be relied upon to produce a laugh. I couldn't do a show without the story about carrying two of John Arlott's large briefcases, both full of claret, up to the commentary box in the Lord's Pavilion. Johnners' description of a dachshund at Headingley is another one that must always find a place, and the Noël Coward and Clive Dunn stories cannot be excluded. I regard my shows as being more comedy than cricket, and I hope to make people laugh rather than to improve their forward defensive strokes, or indeed anything else. We none of us laugh enough and I think we feel much better after a really good belly laugh.

Although I have plied my theatrical trade almost entirely in the UK, I have had one or two extraordinary experiences on the stage in other parts of the world. About five years ago I met an American lady who had been at one of my shows in the splendid Brewhouse Theatre in Taunton. The Brewhouse is the friendliest of theatres although, as I write, its future is sadly in some doubt. One of its incidental joys is that it enables me to stay at the Castle Hotel which is another pre-eminent hostelry. It has been owned for many years by my great friend Kit Chapman, and by his father before him. My American friend thought my show might work in New York, and after going to a great deal of trouble, she persuaded some friends of hers to arrange for me to play four nights at the Laugh Factory, just off Broadway. What a thrill it was to see my name in neon lights above the theatre. Unfortunately, it all went downhill from there. The first show just about passed muster, because she had press-ganged a number of her acquaintances to come along. I doubt they understood a word I said all evening, although one or two seemed to enjoy my voice. Even so, it can only have been a sense of duty which persuaded them to clap at the end. The next night, if we raised double figures it was only just, but I still ploughed through it. We didn't do quite so well the night after that and the theatre was happy to pull the plug on the fourth night. At least it was an experience. When I came back to England a newspaper which had heard about my adventure asked me to write a thousand words about it all. I was too ashamed to admit total failure, and wrote rather a wet piece telling a dreadful fib and suggesting I had just about got by. They did not publish it.

Another interesting evening came my way at the Fridge Theatre in Dubai early in 2012. I had always hoped that my show would appeal to expatriates because it talks about an England that should have a certain nostalgic appeal. I was in the Emirates to commentate for the BBC on the three-Test series being played there between Pakistan and England, and was keen, if the chance arose, to do a show one evening. I was put in touch with Chris Raynor by Eric Brunjes, son of the delightful and ubiquitous Harry and Jacqui, great friends of ours who are each worth a book on their own. Chris and Eric worked for the Fridge agency in Dubai, and Chris was a friend and colleague of a splendid South African lady called Shelley Frost who owned and ran the almost but not quite eponymous Fridge, an unlikely venue above a small warehouse in an industrial part of Dubai. We had little more than a week in which to arrange the show, but the handful of people who turned up seemed to enjoy it, and it was certainly a theatrical experience to compare with those at the Laugh Factory in New York. Blowers Overseas Incorporated may not yet quite have got off the ground, but I am not letting things rest there.

One of the fascinating things about theatrical performances is the sheer contrast it provides with my day job. On *Test Match Special* I am sitting in front of a microphone, with maybe six other people in the box, talking to an audience that could occasionally number millions. In a theatre I am standing on the stage talking to an audience of anything from a thousand down perhaps to less than fifty. It is an entirely different experience when you see and hear the audiences' reaction. In *TMS* there are obviously certain rules to be followed, but it has never occurred to me, even for a second at the height of the most exciting Test match between England and Australia with the Ashes at stake, that I am speaking to an enormous listenership. If you make a joke and there is a ripple of laughter inside the box, you feel you have won. In the theatre you may tell a joke that is a surefire winner, and all you hear from the audience is a cough and a shuffle. It is not a good moment. The one thing you must never do is to tell a joke, then stop and wait for the laughter to follow. If it never arrives, there is a ghastly and embarrassing hiatus which it is not easy to climb out of. You must always go straight on. Should the audience be consumed by laughter, you stop until it dies down and then go back to what you had just begun to say. If a well-tried joke gets no more than a mere snigger, I sometimes wait a moment and say, 'That one went much better in Inverness last week.' For some extraordinary reason this often produces the laugh that never came a few seconds before.

Every theatre audience is different, and you need to watch and listen carefully in the first few minutes. If need be, you can quicken up, or slow down, or go off on another course altogether. I always start a show by saying 'My dear old things'. If that is greeted by dead silence, I know I have a problem. No matter what I say on the radio, I have not the slightest idea whether it has gone down big or not at all. I just have to keep soldiering on. There is another obvious difference too. People turn on the radio because they want to listen to an unfolding story, which you are describing to them. That narrative will hold their attention. But on the stage the narrative is you, and not a game of cricket.

The most extraordinary show I have ever done was at the Albert Hall, of all places. At the end of May 2009, Eric Clapton was performing there for two weeks, and on one of his nights off, Neil O'Brien, who was my agent, persuaded Clapton's agency to put on a show in celebration of my seventieth birthday, which was coming up on 23 September. The idea was that I should do the first half, and then, after the interval, various of my friends would come on and talk about me.

The first to sign up for this was Stephen Fry, another good Norfolk boy. With him at first base, we couldn't go wrong.

Half-term, illness, prior engagements, a first night and a three-day return trip to Australia meant that Rory Bremner, Jilly Cooper, Anne Robinson, Tim Rice and Jeff Thomson couldn't make it, which was sad. But Sir Tom Courtenay came along, as did John Bly from *Antiques Roadshow*; Christine Hamilton, hugely larger than life, terrific fun and married to the imperturbable Neil; Johnny Woodcock; Peter Baxter; the former England opening batsman Peter Richardson; my brother John; and of course Edward Lane Fox, with whom I spent all those years playing cricket at Sunningdale and Eton. They were all interviewed brilliantly by Jonathan Agnew, who found that the splendid ongoing hospitality in the green room meant his footwork had to be quicker than he had anticipated. But he was more than equal to it.

In the week or so beforehand I was given a few complimentary tickets to put around. A few days before the event I had a lunch appointment, and as I had a little time to kill I went into John Brinkley's famous oasis in the Hollywood Road. There were two elegant ladies sitting at the bar and no one else. After a while, as tends to happen on such occasions, we found ourselves speaking. One of the girls was an Italian called Valeria, and the other was a German friend of hers, Marita. We talked for a bit, and then I said to them, 'You must come and see me at the Albert Hall.' They were a little surprised at this, and I was pleased to have such a formidable piece of ammunition up my sleeve – it will never happen again. After I had gone, Valeria told me later, they wondered what I was about, and agreed that because I was playing at the Albert Hall, I was almost certainly a conductor. Marita lived just around the corner, and when she got home she googled me, then rang Valeria in horror. 'He's all about cricket!' she said. But fortunately that did not deter them, and they both came along.

My main memory of the occasion is of when I first arrived

at the Albert Hall in the afternoon. I walked onto the stage down the same passage that Sir Malcolm Sargent, Sir Thomas Beecham, Sir John Barbirolli and so many other famous conductors had used. There was still enough natural light to see the whole of the building. It was huge. The top gallery, which holds thousands, was not being opened, but I still thought, 'How the hell can I play here?' It was breathtaking, bewildering and frightening. Gradually my apprehension subsided, and it became just another theatre. The daylight went, the lights took over, and when we tested the microphone and the lights, all I could see was the glare of the stage lights, which prevented me from seeing how vast the famous auditorium really was.

From my perspective, I was not quite at the top of my form in a rather elongated first half. After the interval, my job was to stand behind a bar on the stage and dispense drinks to all those who had been subjected to the most amiable treatment by Aggers in his best bedside manner. Stephen Fry was of course the star, and he showed what an extraordinary performer he is. He is the consummate professional, and is so charming and friendly with it. He spoke to the audience of three or four thousand people for twenty minutes, and it was fair magical stuff – it must have taken even him a good amount of time to write. He began by giving a list of 'the things that would make any decent person leave England'. They included the winter, Oxford, reality TV, politicians, traffic bumps and 'elf 'n' safety – and a certain tabloid newspaper also got a mention or two. He then went on to list 'what England can offer on the plus side to counter that damning list of indictments'. There were fifteen things, including Radio 4, Cambridge, Norfolk, P.G. Wodehouse, red buses, James Bond and cricket. These were then distilled into a single thing: which turned out to be 'Henry Blofeld'. It was immensely flattering, brilliantly conceived, and delivered in masterly fashion, as only Stephen can. By way of thanks I was able to pour him a huge glass of red wine on stage afterwards, and I think he came back for a refill or two. I can't think of anyone who deserved them more. As seventieth-birthday presents go, it does not get any better than that. And at the Albert Hall too.

I have loved every moment I have spent on stage. Making people laugh is a powerful drug, and I shall go on doing these shows as long as theatres can find anyone to come along and watch them. My one regret is that the two-man show I did with John Bly did not take off. John is the principal furniture expert on *Antiques Roadshow*, and he knows more about Chippendale than Chippendale did himself. He is a man of many parts, with a most engaging sense of humour and great knowledge about so many things. He is also a pretty sharp dresser, as *Roadshow* viewers will know. We were introduced by a mutual friend who saw the possibility of us doing a show together. The *Roadshow* and *TMS* complement each other in many ways, besides having catchy signature tunes. John and I put together a show in which we talked about a range of different subjects, including a number of those things Stephen Fry put on his debit list at the Albert Hall. There was a topical edge to our shows, and we were not always entirely on the side of Political Correctness.

Before we actually took to the stage, I would go down to Tring in Hertfordshire, where John's family has had an antique business since the early 1800s. We would sit in his music room – John still plays a formidable drum in a family jazz band – and rehearse the two acts of our show, then listen to a recording of it and try to produce ourselves as best we could. Lunch was always cooked by John's wife Virginia, who makes as good a fish pie as I have eaten.

The show began with John mixing us both a dry martini, and giving careful thought as to how the perfect dry martini should be made. He loved quoting Dorothy Parker who had said, "I like to have a martini. Two at the very most. After three I'm under the table, after four I'm under the host." After that we sat down, and chatted and laughed our way through two acts of nearly an hour each. John and I worked well together, and the audiences we played in front of were happy to laugh along with us. We played three shows at the 2011 Edinburgh Festival, although the venue, the International Exhibition Centre, was huge, and was probably the wrong place for us. I loved working with John, who is not only enormously clever, but has a lovely, almost inconsequential charm, an indefatigable humour together with the formidable knowledge of furniture that makes him such a splendid performer on the *Roadshow*. He tells the most wonderful stories, too, about antique dealers who have been less than scrupulous, or the cock-ups on the *Roadshow*. He had started on the programme with Arthur Negus, who had put it together in the first place, and John's recollections of Negus brought the great man to life. I chipped in with some amusing gossip from *TMS*, and our shows were well received. Unfortunately, we didn't really get the support I felt we deserved – perhaps we just didn't fire the right people's imaginations – and the show petered out. I still hope we will get a chance to start it up again one day, because it made people laugh.

More recently I have begun another two-man show, with Peter Baxter, who produced me for thirty-four years on *Test Match Special*. We had lunch one day in a pub in Chelsea, the Surprise, where Oscar Wilde, who lived in neighbouring Tite Street, was a regular. On this occasion we were joined by an old friend of mine, Michael Proudlock, and as usual when Backers and I are together we journeyed back and forth down memory lane, telling stories of *TMS* and laughing uproariously. When Michael was finally able to get a word in, he said, 'You two should do this on the stage. People would love it.' That set us thinking. I spoke to Neil O'Brien, and we all had lunch together. Backers and I prattled away as usual, and Neil quickly saw the point. Only a week or two had gone by when he rang to say he already had some bookings.

When Backers and I started these shows, we had done seventy-five years between us on *TMS*. There is no cricket *per se* in the show. We tell stories about the people we have worked with on the programme, some of which have never seen the light of day before. We come at things from different perspectives: I was behind the microphone, while Peter orchestrated everything either from the producer's chair at the back of the box or from his desk in Broadcasting House. The show is essentially comedy, as we share lovely anecdotes about Brian Johnston, John Arlott and all the others. In spite of his blue rinse, Backers is a treat to work with. We bounce off each other well, and as the show is entirely unscripted, we are always surprising both ourselves and the audience with stories we haven't thought of for years, and have never tried out before. Whenever we look at each other and neither of us can think what to say next, we invariably burst into laughter, which is always promising. At the time of writing we've only done about twenty shows, but the feedback has been good, and a fair number are in the book for the future, including 18 at the Edinburgh Festival in 2013.

The eternal question about performing, which I have no doubt will follow me to my grave, is why there should be full houses in, say, Harrogate, Selby, Nottingham, Chichester, Pershore, Pocklington, Axminster and, believe it or not, a few other places besides, and then an audience of barely fifty in some other place that should be friendly, receptive and what I consider to be our sort of area. Maybe it's local economics. Maybe it's the way the theatre distributes posters and promotes the show. Maybe it's one of a thousand other things. Whatever it is, it is a fact of life in the theatre, an ever-lasting conundrum for touring players which is never likely to be solved. The reason I like the stage lights to be so bright is so that it means I cannot see the audience from the stage: I find it much easier to play to empty seats if you cannot see that they are empty.

I almost walked onto another stage by complete chance some years earlier: the High Court. Two former England cricketers, Ian Botham and Allan Lamb, had brought a libel action against the former Pakistan captain Imran Khan, who they accused of calling them uneducated racialists. The case was scheduled to start in the High Court on 15 July 1996, and the week before, I was rung up by Andy Lines, who worked for the *Daily Mirror*, and asked if I would write a daily piece on the proceedings in the idiom of the *Test Match Special* commentary box. I accepted with some trepidation, because I had no idea what I had let myself in for, or if I would be able to churn out the sort of stuff the *Mirror* wanted.

I turned up early on the first morning, and met Peter Allen, the journalist who would be the *Mirror*'s main reporter covering the trial. He seemed terrifyingly young. I was not entirely sure what sort of chap I was going to meet, and suggested we went for a cup of coffee. We got on a treat, and I think Peter was probably as relieved as I was. We found common ground in Norfolk, for Peter had been based in Norwich for a couple of years, working for the *Eastern Daily Press*. On that first meeting we agreed in the loosest possible sense that he would write a rounded report of what went on each day, while I would choose one or two particular incidents that amused, interested or horrified me for my shorter second piece.

We then made our way to Court 13, where over thirteen days the trial would unfold in front of us like a Gilbert and Sullivan opera. The case was presided over by a Mr Justice French, who I felt was never quite sure whether he was on a cricket ground, a football pitch, a golf course or a squash court. In any case, cricket was not a game that came easily to him. Below him to his left was the somewhat patrician figure of Imran Khan, dwarfed, but not in a physical sense, by his advocate, George Carman QC. Carman was a master of cunning who bowled legal googlies that had both opposing counsel and witnesses groping. By comparison, Svengali was the merest beginner. In the right-hand corner were Botham and Lamb, who both gave the impression they thought they were on to a pretty good thing. They were watched over by Charles Gray QC, who in an upright, open way was probably nearly as cunning as Carman, but did not seem it – which may have been his strength.

Peter and I sat in the press seats at the back of the court, not far from Imran's considerable supporters' club. His wife Jemima, who was pregnant, looked glowingly beautiful, and her mother, Annabel Goldsmith, was there every day I was in court, and was always friendly. Her stepbrother, Robin Birley, was also usually there, and her younger brothers Zac and Ben sometimes came too. It was quite a family party, although I don't think they were particularly optimistic about the way the case was going. George Carman was doing everything he could, but the cards seemed to be stacked in Charles Gray's favour, and as the case went on there was a growing buoyancy at his end of the court.

Things began with the usual quiet formality. After the jury had been sworn in, both sides stated their case. Then came a stream of witnesses, who for most of the next two weeks bemused and confused judge and counsel and many others with complicated cricketing technicalities. While the case was being heard, a Test match was being played at Lord's between England and Pakistan. I was commentating on this match and for three days I had to leave the courtroom to Peter Allen. During those same three days certain witnesses who were commentating on the match for television had to take time off to make the journey to Court 13, and take guard in the witness box.

Geoffrey Boycott was one of these, and he was characteristically quick to appreciate the commercial possibilities of his visit to the High Court. He apparently made an impressive appearance in the witness box, resplendent in the clothes he wore for commentary, which were emblazoned with sponsors' tags. I wonder if he persuaded them to pay extra for a visit to the High Court. He will surely have put George Carman right on one or two cricketing points, and probably told the judge a thing or two as well. Sadly, my commentary duties caused me to miss this diverting episode, but it was well reported.

The witness I enjoyed most was the Test umpire Don Oslear. In his rather self-important way, he had the gall to wag his finger more than once at the great George Carman, to whom the intricacies and terminology of the game were complete mysteries. He kept asking Oslear about, and making references to, 'the rules of the game'. Oslear, a stickler for the proprieties of cricket, told him indignantly that cricket did not have 'rules', it had 'laws', whereupon Carman, quite reasonably and conversationally, said that he imagined they were the same thing. This brought Oslear two paces down the pitch, and in effect he said how dare Carman make such an outrageous statement? Laws and rules were certainly not the same thing, and cricket only had laws. Carman was not prepared to take this lying down, and said that for the purposes of this case they could be considered to be the same thing. Oslear went red in the face, looked as if he was going to go ballistic, and vehemently disagreed. Mr Justice French intervened to try to clear the matter up, but Oslear was by no means convinced that the learned judge had got the point either. It was an amusing interlude in which the sublime laws and the ridiculous rules collided head on.

After England had been well beaten at Lord's I returned to my duties at Peter Allen's side. At last it was time for the prosecution and the defence to say their final pieces, and Mr Justice French, who had looked less and less well as the case had gone on, summed up, it seemed strongly in favour of Botham and Lamb. By the time the jury were asked to retire and consider their verdict, George Carman appeared rather like a grey-haired, bespectacled fish which had suddenly found itself swept up onto the beach and didn't know what to do about it. Imran seemed well beaten.

The jury were unable to reach a decision that evening, so we all trooped back next morning. The wait went on and on. Messages came back and forth to and from the jury room, until the judge said a majority verdict would be good enough. By now the suspense was building up. Previously it had seemed an open-and-shut case, but now it had begun to look as if we might be in for a surprise, and there was visibly more life in the Imran camp. George Carman was looking cautiously animated, and was even smiling a certain amount. On the other side of the courtroom there were some worried frowns, although Charles Gray did his best to look as upbeat as possible. Then the word came through: the jury had reached a majority decision. We all went back to our places, and the jury shuffled self-consciously in. You could read anything you chose from their faces. 'Court rise!' came the solemn shout. We did, and Mr Justice French stuttered rather than swept in as he returned to the bench for the last time in this case. The foreman of the jury assured him that they had reached a decision.

'Do you find for the plaintiff or the defendant?' the judge asked. There was an uncomfortable pause, during which a dropping pin would have been deafening.

'The defendant.' The foreman spoke the word tonelessly, almost as if he was frightened of it.

The delight at one end of the court and the consternation at the other was simultaneously both joyous and painful to watch. Imran and company could not believe their luck. If ever there was a moment when such a controlled and unemotional performer in a courtroom as George Carman could have been said to look both delighted and incredulous, this was it. After the financial details had been settled, Imran did not punch the air, although he looked momentarily as if he might. He then left the court in his usual measured way, leaving Botham and Lamb to ponder a likely bill of more than half a million pounds, including their costs and Imran's. Both of them looked as if they had just been bowled by Imran for a duck. Which they had.

Peter and I frantically wrote our pieces in the press room and telephoned them through. We then wandered over the road from the High Court to the George, where Peter told me that George Carman would almost certainly join us for a celebratory drink. Not long after we had installed ourselves there, Peter's telephone rang. After he had finished speaking he turned to me, smiling, and said, 'Great news for you, Henry. That was the office. They loved your piece, and they're going to give you the front page all to yourself. Well done.' Peter, as I came to discover, is always the most generous of men. He wouldn't have been human if it hadn't slightly stuck in his gullet that he had covered the trial brilliantly for thirteen days, only to be upstaged at the end by a ringer. Yet he never complained.

We had a decent bottle of wine and while we were drinking it, Carman came into the bar with a few companions. He spotted me, and came over. 'You're new to this,' he said with great abruptness, almost hostility. 'Everything you hear in here is off the record. Do you understand that?' I couldn't think what I had done to him, but I assured him that I wouldn't breathe a word of anything I heard in that bar. 'I should hope not,' was the uncompromising reply. 'He can be a bit like that when he doesn't know you,' someone said to me later. The next day I rang my brother John, a High Court judge, and told him how Carman had behaved towards me. He chuckled and said, 'I expect that was because he lost his last case, which was in front of me.' Carmen may have felt that one Blofeld after another was more than anyone should have to put up with.

My run-in with Carman was not quite the end of the day. Peter and I decided that a celebratory dinner was in order, so we caught a taxi and headed off towards Knightsbridge. We were tootling down the Mall when Peter's telephone went again. It was his editor, the redoubtable Piers Morgan, about whom Stephen Fry had had a little to say at the Albert Hall. From what I could gather, he wanted to congratulate us both on our coverage. Suddenly Peter said to him, 'We're in a taxi with George Carman, who's coming with us for a drink.' 'Put me over to him, will you? I want to congratulate him,' was Piers' reply. Peter now paid me back for getting the front page. 'Of course. Here he is.' And he passed his telephone to me. I didn't know what to do. I took the telephone and said, almost in a whisper, 'Piers, this is Henry Blofeld. I can't pass you on to George, because he's as pissed as a newt. He's been celebrating hard in a pub by the law courts, and he's asleep. I don't think I should wake him.' This seemed to satisfy Piers, who simply said, 'Oh well, tell him when he wakes up that I'll catch up with him soon.' He thanked me for the piece I had written, said he'd offer me a job if ever I wanted one, but didn't. I returned the telephone to Peter, who was laughing himself silly.

Peter would go on to work for the *Daily Mail*, and then decided to set himself up as a permanent freelance in Paris, rather as Sam White had done many years before when the *London Evening Standard* was his prime concern. I see him whenever I go to Paris or he comes back to London for a visit. Peter is a brilliant journalist, and his by-line appears in a great many publications all over the world. He has become one of Valeria and my dearest friends. I think he may even have forgiven me for getting that front page.

FOURTEEN

Middle-Aged Junkies in Kandahar

It all began at the Weld Club in Perth. Johnny Woodcock and I were staying there in December 1975 to watch the second Test between Australia and the West Indies. It was an extraordinary game of cricket, in which the West Indies gave perhaps the first glimpse of the side they were to become a year or two later. They won by an innings and 87 runs, although they went on to lose the series by five matches to one. Wooders and I were staying at the Weld Club, which was founded in 1871. The club is named after a former Governor of Western Australia, which may suggest that it is stiff, conventional and unsmiling; but it is none of those things. Located in Barrack Street, in the middle of the city, is the most lovely club, with a huge garden (although part of that has now gone to property developers to make sure the club will remain in good financial order for the foreseeable future). The food is excellent, and I always seem to meet interesting people there. Not the least of its joys for me is the lovely twenty-minute walk each morning down St George's Terrace to the cricket ground.

It had been Wooders' billet in Perth for many years, as an old friend of his, Colin McDonald, who lived in the club, paved the way for him to stay there. A year before, when England were touring, he had very kindly done the same for me, and it was to become my home whenever I was in Perth.

Colin, who was by then an old man, was small, fidgety, talked at a furious speed and seldom seemed to draw breath. Colin was in his late seventies when I first met him, and in his time had been a considerable journalist. He was *The Times* correspondent in the Far East and his big moment came in 1937 when he was journeying up the Yangtse River on the US gunboat, the USS *Panay*. The boat had been sent up to Nanking, which was being bombed by the Japanese, to evacuate foreign civilians when it was itself bombed and sunk. Colin was lucky to escape and talked about it all most descriptively. His reports were exclusive and made an enormous impact to the point where they were used by the Foreign Office as the official record of what had happened. Most unusually at that time, they appeared in *The Times* under his own name.

Wooders and I were having dinner together after the last day of the match, having just watched Andy Roberts demolish Australia in their second innings. It won't have been a teetotal evening, and we were probably on our second bottle of something red and delicious from Margaret River or thereabouts when I said to him, apropos of nothing very much, 'With any luck we'll be in India this time next year.' England were touring India in 1976–77. 'Do you know, Blowers,' he replied, 'the last time we toured India, Johnners, Mellers [Michael Melford] and I were going to drive out there.' 'Why didn't you?' I asked. 'Because the wives didn't think it was a good idea,' was the reply.

This set us both thinking for currently neither of us had such encumbrances, and before we had finished our last glass we had decided that, come what may, we were going to drive to India the following year. We played the idea around, wondering how big the party ought to be, how many cars we should take, which way we should go, and who we should ask to come with us. It all seemed too exciting for words, and before we climbed upstairs we had even selected our first fellow traveller. A year before, I had met the most attractive and extrovert lady in Sydney, called Judy Casey. I had been introduced to her by Edward Scott, with whom I had played cricket at Eton, and who was then running John Swire's in Australia. He was as good a friend as I ever had. We had gone out to dinner one night, and I'm not sure now whether or not the first time I saw Judy she was walking across the top of his green Jaguar – although I suppose that may have been after dinner. I hope she had taken off her shoes, in any case. She was tall, with a figure that made strong men tremble, and she had a terrific sense of humour, five lovely children, and a pilot's licence, although I couldn't say in which particular order. She had been married to a relation of Lord Casey, who was Governor General of Australia in the sixties, although she herself was the most un-Government House sort of person I have ever met. We had instantly become friends, and she would undoubtedly provide the colour we would need on an overland expedition like the one we had planned – and no one would enjoy the adventure more. Wooders knew Judy, and was quick to endorse her selection.

So, we had three people, but now we badly needed a car or two. We talked about this often enough in our remaining weeks in Australia, and came to the vague conclusion that we didn't have much choice but to do the journey by Land or Range Rover.

On his return home, Wooders had a great piece of luck. He was asked to dinner by some friends in Hampshire, and one of the other guests was his chum Adrian Liddell, a considerable Hampshire farmer who talked in unmistakeable ringing tones, loved cars – of which he had a remarkable collection – and knew an impressive amount about the workings of the internal combustion engine. When Wooders mentioned our plan to go overland to India in the autumn, Ady sat up at once and said, 'Why don't you let me drive you in one of my old cars?' 'Do you think any of them would be up to it?' was Wooders' reply. Ady bridled slightly at the implied insult, and assured Wooders that any one of his collection would get us there. Shortly afterwards he nominated a maroon-coloured 1921 Rolls-Royce Silver Ghost which he always thereafter referred to as his 'old gal', and we were a good deal further down the road.

Our team continued to be assembled in the most haphazard way. One day in March, I was having a quiet early-evening drink in Boodle's. The bar there has a curving corner to it which was invariably occupied at this time of the day by a jolly acquaintance of mine called Michael Bennett, who would be reading the evening paper, smoking and coping affably with some whisky. He was a stock jobber, had just helped to put the stock exchange on computer, and was in the throes of retiring. He must have been getting on for sixty, was going bald in a mildly distinguished way, and was always full of good cheer as he peered over the top of a pair of horn-rimmed half-moon reading glasses and put the world to rights. He was certainly never short of an opinion. After a while I joined him for a refill. We talked briefly about cricket, which was not really his subject although for some strange reason he got very upset about leg byes, and I then began to tell him about our proposed drive to India. His ears pricked up a fraction, and he leaned over rather more, balancing those glasses on the tip of his nose. I told him how Wooders and I had come up with the idea, and that it would be a stately progress, as Ady was going to drive us there in his 1921 Silver Ghost. Michael got up and went to the loo, saying loudly over his shoulder, 'Stay where you are.' When he came back he ordered another drink, sat down, and shifted round on his bar stool so that he was looking straight at me. 'I've had a terrific idea,' he said. 'Why don't I buy a car and come with you? Two cars would be better than one, and I can think of nothing that would be more fun.'

Michael had made up his mind to invite himself, and he was not the sort of person who would easily change it. We talked for a while about the journey, and he put me right on several points of our planned route. He wanted to know about Wooders and Judy, and was surprised when I told him I had not yet met Ady. By the time we parted company I think he regarded the trip as more his idea than ours, and in his mind he had just about taken over the whole thing. There may have been a slight touch of the Kerry Packer about Michael – although I am saying this now, with hindsight. I had to sell the idea of both a second car and Michael to Ady and Wooders. It seemed to me to make good sense, although I could see that Ady might interpret it as a slur on his 'old gal'.

At that stage, it never occurred to me that the problem would be not so much the cars, as the personalities travelling inside them. Michael and Ady were totally different characters, but they were both used to having their own way, although Michael swept through life with a much broader brush than Ady, who could at times be over-concerned with finicky details. It was a relief that at least they would be in different cars, as Michael would not have fitted, in any sense of the word, in the back seat of the Rolls. They also viewed the adventure in entirely different ways. For Michael and his new Rover, it was principally going to be a light-hearted jolly. For Ady, it was going to be something of an endurance test. Not only was he going to have to drive the old Rolls every inch of the way himself, but he would have to give the engine a complete service every week. Then there were the problems of spare parts, tyres, full petrol cans on the running board, and the sheer physical effort of lugging the big car halfway around the world without power steering. Even on the straightest and flattest roads it would not be able to crack on at much more than fifty miles an hour. I am not in the least suggesting that Ady was not going to enjoy himself – far from it. But his approach to the journey had of necessity to be far more single-minded and concentrated than Michael's. The new arrangement put Wooders and me in an awkward position too. Wooders had found Ady, and I had found Michael – although some might say that he had found me. We therefore naturally tended to support our own corners. In effect, strong positions had been taken up well before the first starting button had been pressed.

We had reached the point where we had assembled two very different cars and five hugely different people. It was a recipe for excitement beyond a doubt, but whether it was one for getting us harmoniously, or indeed in any way whatever, from London to Bombay was a different matter. It already looked as if we had, in the loosest sense, too many drivers and too few passengers. The first time I met Ady, he made it clear that he was not altogether happy that there was going to be a lady in the party, although I was confident that when Judy arrived she would have no trouble setting him straight. But I did not get this right. At their first meeting, Ady made his disapproval pretty obvious. And Judy, always full of bounce, enthusiasm and blonde *joie de vivre*, was more attracted by the broader sweep of Michael's brush than by the smaller, more precise detail that Ady coped with so admirably and made her point abundantly clear.

In fact, Ady's enthusiasm for and obsession with elderly versions of the internal combustion engine was a delight. The Silver Ghost which was going to be our virtual home for six weeks was the pride of his collection, if not of his life – during the journey it was almost as if he was married to 'the Old Gal'. It was clear that this car would make a huge impact wherever we went, and Wooders and I were both thrilled by the prospect of travelling to Bombay in the 'old gal'. It was going to give us so much more than the adventure we had hit upon that night in Perth. While the old Rolls was obviously eye-catching, Judy's bombshell appearance turned a great many heads to the Rover, in which Michael's half-moon glasses perched on the tip of his nose also became something of a tourist attraction, if in a rumbling, more *basso profundo* way.

The planning went ahead through the summer, on a pretty ad hoc basis. Someone suggested we might try to get some sponsorship to help with the costs. Although this was a time when some considered sponsorship to be at least questionable, and at worst vulgar, we held our breath and put out some feelers. There was a heartening, if not especially munificent, response. Air India gave us a modicum of cash, and a send-off party at their offices in Bond Street, at which the Rolls turned up in all its glory and was much admired. The old BBC television announcer Cliff Michelmore was one of those who came along to the party, and he told me that if he had been a bit younger, we would have had a job to prevent him from joining us. Air India also provided some stickers to put on the cars, and promised us more parties along the route, in Frankfurt, Belgrade and Tehran.

Esso opened the batting with Air India – it was a former Oxford cricket Blue, 'Jumbo' Jowett, a friend of Wooders', who led us to them. I don't think they coughed up any petrol, but they came forward with some loose change and some stickers. Coming in first wicket down was probably our best player, Long John Scotch whisky, who gave us a little cash and, much more important, a certain amount of their inestimable product. We had a case or three of forty-ounce bottles, and a case or two of flasks, which hold about a third of a bottle. These flasks came into their own when it was a matter of persuading reluctant or recalcitrant officials at difficult border crossing points to do the decent thing and wave us through. I have never particularly enjoyed the taste of whisky, but when it is the only alternative I try to put a brave face on it. Long John didn't let us down on the sticker front either; both cars were now so plastered all over with them that they looked like a couple of well-wrapped travelling Christmas presents. I couldn't help wondering what sort of impression that would make on the population of, say, downtown Sivas, Komotini, Herat or wherever. But that is advertising for you.

6 October was agreed as the starting date, and we planned to arrive in Bombay on 22 November for the start of the England tour, at which point Wooders and I would have to get our typewriters out and put our heads down.

We left London early in the morning of Monday 6th October 1976. In our caps and Barbours, we must have looked like a party of 1920s explorers. Ady drove his Old Gal while I sat alongside him in the extremely draughty assistant chauffeur's seat, with Wooders in the back reading *The Times*, looking every inch the aristocrat who should once have owned this lovely claret-coloured beast. The partition window, which in the old days would have prevented the juicier pieces of gossip from reaching the chauffeur's ears, was wound up to keep out the draught. This meant that Ady and I were at least spared Wooders' deafness. We were a bit pushed for space all round, and there were piles of luggage on the floor in front of and alongside Wooders, which happily included some of those cases of Scotch which Long John had kindly given us. Wooders made the entire journey in the back of the Old Gal, while I alternated between the back and the draughty assistant chauffeur's lookout post. In the Rover, or 'the Yellow Peril' as it became known, Michael drove with those half-moon horn-rimmed glasses perched perilously, as always, on the end of his nose, making him look like something mildly surprising out of Noah's Ark. Judy, glamorous as ever, sat elegantly alongside him, reminding me of Kay Kendall in that wonderful old movie, *Genevieve*. This would be the arrangement in which we travelled for the whole journey, except for one morning out of Ankara, when Michael was not well, and while Judy drove the Rover I sat in the back with him, assuming the role of Florence Nightingale.

So at last we were under way, even if we had not much idea where we were going. We had hardly got started before we hit our first traffic jam, in New Cross, where the rush hour was at the peak of its form. Wooders leaned forward, wound down the window between us, and gave us his first offering of the journey: 'Good heavens, for a dreadful moment when I saw all those Indians standing at that bus stop, I thought we'd already got there.'

We had three lovely days' holiday to begin with. Our sponsorship duties took us first to Paris and then to Frankfurt. Vineyards, Michelin-starred restaurants (a Lobster Thermidor at Le Cheval Blanc in Sept-Saulx was the dish of the journey), excellent wine and some more than half-decent beer besides. From Germany we proceeded to Austria, perching for one night among the glories of Salzburg. There was a lovely scenic morning as we headed for Yugoslavia, as it still was then, under the tut-elage of Marshal Tito. The winding road took us excitingly through the mountains, climbing round and round, up and up, seemingly forever. It was hard work for Ady lugging the Old Gal round the more or less continuous bends, but good training for what lay ahead. Then it was down the other side, and we had just about got to the bottom when we arrived at a large, round area of tarmac, which was effectively a roundabout. Three roads led off it, and at its centre was a uniformed policeman with his arms outstretched.

For all his sterling qualities, Ady did not star as a linguist. Whenever anybody addressed him in a foreign tongue, he had the delightful habit of saying in those ringing tones of his, 'I'm afraid I have no French/German or whatever.' If the person he was speaking to had no English, it was not a successful opening gambit. On this occasion Ady drove up close to the policeman, wound down the window and said, 'I'm afraid I have no Austrian.' After waiting two or three seconds and receiving no answer, he looked more closely at the policeman, and only then did he realise that it was actually a life-sized dummy. I was travelling in the back with Johnny, as the front was cold and draughty, and the two of us burst into helpless laughter. For a moment Ady seemed a little put out, but it didn't take him long to see how absurd it was, and soon he was laughing as hard as anyone. At every frontier post we encountered Ady always seemed to be saying to the chap who wanted to look at his papers, 'I'm afraid I have no . . .' It became a standing joke.

Later that day we crossed into Yugoslavia, and were soon on the wide trunk road running down to Greece. It was now that we found ourselves in a world of huge, thundering lorries carrying merchandise out to the East. They would stay with us until we got to Pakistan, from which point most of those that had stayed the course took the road on to China. One unnerving aspect of this long trunk road was that every five miles or so we would pass a pile of flowers by the side of the road. These were memorials to people who had recently been killed near that spot, often lorry drivers who had gone to sleep while pushing themselves over the limit: the quicker they completed one journey, the sooner they were paid and the quicker they were able to set off on the next. We later met one driver at the Turko–Iranian border who told us it had taken him only twenty-one days to drive from Bristol to Kabul in eastern Afghanistan and back. I was glad he wasn't giving me a lift.

The lorry culture was quick to embrace us. Wherever we stopped to spend a penny or grab something to eat or drink, there would usually be a collection of parked lorries. The drivers were fascinated by the Old Gal, and would often come over to look at her and talk to us. Ady found himself shorter of languages than ever, but his understanding of sign language was good enough for him to realise that some of the lorry drivers wanted to look under the bonnet. He was delighted to oblige. The drivers were not the only people fascinated by the Rolls. Touchingly, men and women working in the fields alongside the road would take off their hats and wave vigorously as we passed.

The road, which stretched for thousands of miles ahead of us, had an extraordinarily effective bush telegraph. The further we went, the more we found that word of our approach had got around. Petrol stations would be expecting us, and often when we were overtaken there would be a flurry of friendly hooting and waving. Wherever we were, we were always made to feel extremely welcome. This was helped by the considerable number of motorbikes. Their young riders went quicker than anything else on the road, and were particularly responsible for spreading the word ahead. We made many good friends, although sadly we could do little more than pass in the night. But this remarkable camaraderie would be an outstanding feature of the whole journey.

Ljubljana, Zagreb, Belgrade and Salonika went past in a flash, leaving, like a good many other places, not much more than memories of traffic jams. By this time we were getting into the habit of all meeting up in one of our hotel rooms at the end of each day, inviting a forty-ounce bottle of Long John to join us, and mulling over the events of the day. Inevitably the two cars had different objectives. In the Rolls, we always felt we had to be in a hurry, for we had a long way to go, and who knew what hold-ups lay ahead. It was the job of the Old Gal, with her two-wheel brakes and top speed of around fifty miles an hour, simply to get from London to Bombay by 22 November. The Rover, by contrast, could have done the journey in half the time, and found itself somewhat inhibited by its slower companion. Perhaps at about this time we should have agreed to go our separate ways and meet in Bombay. It would have prevented the obvious frustrations suffered by those in the faster car.

But, for better or worse, we continued to travel together. We had an amusing couple of days in the small town of Komotini, on the north coast of Greece, where Ady gave the Old Gal her first full service of the journey. We found a nice hotel on the square, and each evening we sat outside drinking retsina, wine or ouzo and watching what seemed the entire population go for their evening perambulation. They walked around the square in groups, conversing earnestly, plotting, planning, advising, chatting up, talking about the day just ended. Children were playing all manner of games with hoops and balls, and there was a constant ring of laughter. It was the happiest of scenes, and one we often came across in the early evenings the further east we went.

Crossing the Greco–Turkish border was not as difficult or as time-consuming as might have been expected, considering the animosity between the two sides. I don't think we struck anyone at either frontier post as likely fifth columnists, although they might have had a second look at Michael's glasses. The Park Hotel in Istanbul was made elusive by the traffic jams and one-way streets, but turned out to be the kind of lovely old hotel which has a habit of turning up in places where the English once had a significant presence. We spent two days there, and one happy morning inside the Blue Mosque with all its glories. As we were leaving Europe over the Golden Horn, Ady decided to take off his Barbour, and asked me, in the assistant chauffeur's seat, to hold the wheel for a moment. I don't know what happened, but suddenly we lurched to the right, and the Bosphorus beckoned alarmingly before Ady snatched back the wheel. It was the closest shave we had.

The Rolls continued to fascinate almost everyone who saw her, not only other travellers but also the locals. When we arrived in Ankara we found that the main political parties were all holding their annual conferences there, and there was not a single hotel room in the place. As we were edging along in the traffic, wondering what we should do, a teenager appeared who evidently thought the old car was the best thing he had ever seen. We sought his help, and he wrote down a list of about half a dozen hotels. Then he gave us a telephone number, and told us that if we had no luck, we were to ring him at home. Of course all his hotels were full, so Ady rang the number. The boy answered, told us his family would be delighted to see us, and gave us directions. When we got there we discovered that his father was the Quartermaster General of the Turkish Army. The whole family were delightful, and could not have been more welcoming. They invited us to stay the night with them, but as there was only one spare bedroom, it was entirely appropriate that Ady should have it, while the rest of us bunked down on the sitting-room floor. As we were saying our effusive goodbyes the following morning, the General and his wife seemed truly delighted to have been able to help. I think their son would have liked to have kept us for a week, and the Rolls for longer than that.

For the rest of our journey through Turkey it was wet and muddy as we made our way slowly along miles of unmade roads, with stones from the back wheels of the lorries in front constantly being thrown up against our windscreen, making Ady understandably nervous that it might shatter.

This was not our only worry, for Michael was not well. He was a heavy smoker, and an obvious candidate for emphysema, which eventually accounted for him. Now, he was continually short of breath, and his heart was racing. The drama increased one day when it was found that his pills had been put into a bag which had gone on ahead in the Rolls. It was at this point that I spent some time in the back of the Rover with Michael, while Judy drove. That evening, a commercial hotel in Sivas was the scene of a sparky Rolls-versus-Rover contest; nerves were becoming frayed, and harsh words were spoken.

The following day, poor roads gave us a difficult drive through the hills to Erzerum, the setting for part of John Buchan's Richard Hannay novel *Greenmantle*. From there we moved on towards the Iranian border, which took us four hours to reach. There was a two-mile-long queue for lorries, which cars were mercifully allowed to jump, but still the warriors in charge on both sides of the border were not easily prepared to take documents, or our word, at face value, although I dare say the fact that we had no Turkish or Iranian may have had something to do with this. A flask or two of Long John also came to our aid. We left them carelessly lying on the seat and the officials pounced on them and laughingly waved us through.

When we had at last been welcomed into Iran, we drove a few miles to the comfortable Maku Inn near Tabriz. The next day we set off for Tehran, where we were planning to spend four days, to which we were looking forward gratefully as our 'half term'. We arrived late in the morning, and our first stop was Air India where we did our stuff on behalf of our sponsors. They told us that accommodation was tight in the city, and although we rang a great many hotels, we drew a complete blank. Ady then rang a car-collecting friend, Fuad Majzub, an accountant who had made pots of money, to see if he could come up with anything. He was only too happy to help, and offered us the use of his large house just outside the walls of the Sa'dabad Palace. We would have the whole place to ourselves, for he lived in a smaller house elsewhere in Tehran, while his wife and children spent most of their time in Worcestershire. We could hardly believe our luck. When we got there, we found Fuad's butler, Abrihim, waiting for us with something like open arms, and no one enjoyed our visit more or did more to help us than he did. As promised, we had the run of the place, and there were masses of lackeys, including cooks who were kept permanently on their toes. The laundry wallahs had a field day too.

Our four-day break was like a mirage, and it seemed to be over almost before it began. Tehran was still under imperial command, although the Shah's time was running out, and the Ayatollahs were more than just flexing their muscles behind the scenes. We visited a number of excellent restaurants, and lay around Fuad's swimming pool recharging the batteries; Judy got out a smashing bikini. Wooders and I gave the Iranian crown jewels in Pahlavi Avenue the once-over. If you know about such things, these are apparently the best of the lot. Their glittering magnificence is impossible to describe, their beauty difficult fully to appreciate, and their value incalculable. I wonder where they are now, and what happened to them after the Revolution and the fall of the Shah. I fear Ayatollahs do not have crown jewellery, unless it is in their Swiss bank accounts. While we there we had one lovely moment. The alarm bells suddenly started to ring in a pretty serious way, all the doors automatically slammed shut, and the place was instantly heaving with guards, their rifles at the ready. I almost felt as if I was facing a firing squad, but happily it was a false alarm, and after a bit they allowed us to leave – but not before they had had a careful look at each of us as we filed out. I am sure my face is still on file: Blowers the bank robber, to say nothing of Wooders – or perhaps I should have said Raffles.

Meanwhile, Ady spent two days in his overalls attending to the needs of the Old Gal. During our stay Wooders and I were asked to a cricket match being played between the Tehran Cricket Club, who were about to go off on a tour, and some local rivals. We had to be at the ground, at Tehran Airport, at half past six in the morning. The pitch was rougher than one might have expected, and the game had to be finished by midday. At ten past twelve goalposts had been erected, and a game of football was under way a few minutes later. That explained the roughness of the pitch. The game was unusual in that one of the umpires spiritedly joined in all the appeals.

After spending two nights in Tehran, Michael and Judy decided to go on ahead to Babolsar, as they felt that three days on the sea would do Michael's breathing a power of good. The only problem was the road through the mountains, which was hazardous and crowded with lorries. When they arrived, Michael rang Ady, who had spent two days attending to the needs of the Old Gal, to warn him that it had taken them six hours to cover the 150 miles.

We hardly saw our tall, distinguished host, Fuad, until he came to have a drink with us on our last night wearing the smartest of suits. He left us at about nine o'clock; an hour later, an amazing fireworks display began over the wall, in the grounds of the Sa'dabad Palace. It was the Crown Prince's sixteenth birthday, and one didn't have to be Sherlock Holmes to deduce that that was where Fuad – who was said to be close to the Shah – had ended up.

When we left the house the next day, Fuad's butler Abrihim was in tears. He told us our visit had reminded him of the old days, which was touching. The drive to Babolsar was as bad as we had feared. It was snowing some of the time, the stream of lorries was relentless, and they frequently overtook us at terrifying speed. Too often for comfort, we would see a lorry lying about three hundreds yards below us on the side of the mountain, like a stranded whale. It was not a journey for the faint-hearted, but Ady was masterful. I don't think any of us except Wooders had realised just how brilliant a driver he was. He was never better than on that day, and somehow, thanks to him, we reached the Caspian Sea. I hated the journey, because I have no head for heights, and we seemed to be constantly looking down at a sheer drop of several thousand feet. The last forty miles through flat, fertile country was a profound relief.

Babolsar was a flourishing, upmarket seaside resort in the summer, but at this time of year it was splendidly uncrowded. We met up with the others. Michael was looking more like his old Paddington Bear self, while Judy had taken the place by storm, as always, and was the centre of everyone's attention. That evening Ady, Wooders and I enjoyed our caviar and vodka with the sensation that we had passed in a single day from one universe to another, by way of a wall of death.

We moved on the next morning, with Bojnoord in our sights, driving over three hundred miles through lovely, flat, rolling country. You could hardly imagine two more contrasting drives on consecutive days. Bojnoord was not big, and had the friendliest of atmospheres: everyone wanted to help. We had been steered into the town by some delightfully talkative locals who were keen that we should eat with them 'in the open air', so that evening we found ourselves having a barbecue with these weatherbeaten, happy, relaxed people by a roundabout. Although we were not in a part of the world best known for alcohol, there was plenty of vodka about. One of the locals kept shaking Michael's hand and saying, 'We are brothers,' which seemed to be his only English. Michael, who was loving every moment of it, invariably replied, 'This is me.' It was undoubtedly a meeting of great minds. The following day the local director of tourism arrived at our hotel to see us on our way, and promised us all kinds of adventures when we were able to return. What a happy stay we had in Bojnoord, and how lovely its people were, with their beards, considerable moustaches, long flowing robes, brilliant smiles and glorious contentment, all spilling over into a wonderful whirlpool of friendship.

Our next destination was Mashhad, the holy city of Iran, with its extraordinary mosque – alas, we didn't have time to do more than drive round it. Our hotel for the night was surprisingly part of a famous international chain, and as usual, we parked the Old Gal outside the front entrance, hoping that it would rapidly become a tourist attraction and get us a decent discount. The trick didn't work on this particular occasion, but it did flush the hotel's general manager from his lair. He was a good-looking young German called Bruno Brunner, and while he took a shine to the car, the main object of his attention was Judy, who played along splendidly. He organised a party that evening, and 'discovered' somewhere in the hotel, far below stairs, a cachet of champagne which he unleashed upon us. We made sure not a drop was left, and when I was woken up at half past five the next morning, for the Rolls was starting off an hour later, I had a pretty nasty hangover. As we were about to leave, I remembered I had to leave a note for Michael. Not feeling my best, I went back to reception and started to write. I began, 'My dear' – but for the life of me I couldn't think of Michael's name. So I went on 'old thing', and then wrote the message.

Later that day, when the two cars met up for lunch, Michael brandished the note at me and said, 'I have not been called "my dear old thing" since my father died.' And that was where, how and why this silly phrase, which was to become a catchphrase with me, started its life. When the cricket tour started in India at the end of our journey, I found that that 'my dear old thing' came in useful when I was unable to remember a person's name. It gave me a bit of breathing space, during which someone might come up and call whoever-it-was by his correct name, and I would be away.

That hungover morning in Mashhad heralded another, rather trickier landmark: the Iranian–Afghanistan border. When we got there, we found a scene of utter chaos, and we could see it was going to be a long wait. Clutching our documents, we joined the large crowd of waiting people in an elongated Nissen hut. Michael, his glasses inevitably wobbling on the end of his nose, was busily hitching up his trousers when he was surprised to be suddenly embraced by a young Pakistani. He was more than a little taken aback, but then the story emerged. Michael owned a house at Frinton, on the Essex coast, and most weekends he would go down there direct from the City. This young chap had worked for several years at Liverpool Street station, and on many Friday evenings and Monday mornings he had clipped or collected Michael's ticket. Michael of course was unmistakeable, and the Pakistani, who was driving back home, was overjoyed to come across him. It was a lovely coincidence and a meeting of great minds.

We had to wait for more than three hours before we were told we could progress to another packed room, on the Afghanistan side of the border. At this point we discovered that what we had heard in London was true: for some reason the post was controlled by a boy who could not have been much more than twelve years old. It was he who decided in what order travellers should have their passports stamped and be allowed to continue into Afghanistan, and who should suffer another interminable wait. After a certain amount of milling around, with the help of some shrewd queue-jumping, I was able to thrust the letter I had been given by the Afghan Embassy in London in front of the boy. It worked a miracle. As soon as he had read it, he immediately ordered tea for Michael and me. I am afraid this did not make us immensely popular with our fellow travellers, some of whom had arrived hours before us. Anyway, we slurped our tea, and fairly soon we were on our way, this time without the help of Long John.

We drove the twenty-odd miles to the hotel in Herat, where we had a few more dirty looks from some of those who had been waiting at the border. The next day we set off down the long straight road through the bare desert to Kandahar. From time to time we could see collections of huge black tents far out in the distance, the homes of the various desert tribes. Masses of children would venture up to the road in the hope of being thrown boxes of matches from passing cars: the winters here are long and hard, and they needed to be able to light their fires. Michael had bought a hundred dollars' worth of matches in Mashhad, and we threw handfuls of boxes out of the windows. It was wonderful to see the joy on the faces of these children as they picked them up. They could hardly believe their luck as they excitedly ran back to their tents, match millionaires.

We drove 250 miles that day, and found an agreeable hostelry in Kandahar. After dinner, Wooders, Ady and I were walking back across the courtyard towards our rooms when we were accosted by an evil-looking rogue who was determined that we should buy and smoke one of his cigarettes. We were not particularly keen, but he wouldn't take no for an answer, so we paid up – it was not much. The cigarette was lit, and we each had a puff or two. It tasted disgusting, and we all felt dreadful for about two days. Goodness knows what it was. It may have been that as we set off in the Old Gal the next morning to drive the 350 miles to Kabul we were nothing more than a group of middle-aged junkies.

We stayed at an ultramodern Intercontinental hotel in Kabul, which was much like any of its sort in the world. On our first evening the Austrian manager showed us a film of buzkashi, a local game of fierce rivalry and great brutality which involves two teams of horsemen, with a dead goat soaked in water as the ball. To score a goal, a team has to carry this around a marker at their opponents' end of the ground, and then back to a circle at their own end. There are a huge number of players and it is both fast and furious; if a rider falls off there is every chance he will be killed, but no one thinks anything of it.

We were asked along to the magnificent British Embassy, which had been designed to suit the needs of Lord Curzon when he was in Afghanistan in the 1890s. We spent most of our second day in Kabul in Chicken Street, where every tourist ends up in order to buy handsome Afghan coats and other garments. Judy led the way, and put on an impressive display of shopping, turning many heads as she tried on this, that and almost everything else. The shopkeepers must have thought we were a group of suckers, as our efforts to bargain were not hugely impressive; they would have been able to have a good night out at our expense. Even Michael, who was not fond of shopping expeditions, bought something for his lovely daughter Vicky. How awful to think that only a few years later, war would take over Afghanistan, and much of the beautiful city of Kabul would be reduced to rubble. We were so lucky to have seen it as it was.

The Old Gal, which had had a puncture on the road between Herat and Kandahar, pulled out of the hotel car park early the following morning on a day which was to produce the most remarkable scenery of the entire journey. First we negotiated the staggering Kabul Gorge, climbing tall hills and then plunging down into valleys through amazing rock formations. After lunch we encountered the famous Khyber Pass, and the wartorn tribal areas along the Afghan–Pakistan boundary, a home of the Taliban. At the border our letter from London again worked wonders, and on the Pakistan side it was easy. Pakistan were playing a Test match against New Zealand, and the border guards were following it closely, until the Old Gal grabbed their attention. They were amazed and delighted by her, and as so often, the car had a much bigger welcome than we did.

We crossed into Pakistan, and suddenly everyone was speaking English, and we were driving on the left-hand side of the road again. In Peshawar we stayed at Dean's Hotel, another famous old English hostelry. One old bearer put his hands together when he saw the Rolls, and told us that it reminded him of the good old days. I think the sight of Wooders may have jogged his memory as well.

One of the main problems now that we had reached the subcontinent was that when it came to 'hot' food, Ady was in the Johnners' class. Alternatives were not then as readily available as they have since become, but at least he did not quite starve. We drove easily down to Rawalpindi, where beds were hard to come by, and in the end we were put up most comfortably in neighbouring Islamabad by a Wing Commander who was the Air Attaché at the British High Commission. We then moved on by way of Lahore, and finally we reached India itself.

Our stay in Delhi became a round of parties, although we again lost Michael and Judy, who decided to fly up to Srinagar in Kashmir to see what life was like on a houseboat. Wooders now came into his own, because in India he was virtually an honorary Maharajah, he was friends with so many: Cooch Bihar, Pitamber, Dungapore, Gwalior and Pataudi were just a few of them. Then there was the Maharajah of Baroda, who had a house in Delhi, and who had already insisted that we stay with him in his palace in Baroda on our way down to Bombay. We certainly felt we had come a long way from that barbecue at the roundabout in Bojnoord, although that had been only a week before.

In Delhi Wooders was quick to call on another friend, Ashwini Kumar, who was scarcely less influential – not only did he command the immensely important Border Security Force (BSF), but he had played hockey for India and was now a member of the International Olympic Committee. Ashwini, who entertained us royally in Delhi, suggested we should spend a couple of days at Tekanpur, the military establishment where the members of the BSF were trained. He arranged for us to stay in the officers' mess, and we had a wonderful two days watching all kinds of military activities, the best of which was an exhibition of tent pegging. The horses galloped past tents at full speed, and the rider used his lance to spear the peg which held the guide ropes in place, causing the tent to collapse. This technique had been devised to make it easy for the troops coming up behind to capture or kill anyone inside. It was amazing to see the precision of these riders, when they were galloping at such speed. We felt a little let down by Wooders when we had to stay at the State Hotel in Jaipur, a city with a perfectly good Maharajah, but from whom we failed to get a touch. Our quarters at the Lake Palace Hotel in Udaipur were an improvement, but when the Meewar of

Udaipur was nowhere to be seen, we felt that Wooders had again missed a trick.

He recovered himself, though, because in Baroda the palace was our home. There was a quid pro quo for our night there: the Prince, as we had called him on *Test Match Special* two years earlier, insisted that I address the Baroda Cricket Association, which had a huge number of members. At least a five-line whip had gone out, and at about six o'clock that evening they assembled in the great hall of the palace, which was so big that it would have made Westminster Hall look like a broom cupboard. It was packed to the rafters. When the Maharajah's party arrived and took their seats on the stage, the entire hall stood. He then rose and introduced me at some length, and as I walked forward to the microphone, it was to a standing ovation to which the Prince beamed his approval. I spoke for just over an hour as I was asked, and every time I said something that made the party on the stage smile, the body of the hall erupted into gales of laughter. They appeared to be enjoying what I said so much that I was starting to feel particularly pleased with myself. When I had finished the party on the stage applauded, while the hall stood as one man and gave me a standing ovation to end all standing ovations. Eventually I joined the Prince's party, and we moved off to his quarters, where drinks were served. It must have been getting on for ten o'clock when we went in to dinner. Some time after we had sat down, there was a moment of silence, broken by Wooders, who turned to our host and said, 'Now, Prince, of all the two thousand people in the hall tonight, how many will have really understood what Blowers was getting at?' The Prince looked at him, shook his head and said, rather sorrowfully, in his Indiay way, 'Practically no one.' My genius had been kicked into touch.

The Prince arranged for us to spend our last night before

we reached our final destination, the Taj Mahal Hotel in Bombay, at the comfortable guest house of a cotton factory he owned in the town of Surat, a two-hour drive from the city. My last memory of this amazing journey was of Ady tackling the sprawling suburbs of Bombay with the same skill he had shown that first morning in New Cross. He never complained about the driving at any point, however difficult it had been for him. He turned the Old Gal into the forecourt of the Taj Mahal Hotel at almost exactly half past one, and in no time a large crowd had gathered to admire and welcome her. The trip had taken us forty-six days and nights, and for all the momentary disagreements, it was the greatest journey of any of our lives – and one that it has not been possible to accomplish for many years now. We were amazingly lucky to have been able to do it – and in a 1921 Rolls-Royce too.

FIFTEEN

White Vans and Chewing Gum

Old age is a bugger. I take eighteen pills a day, I've gone in the back, and the front too. I've had two new hips. Getting out of an armchair is a hell of an adventure, getting into a bath is worse than that, and I can't get my leg over any more either. It's a bit like finding you are living in the midst of the most permissive society of all time, but when you open the stable door you find the horse is no longer fit to bolt. My days of dancing a waltz let alone the Black Bottom or doing the hundred-yard dash are well and truly over.

This is on the debit side, but there are also plenty of compensations. So many things don't seem to matter as much as they did. The competitive pressures of youth have all but disappeared. I now look at all the things that happened in the days of my upbringing – good or bad – from a more relaxed perspective. I am not so ready to point the finger of blame. Life is exciting, too. There is something exhilarating about the pace of life today and many of its customs, which are so different from those I was brought up with.

In fact, the only real problem these days is the arithmetic. If Shane Warne wants to go on playing T20 cricket at the age of forty-three, he's welcome to it. If he decides to throw the ball at a West Indian batsman, that's up to him. If in jovial retaliation the West Indian hurls his bat furiously down the pitch at Warne, that's his affair too. If it's not all good clean fun, at least it's all good clean commercialism. One-day, and particularly T20, cricket is showbiz, pure and simple. Its only worthwhile job is to raise money, and if it continues to do that, all power to its elbow. T20 cricket has distorted the original and proper game beyond all recognition, so what does another step or two down that road matter? It might even lead a few people on to the proper game. But let's not be holier-than-thou. We live in an instant age, and this sort of thing has an instant appeal. I would be amazed if Warne had not been put up to it, or at least it had been made clear to him that anything he did which would attract the front pages of the next day's papers, to say nothing of the world's television viewers that evening, was more than OK with the bosses. Publicity is the sacred god, and don't let's forget it. No doubt Liz Hurley, Warne's glamorous but gently ageing other half, will put in an appearance some time soon. I for one can't wait.

We are never going to be able to turn the clock back – and do we really want to? Life moves on today at an alarming rate, and what fun it is trying to keep up. We put on dinner jackets and other formal clothes much less frequently than we used to do, but so what? I have some sexy Italian shoes made by a company called Tod. They slip on too beautifully for words, which cuts out all that business of having to bend over and tie those wretched shoelaces, probably slipping a disc or doing something equally painful in the process. My Tods are a mouthwatering mixture of red and white, and I am glad to say they are much admired. A gentleman called Ralph Lauren has made me some pretty snappy shoes too, which would have given my paternal grandmother – to say nothing of Grizel – a good deal more than a go of hiccoughs, and I also have a bright-green pair which might even have drawn a healthy caution from them both. I have lots of lovely trousers in various colours: scarlet, bright yellow, no-messing green, succulent pink, and one or two others. They add much to the gaiety of nations, even if they make my old school chum Michael Tinne shake his well-groomed head in disbelief, or possibly what-has-life-come-to disgust.

(Speaking of Michael, he and his amazing wife Victoria are two of the people who have been more than just good friends for as long as I can remember. Michael has spent much of his life flying off to distant parts of the globe, helping foreign governments solve a variety of their agricultural and environmental problems. Victoria, on the other hand, has stayed firmly put in London, where she has been buying and selling houses for the rich and famous for many years. There can hardly be a decent house in Chelsea, Knightsbridge, Belgravia and the like that hasn't been through her hands at one time or another, and her list of clients reads like *Debrett's Peerage* at the top of its form. She bustles about London in a purposeful, spirited manner in a tiny Smart car in the company of a vigorous, noisy small dog which is aptly named Busy. We all need a Victoria in our lives, and she has been a terrific friend to me, especially when I nearly came unstuck after that heart bypass operation. At another time, when my house was burgled she was soon on the scene, and was spotted squeezing in, head-first through the broken kitchen window. Nothing is too much trouble for her, and dinner at that charming house in Fulham is always a delight, even if she does have a beguiling tendency in mid-August to incinerate the grouse. She and Michael have masses of children, and have probably lost count of the number of their grandchildren. Michael was a distinguished oar in his day, and they still talk about him in Georgetown, Guyana, where he was involved in the rum trade. He reminds me just a little of Noël Coward's

Uncle Harry, who 'loved to go off on missions to rather peculiar climes'. But anyone less like 'Dear Aunt Mary' from the same song than Victoria would be hard to imagine.)

To return to the matter of vibrant hues, I don't mind what they do to one-day cricket, as long as they leave Test cricket alone. My own wardrobe may have an increasing tendency towards the flamboyant, but white is the only colour for clothes and sightscreens in Test cricket. It must be allowed to remain forever as the five-day game's hallmark, together with all other intriguing idiosyncrasies which have gone to make it the fascinating mixture it is. As a rule I walk around the West End of London in all my colourful accessories, and unless convention insists, invariably tieless. But when I go to Boodle's for lunch or dinner I would never consider wearing anything other than a dark suit, a tie and black shoes. Boodle's is the equivalent of a Test match. Eating at a trendy modern restaurant run by a tiresome celeb chef is a one-day, T20 limited-over outing, at which your hair expects to be let down, and it is all the more fun for that. It's no good being too despondent about these things.

The modern age has a great deal to offer, but of course there are some unpleasant aspects to it as well. I live near a clutch – or maybe a creep – of nightclubs which flourish noisily, extravagantly and probably indecently; but maybe it is only elderly jealousy that makes me say that. One of their more unpleasant side-effects is that the pavements around our house are plastered with chewing gum which has been spat out and stamped into the ground. Then there is the ghastly white-van culture – but I suppose you could just about equate that with Warne throwing that cricket ball, or football fans at their bluest chanting in unison.

I may be beginning to sound old-fashioned, but I suppose it is inevitable that the word 'respect' should have taken on a new, watered-down meaning now that we are embraced by a free-for-all society. These days it is every man for himself. You have only to be in a car for a few minutes to know what I mean. I am delighted to wait at the end of a narrow road to enable an oncoming white van to break the land speed record. It would be nice to think that as he passes the driver might be prepared to raise even a solitary finger in appreciation of my patience, but that will never happen. Anyway, we must move on. Those days have gone, and we should have learned by now not to be surprised when the window of a passing car is opened by a beautiful lady driver who delivers a verbal volley that would have embarrassed an old-fashioned costermonger on one of his best days.

Then there is the matter of punctuality. These days, being on time for social encounters has more of an endemic, built-in lateness to it than ever before, while in matters of business punctuality is probably spot on – after allowances are made, of course, for late adjustments made on an ever-smarter mobile telephone. There is still, however, a part of the population that regards those apparently indispensable devices as being beyond the human pale. But just like T20, Tod's shoes (thank God!), white vans and, of course, those dangerous and iniquitous speed bumps, they are here to stay.

I could go on like this forever, but there would be no point. Life has changed, and it is not going to go into reverse. I do believe firmly that as we live in an age which gives us a great deal of fun in so many ways, we must accept the downside, and get on with things just as we did in the days when there wasn't a mobile phone or a T20 bash in sight. But, just occasionally, those of my vintage will reach out instinctively for a piece of the past that they see floating past them, and try in vain to pull it back. Perhaps it would be less stressful not to make the attempt. Drivers lives' today are bedevilled by every sort of speed limit and restriction, but life itself moves at a dizzy pace without a limit in sight. Hey-ho. Oh yes, and if anyone ever again says to me "Have a good day", or even worse, "Enjoy", I will happily go up on a murder charge.

Food and drink, though, have never been better than they are today. The range of both is amazing, and is available at all kinds of restaurants that we could never have dreamt of all those years ago as, without knowing it, we sat in wait for the life-changing 1960s. Think, too, how travel has improved. We can fly almost anywhere in about five and a half minutes. I have been lucky in that my job has taken me to many corners of the globe. I know airports have never been much fun, and have been made considerably less so by Mr bin Laden. When you're having a bad time being searched at a crowded security check, it is more necessary than ever to keep your eye firmly planted on the bottom line: that first rum punch in Barbados, the first plate of Sydney rock oysters, the first glimpse of Rio's Corcovado, the start of an adventure in Vietnam, or maybe just that glass of champagne in the duty-free bar. When it arrives, you will enjoy it all the more. We are becoming more and more global, and it is increasingly necessary to join in – and it is so much fun to do so.

One lovely thing about being in my seventies is that so much has been done to make life easier for us geriatrics and I don't just mean disabled loos. In fact, all those blessed 'elf 'n' safety, compliance-and-risk-assessment busybodies drive me bananas. Political Correctness is another bête noire. I want to be allowed to lead my life as I want. Of course, there is nothing I can do about almost every orifice of my body being filmed continually by these ubiquitous CCTV cameras. Big Brother keeps an eye on Shane Warne too. I cheerfully acknowledge that wet rooms, screwpulls, supermarkets, automatic pepper grinders and automatic everything else save time and injuries, control tempers and make life easier. But does it make me a hypocrite to have an old-fashioned fish-monger and butcher, and to love them – and to have a pre-historic corkscrew?

If I do have a complaint, it is that I find I have far too little time to read. Books longing for my attention pile up all around the house, and I am beginning to fear that many of them will never get read. That does not stop me going into new or second-hand bookshops and invariably coming out with yet another armful. There is something wonderfully compelling and attractive about the physical fact of a book. While I use an electric toothbrush, own a good many electronic gadgets, and have every sort of modern contraption in the kitchen, I am firmly digging my toes in when it comes to a Kindle. I still like to feel a real book in my hands, even if it is a paperback, and to be able to turn its pages myself. A Kindle is much more T20 and white van than the signed second-hand copy I have just bought of John le Carré's *The Spy Who Came in from the Cold*, to say nothing of one of the 350 copies from the limited edition of *Ranji's Jubilee Book of Cricket*. I love bone marrow and tripe too, and I am afraid they are not fearfully avant garde either. And I still like black cherries just as much as I still loathe junket – if things go according to plan, I hope I shall be able to have that one out with Tom one day.

In my old age I have made some great discoveries, and many of them have concerned Italy. I have never known much about the country beyond Julius Caesar, Benito Mussolini and Silvio Berlusconi, but Valeria has already walked into these pages once or twice. As I have mentioned, we met in 2009 in John Brinkley's establishment in the Hollywood Road in Chelsea, and after a slow, watchful start we came together like a couple of well-trained magnets. Unlike any other of the girls in my life, Valeria was immediately interested in what I did in both the commentary box and the theatre, and she rapidly became a great help to me. She has also enjoyed my friends, which is perhaps the best thing of all. She is lovely to look at, and has the sweetest nature – although she doesn't let me get away with everything – and has a dress sense that only Italian women seem to have. She was born in Rhodesia, and having lived much of the first part of her life in various African countries, she then came to London, where she became a significant figure in the fashion industry. She helped open Moschino's boutique in Conduit Street, and was later to run Louise Kennedy's shop in Belgravia, and several other things besides. Valeria is always beautifully turned out, and we do everything together. She comes to all my shows, having suffered my pre-cataract-operations driving through clenched teeth, although she is hoping for better things now. She also accompanies me to most of the cricket I watch, especially overseas. She loves meeting amusing people, staying in good hotels, eating interesting food and drinking good wine. She is a considerable cook, with an admirable Italian bias, and has turned me into a great lover of Italian wine – her family come from Piedmonte, and so, by the happiest of coincidences, do a great many of Italy's best wines. She has shown me many new things, and lots of exciting adventures in Italy lie ahead. I know I have had a number of false starts, but Valeria is truly the most wonderful girl I have ever met. She has transformed my life.

My daughter Suki and her husband Olly, who married in 2005, run the Old House at Home, a delightful, beautifully-situated friendly and brilliant hostelry at Newnham, five minutes west of Exit 5 on the M3, and just a couple of miles south of Hook in Hampshire. They have had their sticky catering moments, including credit crunches, a multitude of recalcitrant chefs, and a fire which put them out of action for over a year. They are now a good deal more than just up and running again. After reopening, they soon achieved a mention in the Michelin pub guide, and they have since graduated to the *Guide Michelin* proper. It is not only the proud father in me who says that this is the result of Suki once again deciding to take charge in the kitchen herself – and her daughterly love is such that she seldom gives me a bill. Having said all that, it really is a brilliant place. Go along and try it, and you'll love it, and Suki too. Obviously, I may not be the most objective witness in this case; but Suki's talents as head chef have been suitably recognised by those who run that famous restaurant guide. Thanks to that helpful publicity, and also to all those clever travel things on the internet, the customers are flocking in.

Valeria and I go down there whenever we can. While the head chef flexes her muscles in the kitchen, Olly, wearing truly exceptional pink socks, presides behind the bar in the most charming, splendidly understated *je ne sais quoi* fashion. He knows the hotel and restaurant trade, as well as his wine list, backwards, and is unusually adept with a corkscrew. He also writes the bills, but don't hold that against him. Someone has to. They have a delightful crop of Latvian waitresses who seldom miss a trick, and a splendid regular clientele: in one part of the small bar, Vic, an early bird, and Maggot, as he likes to be known, have cider-drinking contests. If Vic should be sticking to the beer, Maggot drinks, pretty capably, against himself. The Old House is tucked away in the corner of a typical village green, surrounded by some big houses. My only problem with it is that one of those houses belongs to the son of an old Wykehamist, Peter Stevens, who in 1956, on Agar's Plough, caught and bowled me for nought in the first over of the Eton v. Winchester match. The moment comes back to haunt me at least twice a month.

* * *

I have always been someone who enjoys clubs. I became a member of Boodle's in 1960, and over the years, when I could afford to, I joined two or three others. The first of these was Pratt's, the dining club which belongs to the Duke of Devonshire, where everyone sits at a communal table at which I met people like Sir Malcolm Sargent, Harold Macmillan and good old Willie Whitelaw, and many other politicians. The Conservative MPs who belong to Pratt's like to dine there, because it is not too far from the division bells. All the waiters used to be called George, and they probably still are, and the food was good in an at-home sort of way. It was comfort food, really, and the club claret was rather more than just drinkable. In about 1980 I was elected to the Garrick, which in many ways is the most amusing club in London, but I fell out of bed with my bank manager soon afterwards, and had to resign. The club were sweet about it, and said they would allow me back when I wanted. I eventually took them up on this offer, and returned to the fold, but then I realised that as I only used the club three or four times a year, it would make more sense to resign and let in someone younger. The Beefsteak went the same way.

I still belong to Boodle's – having been a member for more than fifty consecutive years I no longer have to pay a subscription, which is a strong incentive. It is the club in which I was, as it were, brought up, and I love it. The ladies' side is good too, with terrific food. It is presided over by Marcello, with friendly and ample charm, who behaves like an avuncular Italian regimental sergeant major. It suits Valeria and me well.

My other club, which in its way is my favourite of all, is the Chelsea Arts Club. It is fifteen minutes' walk from where we live, the members and the food are splendid, and in the summer the big garden is the best of oases. It is beautifully run, and nothing is more fun than going along and sitting at the big table for lunch or dinner. You never know who you are going to bump into and it is the only club in which I have never been bored. And now I have a family connection: Geoffrey Matthews, my niece Charlotte's husband, has just taken over from the redoubtable Dudley Winterbottom as the Lord High Executioner.

The CAC fields a splendid cricket team, and any technical shortcomings its members may have are more than made up for by their indefatigable and unquenchable enthusiasm. The side is fearlessly led by David Maddocks, who in a match at Eton on Upper Club against the East India Club played one of the greatest innings I have ever witnessed. It took him at least seven minutes to get to the crease, as it had slipped his mind that it is advisable for the next batsman to put his pads on before the wicket falls. He then found that he had taken out two left-handed batting gloves, and spent an age deciding how best to wear them.After all that he was bowled first ball by a slow long hop which bounced twice.

Stephen Bartley, another stalwart of the side, also happens to be the archivist of the Cresta Run in St Moritz as well as the CAC. In the summer of 2012 he arranged for a side which in a pretty loose sense represented the CAC to play two games in St Moritz, where, surprisingly, cricket has been played since 1896. There had been a lot of rain before we arrived, which helped with the acclimatisation process. The first game was played at a school some way out of the town, where the pavilion was so far from the pitch that it was almost impossible to see what was going on. The next day we foregathered at Rolf Sachs's splendid house, which had been the main stand for the Winter Olympics in 1928 and again in 1948. Rolf is the son of Gunther who became probably the most envied man in the world when he married Brigitte Bardot. The peripatetic David Maddocks was the scorer, but had to leave after the first innings to go back to London. Stephen Bartley played a long, patient and pointless innings in a losing cause, while our huge, avuncular host bustled about the place with considerable gusto, and occasional passers-by walking along the road halfway up the hill on the other side of the ground paused every now and then to try to determine what on earth was going on. There was a considerable rally of elderly motor cars in St Moritz that weekend, and it seemed appropriate that a few of them came along with their drivers to watch. I was entrusted with the job of commentating, and as you may have gathered, I was never short of material. It was the kind of weekend that perhaps only cricket could have created, and an adventure which urgently needs to be repeated.

My newest club is the exceptional Club at The Ivy. There is the most delightful and charming informality about it, and its 'browsing and sluicing' is up there with the best. I was steered in that direction by Harry Brunjes, and Fernando Piere, the commander-in-chief, smiled benevolently upon the suggestion. Harry Brunjes and his wife Jacqui are the kindest, dearest couple, and have become wonderful friends. Show business brought them together, and with Harry at the piano, nightingales have never sung more beautifully in Berkeley Square. They have passed on all their talents to their remarkable children. Harry is chairman of the English National Opera, and going with him and Jacqui to the Coliseum, to their splendid house in Sussex or their apartment in London and listening to the best voices of the ENO is an experience it would be impossible to better. Harry is no mean golfer either, and has helped run the affairs of that mighty course at Valderrama in southern Spain. He is a fluent, able and highly amusing speaker on a vast range of subjects, and is successful at everything he touches. It is almost unfair that he should have married such a beautiful girl as Jacqui. Their daughter, Emma, who is in the theatre business, has become a shrewd confidante and adviser.

I am sad that I hardly ever play any bridge these days. I played a lot at Boodle's in the seventies and eighties, but have got out of the habit. My New Year's resolution should be to teach Valeria to play. If I do, it will not be long before she is better than me. I had to give up more energetic pastimes too long ago, when my back began to behave like a Lower Boy. I stopped playing cricket in my thirties, because with my job I was always flat out watching others play the game, and when I had a day off I wanted to get as far away from cricket as I could. Most people who have spent much of their lives on the cricket circuit have been enthusiastic golfers, but I made a conscious decision when I was still up at Cambridge not to play golf. I was a fierce competitor in any sport, and I knew that if I took up the game I would never be able to leave it alone, and would have wasted a significant amount of my life on it. I have never regretted this decision, even though I love watching the Majors on television, and of course listening to Peter Alliss's peerless commentary. I enjoy watching jolly nearly all the big sports on television, although with apologies to Bernie Ecclestone and his progeny, who buy and sell large and ridiculously expensive houses in my part of London with embarrassing frequency, I find it increasingly easy to let Formula 1 fly through outside the off-stump.

Chelsea and Stamford Bridge are too close for comfort, and make movement on a match day almost impossible. A club which lurches from Ken Bates to Roman Abramovich in however many moves it was, must have a misplaced or a pretty weird sense of humour and that is before we get onto the subject of John Terry. I go to Stamford Bridge occasionally with one of my greatest friends, James Lotery, who has a season ticket or two. James owns the World's End Nurseries, a gardening operation in the King's Road which is friendly, accommodating and excellent all at the same time.

James sometimes takes me to Twickenham, which he also attends regularly. This is always an adventure. He drives there from his house in Kensington in what usually seems to be a new Jaguar covered convincingly by at least a year's supply of bird droppings. Just over Richmond Bridge we embark on a perilous short cut which on a good day ends up in a Tesco car park, where the abrasive attendants are quietened down with the help of a few banknotes. We then flock into Tesco's, and buy enough sandwiches and etceteras to feed more than a modest brigade. From there we descend on the stadium, where we have a long climb up the unforgiving concrete stairs until we arrive at the appropriate level. After that, we walk a little further to see if the bar is open yet. It never is, so James goes off to another bar he knows, and returns with an assortment of wobbly plastic glasses. It may not be the committee dining room, but it fills a gap. We will probably run into one or two of James's friends, whose names he can never remember, before climbing some more solid stairs to find our seats.

There is no greater sporting enthusiast than James, who is something like ten days younger than me, a disadvantage I never let him forget. He runs the Middle Balcony Club, who sit, predictably enough, on the middle balcony of the Pavilion for every day of international cricket played at Lord's, although some are a bit sniffy about the limited-over stuff. If he can't get to a game, James listens on the radio in his office to every ball bowled, with a television set alongside for confirmation. Ring him up and ask him how many someone has made, or how many runs England won by, or anything else, and he will give you only the most approximate of answers. Yet no one anywhere will have enjoyed the game more, or will be more full of it afterwards. If all sporting enthusiasts were like James, the world would be a better place. The World's End Nurseries are his alter ego, and his splendid character is in every flower, plant, stone and stick in the place. The only difference between him and the plants is that they drink water, while his tipple is brandy. He is generous to a fault, and one of those rare characters who is a great life-enhancer. Ten minutes of James, and you just can't help feeling better.

All my life I have been a great collector. This began when, over a number of years, I put together a collection of first editions of P.G. Wodehouse, many of them in their original dust wrappers, which are so important to real book collectors. I was never able to lay my hands on a copy of *The Globe By the Way Book*, a compilation of the columns Wodehouse wrote for the *Globe*, a London newspaper in the early 1900s, which is much the most difficult of his books to come by. In the end my bank manager took a stern proprietary interest in my collection, and it was a miserable moment for me when they came under the hammer.

Since then I have turned my attention to the cartoons and caricatures of that famous old Australian leg-spinner Arthur Mailey, one of the greatest characters the game has produced, and whom I have already mentioned when I was playing boys' cricket matches all those years ago in Norfolk. He was a brilliant draughtsman, and I have a number of his original cartoons. He was able to create an extraordinary likeness and impression of character with remarkably few lines. I think particularly of two drawings of the huge Warwick Armstrong, under whose captaincy he began his Test career after the First War. Perhaps it was divine intervention which caused Mailey to take all ten wickets for 66 in Gloucestershire's second innings against the Australians at Cheltenham in 1921. His autobiography, entitled *10 for 66 and All That*, is one of the most entertaining cricket books I have read, and is delightfully illustrated with his own drawings.

For a few years I have been a peripheral part of Lashings Cricket Club, as a commentator at the ground when Test matches allow. Lashings is owned and run by the ubiquitous David Folb. It began life as a pub side in Maidstone, and grew into an eleven of former Test cricketers from all over the world. Each year they play twenty or thirty games against club sides in Britain, and occasionally overseas tours were organised. For a year or two they went out to Abu Dhabi, where they played four games on a lovely ground at the magnificent Emirates Palace Hotel, with the sea on one side and the huge and beautiful palace built recently by the ruler of the country in the background. This ground was the brainchild of Andy Elliott, who hailed from Gloucestershire, ran the Beach Club at the Emirates Palace and bowled unruly left-arm spin. In a short time a presentable pitch was put in place, and although Lashings invariably swamped the local opposition, a great time was had by everyone.

The opulence of the Emirates Palace is impossible to describe: it even has a gold-vending machine in the vast entrance hall. On my first visit I went one night to the hotel's big theatre to watch the Bolshoi Ballet; the following evening we walked to the huge open-air amphitheatre in the grounds and listened to Andrea Bocelli. We were back in the amphitheatre the next night to hear Coldplay. It is that sort of a place. Looking back on it, the Lashings trips to Abu Dhabi were a venture that was unlikely to last long, as so many conflicting personalities were involved. While Hans Olbertz, a German, was general manager, the cricket was seen as an asset to the hotel. When his tenure of office ended his place was taken by a man who was, in every sense, a Young Turk. Although I own some lovely drawings of 'Cricket in Constantinople' in the nineteenth century, which suggests that the Old Turks might have come to the party, the benefit of cricket at the Emirates Palace was not appreciated by this particular Young Turk. Maybe the idea behind it was not sold to him in the wisest possible way. Anyway, Lashings ceased making the journey to Abu Dhabi. I believe that cricket has restarted on that lovely ground, although Andy Elliott who set it all in motion has now moved on.

I must make a special mention of Henry Olonga, for many years a part of Lashings. He is the bravest of men, who along with Andy Flower, England's current cricketing coach, took the field for Zimbabwe wearing a black armband in protest at the atrocities of the awful Mugabe. He is a great human being, and a fine singer whose 'Nessun Dorma' would bring the Albert Hall to its feet. He was also a very good fast bowler. It was because of my friendship with Henry that I was asked to take part in the wonderful festival of cricket put on most years by Arif Naqvi at Wootton House, just down the road from Blenheim Palace. Arif comes from Karachi, and has not done at all badly out of a hedge-funding operation he runs in Dubai. Each year he brings friends, many of them from his university days, from around the world to Oxfordshire, and for four days they play a T20 competition between five teams which are given an assortment of diverting and some-times risqué names. The hospitality is formidable, with marquees and Bollinger everywhere and Arif in the centre of everything, making sure that the whole event is perfection itself.

Valeria and I have been going to Wootton for four years now. Apart from Henry and me, the commentators have included Robin Jackman, Jeff Thomson, Farokh Engineer, Clive Lloyd, Mark Butcher (who brings his guitar with him), Peter Baxter and others. Tony Still runs the coverage too beautifully for words, backed up by the versatile skills of Simon Brooke. I think it is fair to say that the cricket, while whole-hearted, is with one or two exceptions pretty incompetent, but it is all terrific fun, and is for me perhaps the best four days' cricket of the year. The competition is fierce, and the umpires' decisions are always being questioned. The former England umpire Ray Julian organises this side of it, while he himself is organised by his lovely wife Megan. Arif and Fayeeza are magnificent hosts, and have provided me with yet another lovely addition to my cricketing memories.

What, after all of this, has become of Hoveton? Happily it prospers, as the result of an inspired decision by my nephew Tom. At the north end of the estate, King's Wood, which I believe centuries ago had something to do with John of Gaunt, although I am not certain what, stretched from the upland into the marsh for about fifty acres. Tom had the brilliant idea of turning a part of the wood into a children's adventure and theme park, and calling it Bewilderwood. A series of upmarket treehouses were built, and it would take another book to describe all the exciting things there are for children to do. Tom has himself written a number of excellent and exciting children's books about Bewilderwood and the exotic creatures who have lived there. Visitors flock to it, especially in the summer. It has been a huge success, not only saving Hoveton but putting it on a sound footing for future generations. By now my father Tom should have stopped turning in his grave, while Grizel, after an initial sharp yelp of protest, would, first grudgingly, and then enthusiastically, have realised what a fantastic idea it has been. She was shrewd enough herself, and I can see some of her genes in all that has gone to make Bewilderwood what it is.

I still get asked if I would have played cricket for England if had I not run into that wretched bus. I have no idea, and as far as I am concerned from my present perspective, it really could not matter less. I have been exceedingly fortunate, and have had a wonderful, interesting and entertaining life. I hope it is not going to stop any time soon, although I have reached the age at which I find myself writing far too many letters of condolence, each one of which makes me acutely aware of my own mortality. I have been hellish lucky to get away with it so far, and I am keeping my fingers crossed that the Almighty still isn't prepared to face me just yet. I want to write another book or two, and I would love to keep on commentating for a few more years. I hope that the two cataract operations I have just had will make that possible, not only at Test level, but also at the lovely one-day matches at Wootton and those enjoyable Lashings games. There are my theatre performances too, which I enjoy so much that I hope the curtain will continue to rise for a little while longer. I write just as Backers and I are about to descend on Edinburgh for 18 performances at the 2013 Festival. And who knows, maybe there is still time for Blowers, Backers and Bly to end up as a sumptuously alliterative threesome. Also, there are, all over the place, plenty of delicious wines that badly need drinking. But none of these things would be worth it if it were not for Valeria, the only girl I have met who enjoys all these things as much as I do, and who brings something extra to all my adventures.

As a final postscript, I had the best holiday of my life just as the umpire was about to call close-of-play for this book. In April 2013, Valeria and I were invited by an old-ish and much-loved friend, Leon Larkin, whom I had originally met

35 years before in Australia, to stay for eight days at the Grand Hotel Europe in St Petersburg, of which he is the General Manager. St Petersburg must be the most beautiful city on earth. The Hermitage and all those extraordinary palaces, the Russian Orthodox churches, the ballet – we had two extraordinary nights at the Mikhailovsky and the Mariinsky theatres – the visit to the Summer Palace at Tsarskoe Selo and to a local street market to buy delicious Siberian honey, and much more besides. The first night at our astonishing hotel I had the best dinner I have ever eaten – I've had a few to compare too. The menu together with the wines and vodkas they poured for us is reproduced overleaf. Our fifth course that evening, Wagyu Beef, is an extraordinary invention of the Japanese. The beef is reared in Western Australia and the cattle are fed on milk and beer and their tummies are massaged every day. The result is that all the fat dissolves during the cooking and the meat melts in the mouth. What a few days they were. And what a life it has been – and there is still a bit to go – I hope.

Tasting Menu
for Mr. Blofeld and Mrs. De Bruyn
Caviar Bar and Restaurant
April 6, 2013

Beluga Caviar served on scrabbled egg
flavored with white truffle oil and fresh chive

Dom Perignon 2002

Astrakhan oscietra caviar in traditional Russian manner,
with blinis and Smetana

Vodka Beluga

Northern sea composition of scallop, red shrimp, lobster
and salmon and pike Caviar

Gaja Rossj-Bass, Piedmont 2011

Duck liver on a bed of prune and walnuts
complimented with cinnamon emulsion

Capanelle 50/50, Tuscany 2006

Best cut of Wagyu beef with Pommery mustard sauce
and smoked Maldon sea salt

Capanelle 50/50, Tuscany 2006

it was a real pleasure to take care of you.
Dimitry.

General Director
Leon Larkin
Best wishes

was my
pleasure
CHEF

We are gratefull to you for being
our guest and looking forward
to welcome you again!
Yulia Velichko, Senior Butler

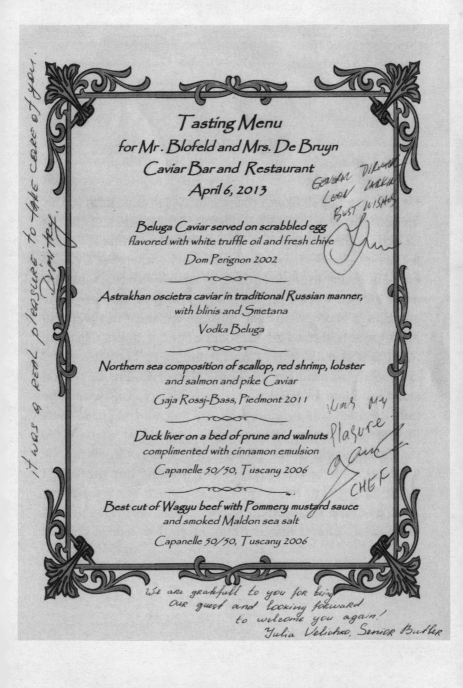

Appreciation

I would most of all like to thank Patrick Janson-Smith for his immense bravery in entertaining this idea on behalf of Harper Collins in the first place. I would also like to thank Patrick for his invariable charm and good spirits whenever I visited him. His ability to smile at times of crisis was remarkable. He never blinked when I kept turning up with yet another paragraph or a photograph that 'must go in', and there was also his invariably shrewd advice. Louise Swannell was a heroine in all that she did, arranging for me to go here, there and everywhere to promote this book. Harper Collins in general and Blue Door in particular were a joy to work with. The tour de force was produced by my splendid nephew, Piers Blofeld, a supreme literary agent who first alerted the publishing world to the possibility of this book, even if he did have a bit of trouble early on working out the VAT. I would like, too, to thank my iPad on which every word was written while it balanced on my right thigh. Its behaviour was impeccable. I never lost anything more than half of chapter nine.

Photographic Acknowledgements

The author and publisher would like to thank the following for permission to reproduce photographs or drawings:

John Woodcock, Peter Baxter, John Ireland, John Springs, Patrick Eagar, and Hattie Miles.

All other photographs are from private collections.

Index

356

358